FROM BOILER SUIT TO BLUE SUIT

AN UNEXPECTED JOURNEY

BOB SANDERSON

Copyright © 2024 by *Bob Sanderson*

All rights reserved. No part of this book may be reproduced or transmitted in any form or by any means, electronic or mechanical, including photocopying, recording, or by any information storage and retrieval system, without permission in writing from the author, except for the inclusion of brief quotations in a review.

Preface

It was the 5th of June 1972, as I waved goodbye to my mother, who was standing by the front gate in tears, my Dad and I left in a taxi to go to Newcastle Central Station. My Mother was distraught as my younger brother David had joined the Royal Navy earlier in the year, and I was now leaving home something she never recovered from. This was a big deal for me, as I had to navigate myself around London, something I had only done once before. We arrived at Newcastle Central Station and located the platform for Kings Cross London. In those days, men did not hug even Father and Son (something I would change with my children), it was very formal, just a shake of the hand, then onto the train with my suitcase, into the unknown.

Arriving in London was very daunting, as I had to get to Marylebone Station for a train to Aylesbury, then onto Wendover. This would be a challenge, as I would have to navigate my way around the underground. To my utter dismay, I managed to get to Marylebone Station and found the train to Aylesbury, then caught the Wendover train. As I stepped off the train at Wendover Station, the sun was shining and it was a beautiful summer day, it was June after all, and I did not know what to expect or whom I would see and meet. I had managed to navigate my way from Newcastle upon Tyne and across London to get this far, which was quite an achievement, I can assure you.

We had written instructions from the Royal Air Force (RAF) careers office to be at Wendover Station for 16:00 hours. The 24-hour clock was still a mystery, but I worked out that it was 4 p.m. As I looked around the station, several others were looking as completely bewildered as I was. It was obvious that they were part of the group joining the RAF.

There were a few boys in the group (yes, we were still boys) and since the girls outnumbered us, we started to introduce ourselves and where we were from. At the time, I had a very broad Geordie accent (which has mellowed over the years, but I still have the Geordie twang to this day), which those from the south found difficult to understand. Around 15:45 hours, a large military bus pulled up, the door swung open, and a Corporal (Cpl) appeared. He was small in stature, quite a rotund-looking chap dressed in the RAF blue serge number 2 second world war-styled uniform. Then he opened his mouth in a noticeable Welsh accent and shouted, 'Right, you lot, get onto the bus'. We all made our way onto the bus with our cases before us. Some of the girls needed help, which we willingly obliged. Once on board, we were on our way to RAF Halton to commence basic training.

I left school at 15 years of age and started working at the local factory of C. A. Parsons, which manufactured steam turbines (at the time, it was the largest factory in the world manufacturing steam turbines) as an office boy. At the age of 16, I started my apprenticeship as a centre lathe turner in a blue boiler suit.

Bob at 16

I am a great believer in fate and how either a single event or a series of events can change your life in ways that you could never imagine. The first event was in 1944 when my grandmother met a sailor and moved to Newcastle from Suffolk. The second event was in 1972, when I joined the RAF to train as a nurse. This book will tell the story of a young boy who was wearing a blue boiler suit working as an apprentice centre lathe turner, transition into the man that I became wearing a blue RAF suit, in what would become an unexpected journey that would shape the rest of my life. I had no idea at the time that I would spend the next 24 years in the RAF and 48 years in nursing.

TABLE OF CONTENTS

CHAPTER ONE IN THE BEGINNING AND BEYOND 1

CHAPTER TWO SCHOOL YEARS 13

CHAPTER THREE C.A. PARSONS 21

CHAPTER FOUR MY BILLY ELLIOT MOMENT! 32

CHAPTER FIVE HOME LIFE 36

CHAPTER SIX MAM 52

CHAPTER SEVEN VERA 58

CHAPTER EIGHT MAUD & OTHER THINGS 60

CHAPTER NINE DEATH 66

CHAPTER TEN NANA 74

CHAPTER ELEVEN DAVID 79

CHAPTER TWELVE JULIE 82

CHAPTER THIRTEEN ESME 85

CHAPTER FOURTEEN RAF YEARS 90

CHAPTER FIFTEEN RAF HOSPITAL, NOCTON HALL 95

CHAPTER SIXTEEN THE SÉANCE CHRISTMAS EVE 1973 105

CHAPTER SEVENTEEN THE EXORCISM 109

CHAPTER EIGHTEEN SECOND YEAR 112

CHAPTER NINETEEN NURSING IN THE 1970S 120

CHAPTER TWENTY WEEKEND CLEANING 125

CHAPTER TWENTY-ONE RAF HOSPITAL COSFORD, 1974–1975 127

CHAPTER TWENTY-TWO RAF HOSPITAL NOCTON HALL, 1975–1978 . 133

CHAPTER TWENTY-THREE RAF LYNEHAM 1978 TILL 1979 141

CHAPTER TWENTY-FOUR RAF HOSPITAL NOCTON HALL 1979 TILL 1981 145

CHAPTER TWENTY-FIVE RAF HOSPITAL WROUGHTON, 1981–1995 149

CHAPTER TWENTY-SIX HOLIDAYS 154
CHAPTER TWENTY-SEVEN RAF HOSPITAL WROUGHTON CONTINUES. 162
CHAPTER TWENTY-EIGHT GULF WAR 1 174
CHAPTER TWENTY-NINE POST-TRAUMATIC STRESS DISORDER (PTSD)AND OTHER THINGS... 191
CHAPTER THIRTY HOME SWEET HOME 194
CHAPTER THIRTY-ONE BACK TO NORMALITY 197
CHAPTER THIRTY-TWO DEPRESSION!!! 199
CHAPTER THIRTY-THREE ROYAL NAVAL HOSPITAL HASLAR, FROM JANUARY 3RD, 1996, TO JUNE 5TH, 1996 204
CHAPTER THIRTY-FOUR LAST 6 MONTHS IN THE RAF 207
CHAPTER THIRTY-FIVE MALMESBURY COMMUNITY HOSPITAL, JULY 1996–MARCH 2000 212
CHAPTER THIRTY-SIX PROJECT MANAGER, SWINDON WALK-IN CENTRE, 1999–2000 218
CHAPTER THIRTY-SEVEN LEAD NURSE OF SWINDON WALK-IN CENTRE 1ST APRIL 2000 TILL 2003 225
CHAPTER THIRTY-EIGHT ABBEY MEADS/PENHILL SURGERY, 2003–2004 229
CHAPTER THIRTY-NINE ADVANCED NURSE PRACTITIONER SWINDON WALK IN CENTRE 2004 TILL 2009 237
CHAPTER FORTY CARFAX HEALTH ENTERPRISE 2009 TILL 2017 240
CHAPTER FORTY-ONE THE FIGHT BEGINS. 247
CHAPTER FORTY-TWO RETIREMENT 255
CHAPTER FORTY-THREE REFLECTIONS 260
CHAPTER FORTY-FOUR MEMORABLE EVENTS 267
CHAPTER FORTY-FIVE ASSASSINATION OF PRESIDENT JOHN KENNEDY 269

CHAPTER FORTY-SIX FIRST MOON LANDING	271
CHAPTER FORTY-SEVEN VIETNAM WAR	274
CHAPTER FORTY-EIGHT THE TROUBLES	275
CHAPTER FORTY-NINE THE COLD WAR	278
CHAPTER FIFTY THE FALL OF THE BERLIN WALL	280
CHAPTER FIFTY-ONE EUROPEAN UNION	281
CHAPTER FIFTY-TWO MINERS' STRIKE	283
CHAPTER FIFTY-THREE DEATH OF PRINCESS DIANNA, AUGUST 31, 1997	285
CHAPTER FIFTY-FOUR GULF WAR 1	287
CHAPTER FIFTY-FIVE 9/11	288
CHAPTER FIFTY-SIX IRAQ WAR	289
CHAPTER FIFTY-SEVEN 7/7 2005	291
CHAPTER FIFTY-EIGHT COVID-19	293
CHAPTER FIFTY-NINE DEATH OF QUEEN ELIZABETH 11	297
CHAPTER SIXTY CORONATION OF KING CHARLES III	298
CHAPTER SIXTY-ONE CURRENT WORLD EVENTS	299
CHAPTER SIXTY-TWO MIDDLE EAST	301
CHAPTER SIXTY-THREE ENERGY AND COST OF LIVING CRISIS	303
CHAPTER SIXTY-FOUR ST. JOHN AMBULANCE	305
CHAPTER SIXTY-FIVE FINALLY	313
CHAPTER SIXTY-SIX SO, YOU THINK IT'S ALL OVER!!!	322
CHAPTER SIXTY-SEVEN AND IT'S DEFINITELY THE END!	333
ACKNOWLEDGEMENTS	351

Chapter One

IN THE BEGINNING AND BEYOND

My life started in a mid-terraced council house in Newcastle upon Tyne on the 16th of February 1953; this was my grandmother's house, who was forever known as my Nana. To fully understand my early years and later life, an appreciation of how my mother ended up in Newcastle needs to be understood, as she influenced my later life. When looking back through the corridor of time, you must be prepared for the bad as well as the good, and there were certainly some bad times sprinkled in with the good.

As previously mentioned, I am a great believer in fate and that a series of events can change everything later in life. The first event happened in 1944 when my Nana met and married a sailor named Charles Summerside from Newcastle upon Tyne, known as Geordie (this was a colloquialism for those living in the northeast of England), whose name was to stay with him for the rest of his life. I will come back to this later.

My mother was born in the County of Suffolk, where she lived in a village called Holbrook. She was born in 1931 in Bury Saint Edmonds Hospital on the 7th of April, she was a very small baby and had to be nursed in an incubator for some time after the birth. She never knew her biological father, as he died of tuberculosis when she was 3 months old. He was only 26 years old.

Mam with her Dad 3 months old

Mam always said that I looked like her father; there is a photo of me with David and Julie in her pram I have to admit that I do look a lot like him.

Bob with David and Julie in pram

Holbrook was a typical country village where everyone knew each other, and life was carefree for those children living and growing up there. Old photographs show my mother sitting on a cart horse with her grandfather

Mam with her Grandad

and romping in the cornfields with her friends, which indicates to me that her life was fun and happy, a point we often discussed later in her life. It was obvious by the way she could recall her childhood days that she loved those joyful times. She would recall watching Spitfires flying high in the sky and seeing the vapour trails of the aircraft when becoming involved in intense dog fights with the German planes.

My Nana, as it turned out, was a bit of a girl and liked male company. As I was looking at some of her old photographs of when she was young, it struck me that she was a very good-looking woman, and I could see why men would be attracted to her. This was to cause some upheaval a few years later when she became pregnant after an affair with her employer, where she worked as his housekeeper. He was a Master Mariner and lived in

Young Walter Rand

Chestnut House, Chelmondiston, which was only a few short miles from Holbrook. After Nana died, I found this photo in a frame when I took it out, the photo had been torn from a photo with the shoulder of a woman just visible on the right side. I have found Walter Rand as a young man, and they are identical, so they are the same person. She must have kept this for a long time.

Old Walter Rand

Due to the shame of getting pregnant as a single widowed woman, my Nana had to leave the village and move to the Isle of Wight, where my Uncle Fred was born in 1936 at 320 Gunville Road, Newport, Isle of Wight. She stayed there for several months before moving back to Holbrook, where my mother resumed her life again with her new brother.

Mam and Uncle Fred

This must have been an upheaval for her, as she had to leave her friends and home for a strange land across the sea. This event was a family secret for many years before my mother discussed it with me. This came as a shock, as I was only 13 years old when I was told about it.

Returning to Event 1, In 1944, my Nana met a sailor who was based at HMS Ganges Shotley, she took all he said at face value and upped sticks with my mother and Uncle and moved to Newcastle upon Tyne. She arrived in the evening following a long and tiring train journey. When they got out of the taxi, a woman was standing at the gate of the next-door house called Mrs. Fox. Her words were, 'Please go he killed his first wife'. My Nana was surprised to hear this, but she never questioned Mrs Fox about this (I have researched Geordie's first wife's death, and she died of uterine cancer in 1942, I am not sure what else went on) and went straight to the front door of 53 Wigmore Avenue, St. Anthony's Estate, Newcastle upon Tyne. She knocked on the door, and when it opened, there was Geordie. Waiting for her was his five daughters and his father living in the house, all of whom he omitted to mention. What was even more bizarre was that they were not married at this point. They were married on the 9th of September, 1944, at the Newcastle Register Office, so she had a chance to go but decided to stay.

Nana and Geordie's wedding

My Mother never really recovered from this shock and the subsequent years living there, but Nana stayed and was married to Geordie for 44 turbulent years.

They would fight like cats and dogs. Geordie was miserly with his money and would not give Nana adequate housekeeping but would willingly buy her gold bracelets and expensive rings. He had a bureau, which he kept locked all the time, as he had bags of money inside, mainly half-crowns, two shillings, and sixpence (8 would equate to £1) in old money and about 12½ pence in new money. He would spend hours counting the money. He was a modern-day Scrooge.

Nana and Geordie just before he died

On the weekends, he would go to the local public house and have too much to drink. When he arrived home, he would expect his dinner to be on the table, if he did not like what he was given, he would throw the plate across the room. He got his comeuppance later in his life when I was older, and he was an old man, so I protected Nana from his rage. He was warned of the consequences should he misbehave. What was odd about his behaviour he always gave me pocket money on a Saturday, which was 2 shillings (10p in new money), which at the time was a lot of money. He would enjoy squeezing my knee if I was sitting at the table then he would stir his tea and put the hot spoon on the back of my hand, completely mad.

My Father was born in 1925 in Newcastle upon Tyne. He worked in the shipbuilding industry as an electric welder, and his childhood was also interesting and shaped how he would be as a father. My Dad was born at 6.30 p.m. on the 1st of March, 1925, his twin brother George was born at 6.35 p.m. on the 1st of March, 1925, at 30 Fairless Street Byker. Dad was the smallest of the two babies and was not expected to survive, so his brother was given all the immediate attention. My Dad was so small that he was put in a small box wrapped in a towel and put in the oven to keep him warm. Again, as fate would have it, my Dad survived this ordeal, and sadly, his twin brother George died on the 6th of March, 1925, at the age of 5 days old.

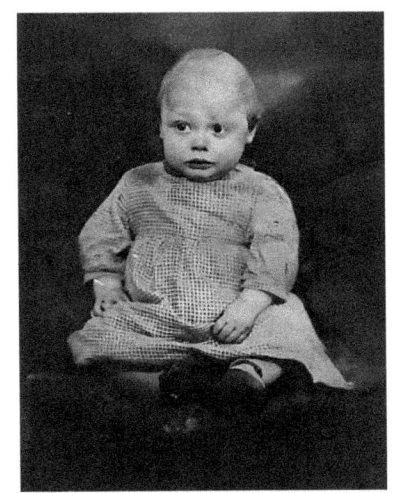

Dad as a baby

My Dad was always the fighter he needed to be, as most of his early years, he had to fend for himself as his older brother Bobby (Robert was his real name) was very ill with rheumatic fever and needed lots of care and attention, which resulted in Bobby being sent to The Children's Rest in Liverpool. This was a Charitable Hospital for Sick Children and was funded by the City Councils where the child was living; in Bobbie's case, it was Newcastle City Council. Bobby died at the age of 12 years old on the 23rd of July 1936 of cardiac failure and rheumatic fever. His Mother (my grandmother) was with him at the time of his death. I can't imagine

Dad left Bobby right

what it must have been like to lose not one but two children. My Dad often talked about Bobby and how he used to get involved in fights to protect him; oddly, he never mentioned the death or the funeral. Dad did not have a very good childhood; he told me of times when his Father would use a belt on him as punishment. For most of his younger years, he was looked after by his Aunts, as his Mother was away in Liverpool. I tracked Dad down on the 1939 Register, where he was 14 years old and working as a Butcher's Boy.

When I was researching my family history, I contacted Liverpool Central Library to see if they had any information on the Children's Rest Liverpool. On the day I contacted the librarian, she said, 'This morning, they had been sent a yearbook for the Children's Rest'. She sent me a copy, and when I read through it, I could not believe it. There, he was listed as a patient, Robert E S (Robert Edward Sanderson, same name as his father), with the comment improving, but sadly, that did not continue. It was just a chance email, but it resulted in pure gold dust.

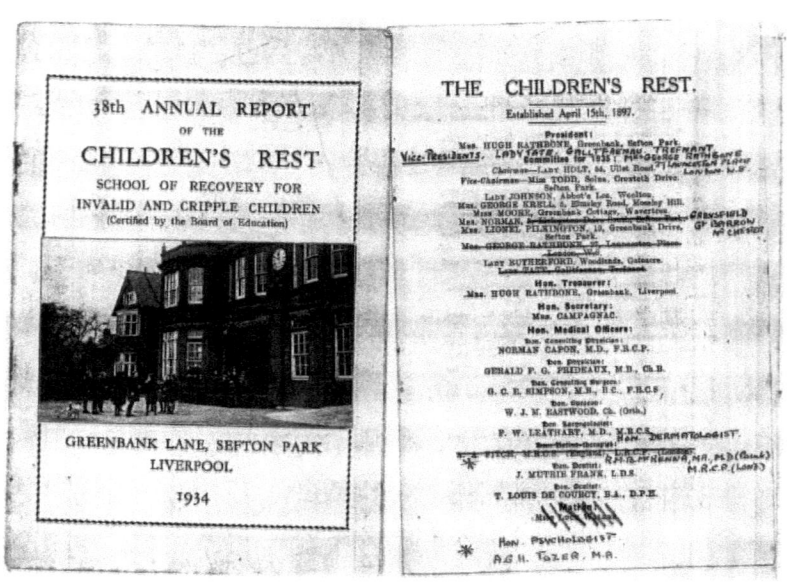

Children's Rest yearbook

Name.	Age.	Disease.	Admitted.	Remarks.
James K.	10 1/12	Rheumatism	April 29, 1933	Discharged July 27. Improved. Removed against medical advice.
Frank B.	9 5/12	Congenital heart deformity	May 18, 1933	Satisfactory progress.
Granville D.	12 4/12	Rheumatic Endocarditis	May 18, 1933	Condition satisfactory.
Mary E. B.	13 7/12	Subacute rheumatism	June 6, 1933	Improving steadily.
Emily S.	13 7/12	Rheumatic Endocarditis	June 8, 1933	Condition shows improvement.
Freda L.	12 1/12	Rheumatic Endocarditis	June 30, 1933	Shows great improvement.
Thomas E.	11 5/12	Congenital heart deformity	July 3, 1933	Very good progress.
Julia M.	14 1/2	Rheumatic Endocarditis	Sept. 12, 1933	Removed against medical advice, March 23. Much improved.
Winifred D.	11 7/12	Rheumatic Endocarditis	Sept. 12, 1933	Removed against medical advice. Improving well, August 25, 1934.
Irene C.	10 5/12	Spinal caries (L.)	Oct. 31, 1933	Improving.
George N.	10	Rheumatic Endocarditis	Dec. 6, 1933	Progress satisfactory.
John A. F.	12 5/12	Chorea	Jan. 18, 1934	Recurrent chorea. Improving now.
Irene C. R. B.	7 1/12	Rheumatism	Jan. 31, 1934	Removed against medical advice, September 22, 1934. Much improved.
Doris M. D.	7	Congenital heart deformity	Jan. 27, 1934	In statu quo.
Louie R. C.	14 5/12	Rheumatic Endocarditis	Mar. 23, 1934	Steady progress.
Margaret C.	9 1/4	Rheumatic Endocarditis	Mar. 23, 1934	Improved generally.
Ellen M. F.	8	Chronic Bronchitis and Debility	April 25, 1934	Shows slight improvement.
Dorothy B.	9	Rheumatic Endocarditis	April 27, 1934	Improvement marked.
Eleanora C.	9 5/12	Rheumatic Endocarditis	April 27, 1934	Improving.
Elsie G.	11	Rheumatic Endocarditis	April 27, 1934	Much improved.
Robert E. S.	10 1/2	Rheumatic Endocarditis	April 27, 1934	Marked improvement.
Mary F.	12 7/12	Rheumatic Endocarditis	May 7, 1934	Progress steady.
Nellie F.	10 1/2	Rheumatic Endocarditis	May 9, 1934	Condition improving.

Childrens Reast yearbook

Mam and Dad wedding day

Grandma and Grandad Sanderson

Nana and Geordie

Group photo of wedding day

Mam met Dad at a dance and was married in 1950. I suppose they had all the hopes and dreams of a young couple living in the post-war period. However, rationing was still in place and housing was in short supply; hence my parents lived with my Nana (the 5 daughters had left by then and Geordie's Father had his own home). This was common practice at this time, and that is how I ended up being born in my Nana's house.

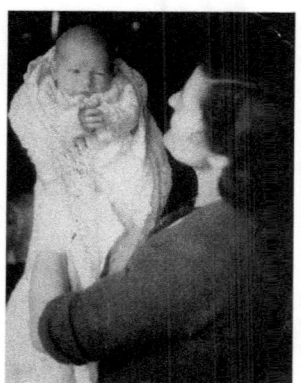

Me with Nana

There are always those family stories that become myths and legends. One such story was that Geordie's Father committed suicide in the same house where I was born. Again, while researching my family history, I investigated this, and surprisingly, he did commit suicide by hanging himself (true), not in the house I was born in (myth), but in his own house. I requested the death certificate, which was very graphic; everything was written down. It said he "died of strangulation while the balance of his mind was disturbed."

Geordie's Father death certificate

Although I never knew him, he must have been in a state of despair at the age of 76 to commit suicide (mental health was not talked about in the 1950s as it is today, and treatment was limited). Looking for more information, I emailed the Coroner's Office at Newcastle Civic Centre, and to my astonishment, they sent me copies of the suicide note, which is very faint. I need a specialist to look at this, copies of the police and doctor's reports, a copy of Geordie's statement to the police as he found him and a copy of the inquest

Up north, the kitchen is called the scullery, and the living room or lounge is called the kitchen. He hanged himself by tying a rope to the pantry door handle inside the kitchen. The door had a doorknob on the inside, to which he fastened a rope before hurling it over the door. He constructed a noose, stood on a stool put the noose around his neck, and kicked the stool away. Given that the death was by strangling, it must have been a terrible one. When Geordie went to check on his father after not hearing from him in a few days, he discovered him hanging from the pantry door. I have no idea how this would have affected Geordie or what it must have been like. He bequeathed £199 and 13 shillings to Geordie in his will.

Chapter Two
SCHOOL YEARS

We moved from my Nana's house to a brand-new flat at 76 West Farm Avenue, Longbenton, when I was 4 years old (this was on the far east side of Newcastle). This was a council flat; they were 3 stories high, 12 flats in each block, and they were built to form a quadrangle with a large green field in the middle. We lived in the middle flat, with a balcony looking out onto the green. I used to play cowboys and Indians on the green with the other children; we had the cowboy and Indian suits, which made it more realistic. Mam had a friend who lived on the ground floor

Bob at 5 playing cowboys and Indians

called Beaty Tonge. Beaty was rough and ready, and as a single parent of two boys, she would do anything for you. This is what people were like in those days. I used to go down for my tea; she made great sausage eggs and chips with lashings of brown sauce. The only other person that comes to mind is a lady called Mrs. Fitzpatrick. She was an old woman with long grey hair who lived in the block to the left of ours. She also had a middle flat and grew loads of geraniums in pots on her balcony. In the summer, her balcony was a sea of red flowers. I now grow geraniums in the summer months, and I often think of her from all those years ago.

I started school at 5 at Gothland Avenue Primary School in Longbenton. I don't have many memories of this school, as we moved house not long after I started school. We moved back to Wigmore Avenue, number 42. Nana lived just across the road from us. This meant I had to go to Wharrier Street Primary/Junior School. The school was run by a Headmaster called Mr. Hall. He was a small man with a loud voice. He would always stand at the school gates every morning, checking the children as they walked through the main gates. I would imagine that he would have been an officer during the war. He was very smartly dressed, always wearing a bow tie, and had high standards, which were reflected in the school. He was also a Justice of the Peace (JP) now known as a Magistrate. I did not enjoy my school days as I was not that clever and hated the morning mental arithmetic tests as I could never get them right. As such, I was ridiculed by the teacher and other pupils, which caused even more stress.

Corporal punishment was commonplace; it consisted of 4 or 5 12-inch wooden rulers held together by the teacher, and he or she would slap the back of your thighs till there were welts present. You did not want too many of these punishments. I have often wondered if this was part of teacher training, as in those days, it seemed to come very easily to some of the teachers at the time.

If you were really in trouble, you were sent to the Headmaster for him to notch up the punishment to the next level. This was a leather belt about 18 inches long. At one end, there were cuts in the leather to give tails, this hurt the most. You had to hold out your hand and were given six of the best (as it was called), then sent back to your classroom. This was going on daily, and no one batted an eyelid. It was an acceptable practice in the 1960s.

However, it was while in junior school that I was introduced to local politics. One of my teachers, Miss Jenny Collins, parents were both local Labour Councillors, Tom, and Margaret Collins. During the local elections, I would help with delivering leaflets to the local estates, and on the day of the election, I would stand at local polling stations to ask for the voting number. These would be sent back to the local constituency office so they could be checked off against the electoral register, so we would know who had voted. In the evenings, I would go around with Jenny in her car to knock on doors to ask the people who had not voted if they wanted a lift to the polling station. I would continue with helping until I joined the RAF in 1972.

I found this period a great learning experience, and I gained a good understanding of local politics. As I got older, I attended several local counts, which was extremely exciting. To be fair, there was no chance of the Collins being unseated as they were in solid Labour areas. The local MP was also Labour, again, this was a safe Labour seat and still is. It was an expectation that when you were old enough to vote at the time, which was 21 years old and then reduced to 18 years old in 1969, you would just vote Labour. It was only when I left Newcastle that I was exposed to other political views. Jenny kept in touch with Mam and Dad for many years. She was a wonderful person and an excellent teacher. 10th of April 2024 I have just seen on Facebook that Jenny has sadly passed away aged 82 years; she lived to a grand old age all of the posts spoke very fondly of her which was nice to read.

I failed the 11+, so I was condemned to a Secondary Modern School, which was next to the Junior School, so the move was straightforward enough, however, the school was an all-boys school with all male teachers and was very confrontational. Several local thugs revelled in bullying the first-year boys. This period of my education was awful, I hated every minute of it. I did not learn much as the classes were disrupted by the bad behaviour of some of the thugs. The teachers would throw the blackboard rubber or pieces of chalk at the perpetrators to regain order. My best friend was Richard Allison. We were friends until I joined the RAF, then we lost touch. He was a bit of a wide boy, noticeably confident and mature for his years. We would go to the pictures (cinema) on a Friday, and he had a clever idea to get one of us in for free. The plan was that one of us would buy one ticket, this would be Richard, and I would go to the window of the toilet, and Richard would give me his half of the ticket, so we would get into the pictures for the price of one ticket. Unfortunately, back in the day, most picture houses had a uniformed Commissioner monitoring the door, and we got caught just as he was trying to retain us. Richard punched him in the stomach, and we escaped. I never did this again. To be honest, it was not expensive to get into the pictures. We would go on a Friday or Saturday night. There were two films, always one Western film, plus Pathe newsreels. In the 1960s, these were short clips of news from around the world that were great to watch. At the end of the last film, the National Anthem was always played, and everyone stood up.

I got 2 shillings and sixpence (half a crown) in pocket money (that trebled when I was doing my paper rounds). The cost of a ticket to the pictures was 1 shilling and threepence, which left enough money for 5 cigarettes (Cadets) and a packet of chips, which we ate on the way home.

I am not a great swimmer, as I have a fear of deep water. Then, I suddenly remembered how we were taught to swim. The school did not have its own pool, so we had to walk to Walker Swimming Baths, which was about 15 to 20 minutes' walk. When we got there, we had to line up at the deep end and either jump in or be thrown in by the physical education teacher. This is the source of my fear of deep water. I was thrown in and had to be pulled out as I panicked and started to swallow water.

This was common practice at the time. I did go back to the swimming pool during the summer holidays with some of my friends. We used to walk from our houses and spend a couple of hours in the pool. I stayed in the shallow end (I still do this today; the pool I use today is 1.2 metres deep, which is perfect). On leaving, we were always starving, which meant a short trip to a small corner shop next to the pool to buy a penny loaf. The shopkeeper had a large, uncut white loaf and would slice off a large chunk of bread for a penny, which we would eat on the way home.

At around 13, I caught a significant chicken pox infection and was off school for 2 months, which put me back further. I still have my school reports from the time, and some of the comments from my teachers were not very helpful.

Bob's school reports December 1964

Bob's school reports July 1965

Bob's school reports December 1965

Arithmetic was still my downfall. I had decided that I would leave school at 15 and get a job, and then, unexpectedly, the government brought in a new school system called the Comprehensive Education System. This was supposed to enable bright pupils to flourish and support the less able. So, at 14, we had to change schools and were sent to a brand-new school called Benfield Road Comprehensive School, which opened in 1967. To get there, I had to get a school bus, which was a pain. Luckily, I had a school bus pass, which gave me free travel.

As my mind was made up to leave at the end of the term, I did not get much out of this new school system. Unfortunately, all that happened was that the thugs were exported to the new school and continued their reign of terror. There was one thug called "Toad Eye" he was cross-eyed, hence his nickname. He would walk along the corridor with his entourage of thugs and, at random, kick other pupils between the legs, which was bloody painful (as I was one of his victims) and another reason to get out of this place.

The school now had girls and boys together, which did cause problems, as you can imagine, bringing 14-year-old girls and boys together when the hormones were flowing. There was lots of snogging going on behind the bike sheds. I know it is a cliché, but that's what went on. I left school with no qualifications, which caused me problems later in life.

So, I started to look at jobs. In the 1960s, jobs were plentiful in shipyards and local engineering companies. I applied for an apprenticeship at C.A. Parsons, which at the time was the world's largest manufacturer of steam turbines. I was offered an apprenticeship but had to work as an office boy till I was 16 years old, as you had to be 16 to start an apprenticeship. During my time as an office boy, I observed the inner workings of the company and gained valuable insights into the industry. This experience allowed me to develop a strong work ethic and a desire to excel in my future apprenticeship at C.A. Parsons. It was a challenging period, but it allowed me to build a foundation of knowledge and skills that would serve me well in my future career as an apprentice at C.A. Parsons.

Chapter Three
C.A. PARSONS

C.A. Parsons was a prestigious engineering company sited along the top end of Shields Road Heaton in Newcastle Upon Tyne, there were acres of it. If you were offered an apprenticeship at Parsons, you were part of an elite group of young people starting out in their working lives, at the time, it was seen as a job for life (so they thought), as they only took in 60 apprentices a year.

Following an application and interview, I was offered a position but had to work the first year as an office boy as I was only 15 years old and could not start my apprenticeship until I was 16, which was 5 years in duration. I was assigned to the mechanical engineering office, which was a massive department. Once I got into the job, it was a fascinating insight into how the turbines were made. I had to go on day release to Newcastle Technical College to study mechanical engineering, science, maths, and physics. This was my worst nightmare as I cannot do maths!

However, the men in the office were an immense help and a fabulous resource. I learned more from them in 12 months than I did in all my school days. I passed all my first-year examinations, which included maths and physics!

NORTHERN COUNTIES TECHNICAL EXAMINATIONS COUNCIL

This is to certify that

ROBERT FREDERICK SANDERSON

was successful in the following examination(s)

GENERAL COURSE IN ENGINEERING
First Year

...
Science	Credit
Mathematics	Pass
Engineering Drawing	Pass

...

SESSION 1968-69

SECRETARY TO THE COUNCIL

First year General Course in Engineering results 1968/69

Mechanical Engineering Technicians results 1969/70

Mechanical Engineering Technicians results 1970/71

As an office boy, you were at the behest of the men in the office and others. There were some lovely ladies that worked there and would look out for you, one in particular called Sue who was a typist was lovely we got on like a house on fire.

We had to run errands into the machine shops with blueprints for the machinists. You would take the opportunity to meet up with the other office boys to have a quick fag and a cup of tea. There were two big machine shops called the light and heavy machine shops. When you first had sight of these monoliths, it was mesmerising, after several weeks, it became all too routine.

The light machine shop had smaller machines, lathes, capstan lathes, and boring machines, the heavy machine shop had massive turning lathes that would turn raw steel into these long rotor arms that would hold the turbine blades. It would take days for the lathe to turn the full length of the steel, and the turner would sit on a small chair attached to the lathe so he could monitor the process. The turners would work, day and night shifts just watching this machine. The large swathes of metal swarf would twist and turn as it became detached from the steel being turned. Swarf was deadly if you were not careful, as it was razor sharp, and if you became tangled in it, you would suffer appalling injuries, which often happened. Looking back now, I do not know how these men did this job of just sitting and watching a machine turn this long piece of raw steel into a rotor arm for a turbine. It would have driven me mad!

The time spent as an office boy was great fun, we were able to get out and about all over the factory, meeting different people. This was helpful in future years, just getting to know how things worked and who to ask for help. We worked out of the main office block, which housed all the support departments that allowed the factory to run smoothly. There was this lift called a paternoster. A paternoster lift is a passenger elevator that consists of a chain of open compartments that move slowly in a loop up and down inside a building without stopping. Passengers can step on or off any floor they like. One of our challenges as office boys was to remain on the paternoster until it disappeared into the upper workings, where the carriage was moved across and started to go down the other side. It was scary the first time that I did it. There was also a large Xerox photocopier in a room, it was massive. This was the first time I had seen a photocopier. It was our job to do the copying. The worst job was copying the annual reports, as they had to be collated by hand and then stapled together no automatic sorting! During the day, there would be a tea lady who would bring tea and cakes to each office within the block. Ah, the good old days no drink machines then. The Office Boys' days soon were over, as at 16, I had to move over to the Apprentice Training School to start my apprenticeship.

It is hard to imagine today, but back in the 1960s, jobs were plentiful, with most, if not all, offering apprenticeships. For those that remember the era, the general feeling is that the 1960s was an enjoyable time to be alive. The swinging sixties are remembered as a fun-packed, carefree optimistic decade characterised by the Beatles, Rolling Stones the mini skirt and the mini car. England's win in the 1966 World Cup. There were plenty of jobs for those who wanted them. School in the 1960s was a unique experience from children of today where digital technology has encroached into every aspect of our lives. In the sixties it was "talk and chalk" with the teacher at the front of the class and the pupils sitting at lift-up desks (with ink wells for your pen which was dipped in ink from the well) facing the blackboard, how times have changed. It was quite common for a Father and Son to work for the same company. There was no expectation of further education or university, so most young boys learned a trade via the apprenticeship route.

When you first enter the apprentice training school, you don't have a clue what you want to do. Over 6 months, you would be exposed to all aspects of engineering. Initially, I wanted to be an electric welder like Dad, but as it turned "pardon the pun" out, I settled for a centre lathe turner, not sure why. Dad was clear that I would not go to the shipyards, which was lucky as I did not want to work there either.

Dad worked at Walker Naval Yard, which dates back to the war years when the company that took over the yard was Vickers Armstrong. Numerous ships were built between 1931 and 1971. The yard was suitable for the construction of large ships up to 1100 feet in length. During the war years, many naval vessels were built on the Tyne, including HMS Sheffield and HMS Hermes. In the post-war period, Vickers Armstrong embarked on a modernisation programme at their Newcastle Yard to prepare for prospective work on passenger and cargo vessels.

The Walker Yard formed part of a merger deal made by Vickers Armstrong with Swann Hunter Shipbuilders, in 1968, a new company was formed, Swann Hunter and Tyne Shipbuilders.

So, my choices were limited to either shipbuilding, making steam turbines (not much of a choice) or working for the Central Generating Electric Board, but this was a nonstarter as I did not like heights and scaling electric pylons was not appealing.

In the mid-1960s, there was an expectation that you would leave school and get a job to contribute to the family income and pay your way.

My first wage packet was £3 6 shillings and 8 pence (today's money is £3.34). My Mother had £1 for my "keep", which was a third of my wages. At the age of 16 years old, I embarked on what was to be a 5-year apprenticeship, learning how to be a centre lathe turner.

The first 6 months in the apprentice training school were spent being exposed to all aspects of basic engineering, where you were taught all about the different processes and all the different machines that you would come across, including centre lathes, shaping machines, grinding machines, electric welding, basic electrics, and capstan lathes. At the end of the 6 months, you had to choose which area you wanted to specialise in.

Apprentice Training School C.A Parsons 1960s

For some reason, I do not know why I chose to be a centre lathe turner. It was the best of a bad job, as I was beginning to question why I was doing this. The next six months in the training school were spent on the machine of your choice, the lathe in my case. There was a group of us that wanted to be Turners, which helped us, we would be given various tasks to perform and make different items of tools to learn the various skills needed to be a Turner. I remember making a vice that had numerous different components, e.g., we had to learn how to make screw threads and how to use a micrometer, the tolerances were +/- one thousand of an inch.

We needed to be taught these skills, as we would be sent to one of the machine shops in our second year. In Parsons, there was a heavy machine shop and a light machine shop. I would be sent to the light machine shop. Both sites were massive and seemed to stretch for miles. The noise was hellish, but no one wore ear defenders. The factory was about 3 miles from where I lived.

In those days, we could not afford a car, so it was either walking or cycling to and from work. I used to walk to work, as there were several of us who would walk and meet up. I would meet up with Tommy first, then Frank and John. There was the normal chatter about the football (which I had no interest in) or about the working men's club and how many pints they had drunk over the weekend—inspiring stuff!

When you arrived at work, you had to clock in using a clock card, which went into a machine with a clock built into it so the time you arrived and when you left could be logged. Your wages were based on your clock card times. On arrival, there was a gentle hum around the place from the night shift, shutting down their machines. Work-life was centred around a ringing bell, at 07:25 a bell would ring. This was the 5-minute warning as work started at 07:30 on the dot. When the 0725 bell went, you could hear an increase in the noise levels as all the machines were starting up again and ready to go on the 07:30 bell.

We all had a work's number, mine was 11383, and we were issued six brass discs with your number on them. This was for borrowing tools from the store. You handed over one of your discs for whatever tool you needed; your disc was returned when you gave the tool back to the storeman. The main things you borrowed were specialist cutting tools, a micrometer, and a Vernia gauge. Both instruments were to measure your work as you would be working from a technical drawing, and it had to be correct. A micrometre is a precision measuring instrument used to measure dimensions with high accuracy. It consists of a calibrated screw that moves a spindle against an anvil. The spindle is attached to a thimble, which has a scale engraved on it. A micrometeer measures external measurements to +/- one-thousandth of an inch. A vernier gauge is a precision measuring instrument used to measure linear dimensions. It consists of two graduated scales, a main scale and a vernier scale. The main scale is marked with evenly spaced divisions, and the vernier scale is marked with a smaller number of divisions that are spaced slightly differently.

All your work had to be checked by one of the checkers. These men wore white coats with red collars and would either accept or reject your work. There were also men wearing white coats and blue collars; these were the foremen.

Going back to the bell, the next bell was at 09:20, which was the start of your 10-minute break. We all brought a flask of tea and something to eat. I always had a Twix bar (which was twice the size as it is today) with my tea, along with a copy of the Sun newspaper to read. The dinner break was from 12:15 to 12:45. We all had a large wooden toolbox, which we sat on to eat our bait (sandwiches) and read the paper. A series of bells controlled your life; work ended at 16:30.

My first day in the light machine shop was horrendous. As apprentices, you were at the mercy of the older men. They would do things to apprentices, this was called the initiation, and today it would be called assault or sexual abuse. Looking back at this time, most of the older men were obsessed with the crotches of the younger apprentices. They would grab you between the legs and squeeze your testicles, then try to gauge the size of your penis and testicles. This was not a great an experience as you could imagine. They would describe in graphic detail the size of people's genitalia, as this was widespread practice, and no one challenged it as this was part of being an apprentice.

Health and safety were not good either, as there were numerous accidents. Working on a lathe was not for the fainthearted, as there were many ways in which accidents could happen. The commonest was being pulled into the machine by bits of loose clothing being caught up in the revolving part of the lathe. There were stories of people being scalped due to getting their hair caught in the machine, so we all wore woolly caps, as long hair was all the rage at the time.

Eye protection was inconsistent, so it was common for bits of metal to fly off into your eye. Brass was the worst, as the waste came off in small bits. The other lethal aspect was something called a swarf. This was the waste metal strip that came off the tool head again. This was razor sharp, so you had to be careful not to get tangled in it as it would rip through your skin like a knife through butter. Then, there was the coolant called white water. This is what you used to keep the tool head cool while it was cutting through the metal. This stuff would get on your hands and could cause dermatitis and skin irritation.

I soon realised that I was a square peg in a round hole. I began to hate working at the factory. It was the same thing day after day, you went to work and were given a job card with the work you had to do that day. Each job was then checked by the inspector (the man with the red collar). If it was wrong, you would have to do it all over again.

It was becoming increasingly obvious that this was not the place for me. I think in the end, I had what I call my "Billy Elliot moment" when I saw all the old men coming out of the factory gates with bent backs and wearing flat caps, looking like matchstick men from a Lowrey painting. They all looked completely worn out and knackered. I thought I could not do 50 years of this; I would go mad. I did not want to be a *"Ballet Dancer,"* but there must be another way to earn a living.

I should not have said I would go mad; the following morning, I woke up and could not get out of bed. My mother called the doctor, who visited me at home. He prescribed some sleeping tablets (Mogadon) and an anxiolytic (for anxiety, Librium), and I was referred to a psychiatrist for an assessment. It was some kind of 'psychotic episode', the doctor said to my mother. As I did not want to go back to the factory, my mind just shut down. But the answer was becoming increasingly clear, I had to get out of the factory.

I was off work for several weeks but had to go back as I had nothing else to do, and being unemployed or sick was not an option.

Chapter Four

My Billy Elliot moment!

The day was like all those other days that had gone before; it was grey, cold, and wet. The 45-minute trek to work that I had walked hundreds of times before was becoming harder and harder to do. On the way, I met up with two friends, and we walked together, talking about the weekend and what we had done. Tommy and Alan were just the same, talking about the football game on Saturday, which was Newcastle United.

What was I becoming? Where was my life heading? I had tussled with these thoughts for some time, as I was now becoming like the rest of them, an automaton in the world of flat caps, blue boiler suits, donkey jackets, grease, and oil. As I approached the factory gates, it was the sight of all those men, young and old, pouring into the gates like ants returning to their nest that made me think about the future course of my life.

I am not sure why that day was the day I saw my life fast forward to those older men with their flat caps and bent backs, looking like images from a Lowrey painting. I was entering the world of the machines that dominated my life and what had become a living hell with the noise of the bell that summoned the workers to their workplaces. At 07:25, the first bell sounded. This was the 5-minute warning bell before the working day started. These 5 minutes were for the machines to be turned on. The hum of the motors warming up became louder and louder, which reached a crescendo as the 07:30 bells clanged above the noise.

I suddenly realised that I could not do this anymore. I had nothing in common with this life; I was different. I hated football and loathed the working men's club, and now I hated my job. I was following the same path as my Father and Grandfather. I was doing what was expected of a Northern man in the 1960s, which was to work in the factory, watch football on Saturday, then spend the weekend drinking in the club. This was not for me. I needed to get away from all of this.

Walking home, my head was awash with all these thoughts. I was desperate. What could I do to break free from this living hell I hated every second of the working day? The factory was a hard place to work, with hard men who were crude and rough. As a young apprentice, you were a lackey for the older men. Looking back on some of the practices that went on, they were sexual abuse and assault. Then there were the men in white coats with red collars; they were the inspectors who checked that your work was up to standard. Again, as a young apprentice, you lived in fear of these men.

Thank God it was Friday night, another week over. My salvation came that weekend, as by chance, I was reading the evening paper, the Newcastle Evening Chronicle, and there was a route out of this misery. I saw an advertisement for the Royal Air Force (RAF), where they were recruiting people to train as nurses. I had always known I was different from some of my friends. I had a caring side to me, not aggression. I hated all the macho things that went on. This was worth exploring. I went to the recruiting office on Saturday, and I did it; I started the process of joining the RAF. There was a process to go through first, a written examination to check your literacy and numeracy, a medical examination, and an interview in London with the Chief Matron.

For me, this was a daunting task as I had never been out of Newcastle, but this was my chance to make a different life for myself. For the first time in years, I could see another life away from the flat caps, boiler suits, and grease.

I was sent a travel warrant to get to London, which I managed to do. I successfully passed the interview with the Chief Matron and was accepted as a pupil nurse in the RAF. I signed on the dotted line and joined the RAF to start on the 5th of June 1972. The only thing left to do was to tell my Mother; she knew that I was applying to join the RAF, but once I broke the news that I had joined, it was a different matter. There were tears and lots of debate about my reasons for leaving home. Mam could only see the negatives in that she was being abandoned; she could not see the positives for me. But I stood firm and embarked on what was to be a long and enjoyable career of some 24 years in the RAF.

I qualified as a State-Enrolled Nurse (SEN) in 1974 and went on to become a Registered Nurse (RN) in 1989. I retired from the RAF in 1996 as a Warrant Officer (the highest non-commissioned rank of which I was immensely proud)

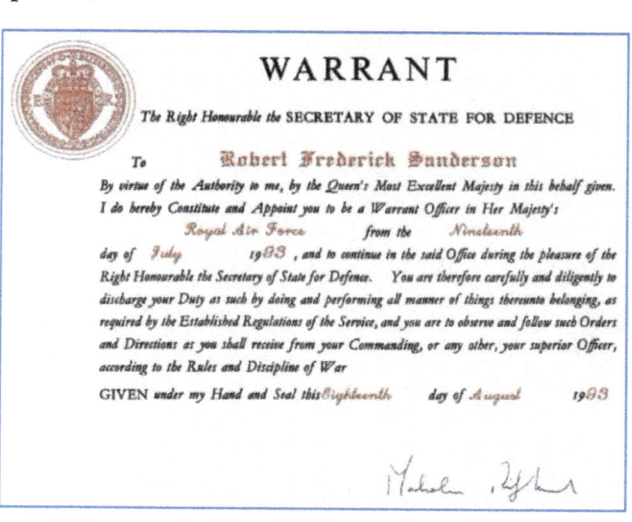

Warrant Officer Certificate 1993

after serving for 24 years. I continued to work as a nurse in the National Health Service (NHS) until I retired in 2017. As I write this, I am in my 48th year of nursing (I extended my career by 2 years on the COVID-19 register). During this time, there have been many changes in nursing, some for the better and some for the worse. Throughout my nursing career, I have witnessed significant advancements in medical technology and treatments, which have greatly improved patient care. However, I have also observed the increasing challenges and demands placed on nurses, such as staffing shortages and heavier workloads. Despite these changes, my passion for nursing remains unwavering, and I am grateful for the opportunity to have made a positive impact on countless lives.

Chapter Five

Home life

I lived at 42 Wigmore Avenue, St. Anthony's Estate, Newcastle Upon Tyne. Nana lived across the road at number 53.

View from our house

At the end of our street, Walker Road, the main road into Newcastle, was bustling with activity. It was lined with various shops that catered to the needs of the local community. One of the prominent shops was the Green Grocers, where the vibrant display of fresh fruits and vegetables enticed the shoppers; their high-quality produce, was always a delight to buy. Mr Peace the Butchers had an array of high-quality meat. Mam never bought her meat from Mr Peace as she had the butcher come to the door. Nearby, the Handy Shop was a treasure trove of odds and ends, from toys to haberdashery items, screws, and nails. And then there was Mr. Goldwater's chemist shop, where he would concoct remedies for various ailments, often resulting in foul-tasting liquids with corks in the bottles.

Just around the corner was a small betting shop where Dad would put his bets on the horses on a Saturday. The shop was tiny and just consisted of a small counter with a wire mesh grill, presumably to deter thieves. The place was always full of cigarette smoke, and the punters would congregate in huddles to listen to the horse race over a small squawk box (a device that broadcasts the horse races). Dad never put his own bets on; it was either Nana or me as I got older. Next to the betting shop was the Birds Nest Club, where most of the men spent the weekends and evenings.

Every estate has notorious families, and we had several who were always in trouble and causing problems with neighbours. Along with these people, others were well known. There was one old man who went to the pub every weekend. The problem was that he lost his leg during the war and had an artificial leg. He would stagger down our road and sit on the wall opposite our house, and without fail, he would fall backwards onto the ground and could not get up, so me and Mam would go over to pick him up.

We moved back to Wigmore Avenue to a house with a large garden. Thank God we were away from those bloody flats. There was a positive outcome to this move, which was living opposite Nana. We lived in a terraced house that had six houses in the block (built around the 1920s and 1930s). There were two arches in the block, one joining our house from 42 to 40 and 44 to 46. These were like a tunnel that allowed you to walk from the front to the back of the house. They also gave access to the bin men, who took great delight in throwing the bins through the arch.

At the front of the block were two greens, that's what we called them, they were essentially two areas of grass. The green outside our house was just grass; the other one had three trees planted within it.

Bob on green

So, the green outside our house was the one of choice for playing football, and soldiers usually doing WW2 re-enactments of Germans and British. The bottom green was policed by this very miserable woman called Mrs. Burns. She would come out and chase the kids off the green, and especially if we were climbing the trees, she would come out of her house and tell us to 'bugger off' or she would threaten us with the police or telling our Dads. I had a lovely dog called Major; he was a cross Labrador with something else. He was my dog.

Bob with his dog Major

I would take him out for a walk every night with mad Stan next door who had this equally mad cross Border Collie called Glen we would walk to the park and let the dogs run around. To be fare Major and Glen got on great. After the park we would take the long way back home we would be out for 2 hours. When I joined the RAF and was coming home on leave Major would sit all day looking out of the upstairs window he knew when I was coming home, do not know how he knew. Sadly, he had to be put down as I was not there anymore to look after him. One of my cousins came to see Mam and Dad with their little girl something happened, and Major snapped at her and nipped her ear so that was his death warrant signed. I was terribly upset about this. Why did Mam not put Major in the scullery as he was not used to young children. This was a convenient way out for Mam and Dad as they could not take Major out for walks.

There were very few cars on the street, we never had a car. Our next-door neighbour had a car, Maud, and John Anderson (she was the Mrs. Bucket! of the day). John had his own furniture removal business, and his van was always parked on the street outside of their house. He had a Ford Consul with column gears, which was always a fascination when I used to go out with them. He later changed the car to an Austin A40, a green one. This was involved in an incident one Friday night. I always stayed at my Nana's house on Friday nights. She would make cocoa with hot milk and sometimes put a drop of brandy in the cocoa. We would go upstairs to bed by the light of a candle in an enamelled blue candle holder. God knows why, as she had electric, but she maintained the use of a candle. She had long grey hair, which she would brush before going upstairs. She always wore a long white cotton night dress. She had two single beds in her room, which was at the front of the house. It is only now that I am thinking back. She never had a double bed, so she never slept with my Step-grandfather. That is another story!! He worked for British Rail at weekends, so I would stay when he was at work. There was still a gas streetlamp outside Nana's house (which shone into the bedroom). I can clearly remember a man with a long pole, which he used to light the gas light. This was soon changed to an electric streetlight.

Anyway, back to the night of the incident, John, for some reason, had not parked his removal van on the street that night, just the car. Nana and I woke suddenly due to an almighty bang. We looked out of the bedroom window, and John's car had been hit by a large articulated truck and was wrapped around one of the trees on the green. The whole street was out, (it was about 1 o'clock in the morning) looking at the carnage following the crash. There was no sign of the driver of the truck. Maud called the police, as she was the only one with a phone in the block. It transpired that three drunken youths had stolen the truck, luckily, no one was hurt, but it gave everyone something to talk about for weeks to come.

Nana had to take in lodgers to make ends meet, as Geordie, as we called him, my Step Grandfather, would not give Nana enough housekeeping money, so she had up to three lodgers at a time, two in the back room and one in the other small room at the front of the house. This was where long-term lodgers slept. There were some odd characters over the years, one was Tommy Irvine, who worked as an accountant at a large department store in Byker. One evening, there was a knock on the door. Nana opened the door, and two police officers were standing on the path, asking 'if Mr Thomas Irvine lived there'. They arrested Tommy, never to be seen again. He had been embezzling the company out of thousands of pounds for years.

Nana had various lodgers with her over the years. Manfred was a lovely man. He was German and worked for a local company. He wrote me a lovely letter when Mam died, which was very nice of him given that it had been about 30 years since I last saw him. There was a long-term lodger called John O'Brien, who was a joiner who worked for Newcastle City Council. He lived with Nana for years (he even had his own chair) until he died. He was an odd character, but he was pleasant enough. He had a bag of tools he would carry on his shoulder and walk around the estates to do minor repairs to council houses.

Tommy Irvine

Money was tight in those days, and Nana had to do anything to earn a little bit extra. Her next venture was homeworking, making party items, hats, blowouts, papier mâché noses, masks, you name it, they would make it. The company was called "Banghams," and they delivered all the raw materials once a week. There were boxes of stuff, including a big tub of white liquid glue.

The pay was verging on slave labour, 35p for 144 (one gross) of any products, so you can see you had to make a lot of these items to make any substantial money. So, both Nana and Geordie would spend all day making this stuff. To be fair to them, they churned out boxes of party products. Then Mam and Dad started to make them. It did not take long for the house to be packed with boxes of crepe paper hats, which had to be made up with a silver disc glued to the front of the hat to hold it together. The worst things were these things called blowouts. They were comprised of 4 pieces, a small cardboard tube, a plastic whistle, a feather, and a strip of coloured paper about 12 inches long by 1 inch wide. There was a long wire strip running down the centre, which had to be put through a machine to bend the wire, causing the strip to curl up. In one end, a cardboard tube was glued, followed by the plastic whistle, which was glued onto the cardboard tube, and at the other end, a feather was glued, so when you blew the whistle, the blowout would uncurl, causing a whistling noise, and the feather would pop out the end of the blowout. It did not take long for the house to be completely taken over by the party products feathers and glue everywhere.

Dad stopped work at the age of forty-six due to a back injury he sustained in the shipyards (this would dominate all our lives until my Mother died). He was an electric welder, which caused him numerous health issues, including chronic chest disease besides the back problem. This meant the only income was Dad's sick pay, known as "Giros", which came once a week and had to be cashed at the local Post Office. Mam would never go out anywhere (though strangely, I was taken to see the Beatles film A Hard Day's Night at the Newcastle Odeon in 1964). Something happened to her when she was younger, she witnessed an accident while on a bus, which seemed to be the root cause of her phobias or fear of going out. This was problematic as when we needed new clothes, she was not able to take us out to get them, however, she found a workaround that suited her, she would have the shops come to her.

There was a man with a van who would come to the house called "Powell's" who had all the clothes that we would need, shoes, shirts, and socks. He had the lot, and she paid him weekly in those days, this was called "tick". The other thing she would do would be to buy Provident Cheques, which again were paid weekly, which I could take to the shops to buy my own clothes, this was mainly when I was older. She managed to live quite simply by everyone coming to her, the butcher would come once a week. I remember him being a small man with a pointed nose, and he smelled of dried blood. She bought this ghastly "butcher's sausage", which was bright red and full of offal and fat. We would live off mince and dumplings, liver, and sausage, apart from Sundays. The Ringtons Tea man would deliver the tea sorted!

On Sundays, we always had brisket. Dad would cook Sunday dinner, which started the night before preparing the mushy peas, which we had every Sunday. Mam bought dried peas, which had to be soaked overnight using a sodium bicarbonate dissolving tablet. In the morning, the peas would have expanded to twice their size, they were brought to a boil and simmered till they went mushy! Dad made Yorkshire puddings and roast potatoes; he was a very good cook. During his national service, he was a cook first class with the RAF in India, where he did his national service.

Dad doing his National Service in India

He wanted to carry this one when he came back, but his father made him go back to the shipyards with him to finish his apprenticeship.

Dads Certificate of Apprenticeship 1945

What a waste, but this was how things were at the time, sons would not argue with their parents.

Dad would sometimes make broth using ham, split peas, onions, and carrots. It was nice. We did live in a straightforward way due to the lack of money, but we never went without food. Nana would also bring over food, she made this cracking beef mince pie it was moreish. Mam had her hair done by Carol, who would come to the house to do this, so again, she managed to get things done without going out.

I would do the shopping with a friend called Esme. She was a SEN who worked as a District Nurse. She would pop in every day for a cup of tea and a cigarette. We all smoked in those days, me included. Esme smoked Sovereign Mam smoked Embassy I smoked anything I could get my hands on. This was the mid-sixties, my sister was born in 1964, so I was 11 years old, so I had to grow up very quickly to support Mam and the house. This was the time when the first supermarkets were opening. The first one was called Fine Fare. Mam would give me a shopping list, and Esme and I would go shopping as she had the car.

When Dad was working, he would get up for work at about 6 a.m. and have the same routine every morning, a strip wash and shave in the kitchen sink, always in his vest. He would make a bacon sandwich for his breakfast, he would cut off a small piece to eat, then wrap the rest in a waxed bread wrapper for his bait (northern for food) at work. He would then make a flask of tea. Mam would still be in bed. He would cycle to work, in the Summer months, I would get up with him and have a ride on his bike before he went to work, as I did not have a bike. It is funny the things you do, which at the time seemed perfectly normal but today would seem weird. Looking back on this time, I was yearning for a bike of my own, but Mam and Dad could not afford to buy me one. I did eventually get my own bike, as Nana bought me one. It was a Hercules

Bike top-notch, as I had a paper round in the mornings (I would be up at 06:00 to deliver the papers before school) and evenings, so I needed a bike. I was saving up to buy a greenhouse. I know it may seem an odd thing to do at 14 years old, but this was my passion for gardening and growing stuff and still is.

Once I had my bike, it gave me the freedom to go out with my friends during the summer holidays. We would be out all day on our bikes, only returning home around teatime when we were hungry. To be fair, the roads were quiet, unlike today. We used to cycle miles up the coast road and through the old Tyne Tunnel.

Dad with Bob in his greenhouse

Mam would get up shortly after Dad had left for work to get breakfast for me and my brother, then off to school. School was just a short walk from our house, so we could walk to school ourselves regardless of the weather, hail, rain, snow, or sunshine. The schools never closed due to inclement weather.

Our house had a scullery rather than a kitchen, as up North, things are called something different. The kitchen was the lounge or sitting room. There was still a black range in the scullery, which backed onto the open fire in the kitchen. There was a Belfast sink, a wooden drainage board, some cupboards, and not much else. Mam used the gas oven as a source of heat in the winter months. She would light the oven and leave the door open so the heat would come into the room.

Breakfast was always bacon and eggs, and if me and my brother started to argue, Mam would slap us with the fish slice. We would get dressed first, then have a wash due to the cold. We would have a bath once a week on Sundays, using the same bath water. We all sat in the kitchen together to eat (we did not have a table, so we used the stools from the scullery to eat off) and watched television. I suppose, looking back, there was more family time together than there is today.

Our bedrooms were freezing in the winter, and the windows were covered in ice with the net curtains sticking to the glass. The only heating we had was paraffin heaters, which smelled and caused a lot of condensation. The smell of paraffin would emanate throughout the house during the winter months, as this was the only form of heating that we had apart from the coal fire in the kitchen. There were two types of paraffin in the 1960s, Esso Blue and Aladdin Pink Paraffin. Dad would buy the pink paraffin, which was delivered to the door. He had a 5-gallon drum that would be filled up from the van. The paraffin was kept in the shed, and then he would decant the paraffin into a smaller container that would fill up the heaters. We had various types of paraffin heaters over the years, and Dad would carefully look after them, including the wicks, which he cleaned regularly with his wick cleaner.

Then, in the 1970s, the council started a modernisation programme that would put an end to cold bedrooms, coal fires, and the dreaded paraffin. The downside to this was that we had to lose the small bedroom (it was lucky that me and my brother were leaving home), which would become the bathroom, and the downstairs bathroom was knocked out to make a larger scullery (kitchen). Then we had the luxury of a gas fire (with North Sea gas) and marvellous central heating. Dad was a stickler for turning off the lights if there was no one in the room. This is a trait that has rubbed off on me. I go around turning off the lights.

What I need to uncover is how my Mother went from a confident, good-looking Nursery Nurse to a lifelong recluse who died very young, at 66 years old, of aortic stenosis

Mam as Nursey Nurse

She spent years frightened to go out of the house and would not travel on a bus. The only two times she left Newcastle was when Mam and Dad were invited to a Royal Garden Party at Buckingham Palace (they set up a local disabled group and were nominated by the local councillor to attend the garden party) and when her first Grandson Andrew was born, at the time we lived in Lincoln. They managed to get the train to Lincoln, which was not an easy journey as there was a change at Newark, which was a cold, desolate station. Apart from these two occasions, she never left Newcastle again. She became a prisoner in her house,

Mam and Dad at Royal Garden Party

which worsened after my Dad had his first heart attack. She was terrified to leave him alone in case he died.

Mam and Dad had 4 Grandchildren and 4 Great-Grandchildren, sadly, only Dad saw Joe his (now 25 years old) Great-Grandson just before he died. Andrew (Grandson) took Joe to see Dad in the hospital, which was a lovely thought. Mam never saw Joe.

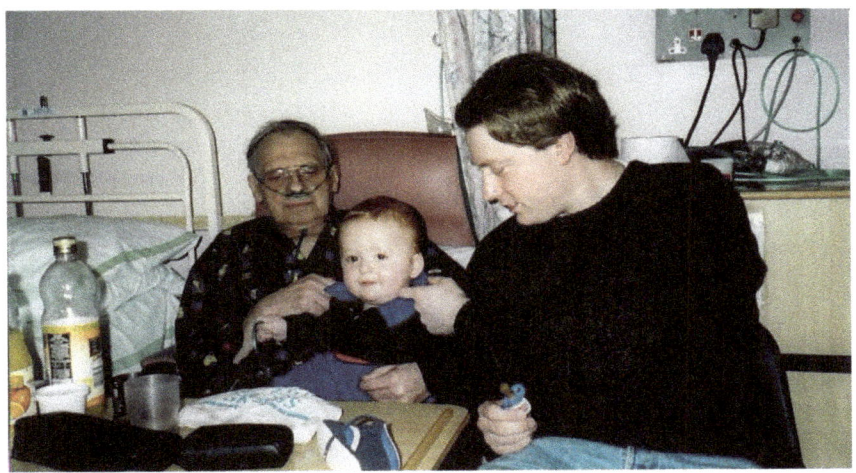

Dad with Andrew and Joe just before Dad died

Mam lived in constant fear that Dad would die before her, as she would never have coped without him. Ironically, she died suddenly before Dad on the 13th of December 1998. I spoke to her on the 12th of December 1998, which was a Saturday evening. She was in bed with various problems; she had aches and pains due to a broken ankle (some 10 years ago), which became a major issue over many years. I told her that 'she must get up as people die in bed'. She died that night in her sleep.

To fully understand the issues, it is important to look at the history of my mother. When Andrew was a baby, we were posted to RAF Lyneham in Wiltshire from RAF Hospital Nocton Hall in Lincoln. Unfortunately, there were no married quarters available at RAF Lyneham, so Mary and

Andrew went up to Newcastle to stay while a married quarter became available. Unfortunately, this did not go well. After a while, there were tensions, as Andrew did not sleep well and was awake a lot at night. There was also the question of money, as Mam was asking for money to support Mary and Andrew. I did send up money regularly, but it became a big issue and not enough. What finally happened was that Mam opened a letter that I had sent to Mary, which resulted in a breakdown of our relationship for a couple of years.

When Mary and Andrew came home to RAF Lyneham, Mam was washing the bed sheets that they had used. She tripped, going down the back steps while hanging out the washing, which resulted in her breaking her ankle. She was in plaster for months until the fracture was healed. The "ankle" became the focus of her life, which she used as a weapon for years, which again caused tensions. Sadly, the ankle caused her demise, as she was always complaining of pain, and whenever she saw the GP, it was the ankle that she focused on. She did not tell the GP that she was getting increasingly short of breath and started using Dad's inhalers, which did not help with the problem as the issue was with her heart, not her lungs. After she died, I saw a photo of her, and she looked ghastly.

No one else recognised how ill she was, as she was always crying wolf. The other issue was that she was terrified of hospitals, which caused her much distress. I never got to the bottom of this phobia.

FROM BOILER SUIT TO BLUE SUIT

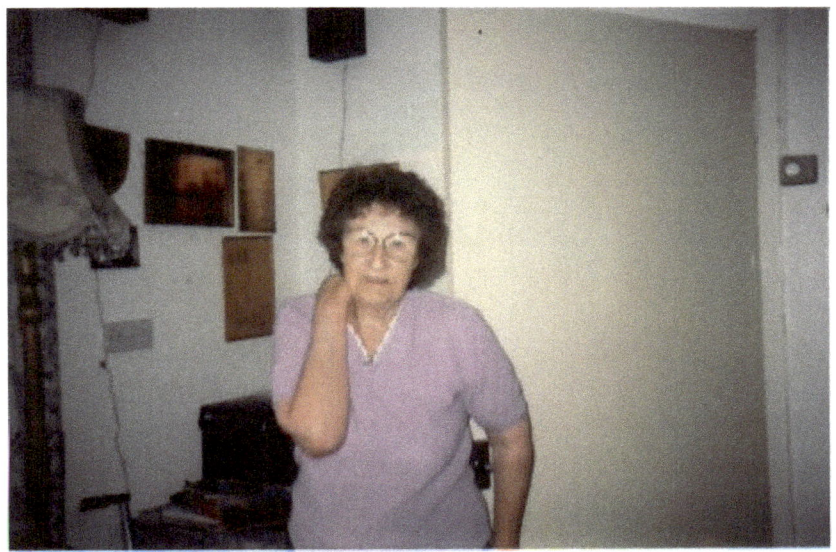

Mam looking ill 1998

Chapter Six

MAM

I was very close to my Mother when I was young. I would keep her company on Friday, Saturday, and Sunday nights when my Dad was out at the Buffs Club. Mam and I would watch TV and play cribbage. I was very good at it in the end. It was obvious Mam was lonely and needed company, but this should not have been put on my shoulders, as it was not fair and I felt I had no choice, so I did not go out much with people of my age. Mam also loved Christmas, and we would put up lots of decorations. She would buy crepe paper of different colours, then we would cut about a 4-inch-wide portion from different coloured crepe paper, then we would put small cuts along the two long sides of the crepe paper, join two different colours together, pin one the end to the corner of the ceiling using a drawing pin, then twist. This would make a lovely crepe paper streamer, and we would repeat this all around the room. Balloons in each corner of the room would finish the ceiling decorations. We had the same Christmas tree for years, but every year the lights would not work, so I had to go and get replacement bulbs from Woolworths (remember them) as they were just screwed into the bulb holder. Mam and I would make sausage rolls and mince pies on Christmas Eve. Our presents were never wrapped in Christmas paper, we had stockings, and we always had a tangerine, apple, nuts, and chocolate in the stocking. Our main presents were left at the end of our beds. We had Christmas dinner at Nana's house every year, as she cooked a great feast. Dad's brother, Uncle Alan, would often spend Christmas Day with us.

He was part of a pop group called the Gamblers; they were formed in 1959. Uncle Alan played the bass guitar. The Gamblers did a lot of local gigs around the Northeast. Uncle Alan always tells the story that they were playing at the Majestic Ballroom on Westgate Road Newcastle in 1963, and the Beatles were playing their first live show in Newcastle. So, the story goes, Uncle Alan lent John Lennon his winkle picker boots, as John Lennon had a hole in the sole of his boots.

Unce Alan

The Gamblers were one of the most popular groups in Newcastle in the early 1960s. They played a residency at the Majestic Ballroom on Westgate Road from 1961 to 1963, and they also toured extensively throughout the UK. The group released several singles, but they never achieved national success. They became Billy Fury's backing group and made a film called I've Got a Horse. The Gamblers' sound was influenced by a variety of genres, including rock and roll, rhythm and blues, and soul. They were also known for their flamboyant stage shows. The Gamblers never made the big time, so they spent a lot of time in Germany and playing around Europe. They released several singles on the DECCA record label. The only song to make the charts was You've Really Got a Hold on Me. So how cool was this having an uncle as a pop star? Unfortunately, Uncle Alan died at the young age of 53.

poster promoting the Gamblers

Record sleeve cover with Uncle Alan

Do you remember my schoolteacher, Jenny Collins? She eventually left school teaching and got a job on the Hughie Greens quiz show Double Your Money (1955 to 1968) as a researcher for setting the questions. She was quite good at promoting the Gamblers when she could. I remember one contestant losing £1000 because he did not know who Billy Fury's backing group was!

When I reached 18, I went with Dad a couple of times to the Buffs Club. It was dire to start with; there was a 40-minute bus ride to the club. The exterior was drab, with just a door and a sign over the door with RAOB, which means the Royal Antediluvian Order of Buffalos

Bob's 18th birthday

(RAOB), which was one of the largest fraternal organisations of the late 19th century. The order started in 1882 and is still known as the "Buffs" to its members. I remember Dad having a lapel pin that indicated that he was a member. Anyway, going back to the club, when you walked into the club, the doorman was generally a member who would check your membership card. If you did not have one, you had to be signed in by a member.

Dad would sign me in as a guest (I never wanted to join), and then you went into this large, smoke-filled room, as in those days, most people smoked, including me. Dad would only smoke if he was having a drink, so he only smoked on Friday, Saturday, and Sunday. There was a blue haze filling the room with the smell of stale beer. Virtually all those in the room were men, hence the name Working Men's Club. There were a variety of age groups, but the vast majority were older men (50+). Most wore flat caps. Dad would always wear his jacket and trousers with a shirt and tie and his overcoat, and then he had a trilby hat. To be fair to him, he always looked very smart when he went out.

What I could not understand was why the men would sit in huddles at tables just drinking this awful beer called Federation Ale, which was brewed locally by Northern Clubs Federation Brewery Ltd. I could not get on with beer when I was young; it made me feel nauseous and bloated, but you had no choice but to drink this stuff if you were in the club. The only entertainment, if you can call it entertainment, was cribbage or dominoes; they would sit for hours playing these games. On Saturdays, there were what were known as "turns." These were generally singers or comedians. Then there was the lottery, which you had to enter. I hated every minute of this (the square peg in the round hole was present again). I looked at these men, many of whom were working in shipyards or coal mines, and I thought again, Is this it? It looked to me like, if you stayed in this culture, you would end up like the rest of them, sitting in a smoke-filled room drinking and playing dominoes. Conversation was very limited as well, mainly around football and Newcastle United Football Club. I knew I had to take drastic action. Otherwise, I feel I would have significant mental health issues, as I was predisposed to mental health problems, which lured its ugly head some years later. The vision in my head was that working in a factory all day and then ending up like the numerous old men was not a situation I was willing to do, so I made my decision to join the RAF to enable me to train as a nurse.

My Mother would struggle for the remaining years of her life with both me and my Brother leaving home, she did not see the positive aspects of trying to better ourselves. It was just after we left home that she started losing a lot of weight, she looked ghastly, as though she had cancer. Thankfully, it turned out to be an overactive thyroid gland, which was easily treatable with tablets. Unfortunately, my mother revelled in this, as she had something wrong with her, and she focused every aspect of her life on this illness and other medical problems.

I think this was partially due to my Dad not being a good health for many years. He had suffered for years with lower back pain, which eventually stopped him from working. He was signed off as permanently sick by his GP. The GP was called Dr Pearson, he was an old-fashioned GP, his background was being a doctor in the mines, and he understood the working class. If he was passing the house, he would pop in for a chat to see how things were going and have a cup of tea with Mam and Dad. I think he knew that my mother was a complex person. He used to call Dad Willie; he was a very caring GP. However, with the benefit of hindsight, some of the drugs that were prescribed in the late 1960s and early 1970s would be questionable now.

Dad was on diazepam (Valium) as well as sleeping tablets called Mandrax (the drug was withdrawn in the 1980s) as they were powerful sedatives and hypnotics. Mandrax was mainly used for insomnia but became a recreational drug in the 1970s. I suppose, at the time, it was not known about the long-term consequences of such drugs. Today, there are still people addicted to Valium, as it was widely used for the treatment of anxiety, mainly in women.

Chapter Seven

VERA

Talking about Mandrax reminds me of our next-door neighbours, who were an odd lot. Stan and Vera, Stan had a personality disorder, but Stan denied this. It was only when he told me what tablets he was taking (Nardil) that I looked them up and found out what they were used for. He used to tell everyone they were heart tablets, but they were antidepressants. Again, looking back, it explained a lot about his behaviour, he could fly off the handle at the slightest thing. They had two young boys and a mad dog. His wife, Vera, was lovely but had to put up with a lot with Stan.

Vera worked as a cleaner at Boots the Chemist in Newcastle City Centre. She would start around 05:00, so there was nobody else there (this is relevant as we go on). In the summer months, she would sit on the back doorstep. Each house had three large steps up to the house, so they were ideal to sit on, especially in the summer months as the backs of the houses were south facing, so they got the sun all day.

Going back to Vera, as a way of coping with Stan, she would sit on the back step drinking Whiskey Mac, which was a cheap drink consisting of whiskey and ginger wine. You could buy this from the local off-licence, these were the days before supermarkets sold alcohol. There was an off-license called the Wine Bin next to the Gloria Bingo Hall (which used to be a cinema but closed when bingo was all the rage). This is where she bought her drink.

Returning to poor Vera, she was constantly pissed in the summer months. She would sit on the back step when she returned from work around 9 a.m. until about midday drinking, then one day, she confessed to my mother that she was taking tablets from boots called Mandrax. So, she was taking Mandrax and drinking alcohol, a lethal combination. When I came home on leave, she told me that she was helping herself to Mandrax from Boots while she was cleaning (I tried to advise her that this was not a good idea). At the time, all tablets were loose, unlike today, where they are in blister packs. It amazed me that she was never caught. It was quite sad to see her sitting on the back step in a state of drunken and drug-induced stupor, as this was the only way she could cope with life and Stan. She did stop doing this when Stan died!

Chapter Eight
Maud & Other Things

The other side of us at number 40 was Maud and John. Maud was the Mrs. Bucket of those days. John had been a prisoner of war with the Japanese. He was very thin and always looked ill. He had a skull-like head with the skin being very taut, so all his bone structures were very pronounced, and his eyes were protruding. He had his own furniture removal firm, and the van was always parked on the road in front of the houses along with his car. They were the only ones with a car and a telephone. The house was spotless. Maud worked in a large department store in Newcastle, selling freezers, which were just becoming more accessible. Maud had a large chest freezer!

She had two sons, John and David, John was in the RAF, and David was the same age as me. We both went to the same school and were friends of sorts, falling out and then making up again as boys do.

Next to Maud at number 38 was Billy and Sarah Swann they were a young couple and were very pleasant. I became a good friend of Billy and Sarah would come around to our house on a Friday night. Billy unfortunately had seizures, which could happen at any time. Sarah and Billy had two daughters, Sharon and Lynn. We had some great fun in the summer months with hosepipes having water fights

Maud left Sarah middle Mam right

Billy left John middle Dad right

Next to Stan and Vera at number 46 was Mrs. Churnside. She was small and thin with a wrinkled face, and her hair was always tied back in a bun. She could walk very fast but was a busybody, always gossiping. She used to help lay people out who had died at home. She lived with her daughter Annie, her husband, and their daughter Susan. Annie was a small woman as well. Mrs. Churnside and Annie always wore a wraparound apron, they never took them off. I assume they washed them. Annie was quiet and did not engage in chatting.

We had quite big back gardens, most of us had a lawn of some description. Annie's lawn stretched the whole length of the back garden. She used to cut the grass with a pair of shears. She did not have a lawn mower; it would take her hours to do this.

Next to Mrs Churnside was Mr and Mrs Petch, I never knew their first names. Those days, you showed respect for older people, as you would get a slap from your Father if you were disrespectful or cheeky. Mr Petch was a Sergeant Major in the army during the war. He was a tall, well-built man, his shoulders pulled back straight, and he would always wear a white vest while in the garden. When they went out, they were always very smartly dressed. All the front gardens had privet hedges, which were always kept smartly cut using a pair of shears. Most people took pride in how their front gardens looked.

Our house was always a mess, it resembled a scene from "The Royal Family," which was a TV show which ran from 1998 to 2000. There was clutter everywhere; if there was a space, something was put there. The scullery was the worst place, it drove me mad, as nothing was put away. The scullery was a small room with an old black range on one wall, which backed onto the fire in the kitchen (remember, the kitchen is a sitting room). This took up a large amount of room for no purpose, as we had a gas cooker on the opposite wall and a Belfast sink with a wooden draining board. Completing the amenities was a small drop-leaf red Formica table placed next to the old range. In the winter months, it was bloody freezing as we had no central heating, so Mam would light the gas oven and leave the door open to heat the scullery. When we were all in there, you could not swing a cat. The gas was paid for by putting a shilling in the gas meter (5p in new money). The gas meter was hidden away under the stairs, so I had to get down to feed the meter with shillings. There was a Morphy Richards fridge and a Hoover Twin Tub washing machine squashed into the scullery as well. Unlike today, washing was done on a set day, generally Mondays, washday was a state of chaos, with dirty clothes all over the floor. Then, when the weather allowed, the washing was hung on the washing line, which stretched the whole length of the garden. In the winter and rainy days, the washing was hung on something we called a "pulley," which essentially was a set of wooden slats fitted on either end through a cast iron holder. This was attached to the scullery ceiling and could be pulled up and down by a set of pulleys, hence the name "pulley." No tumble dryers those days!

Eventually, in 1970, the houses were modernised. Out went the coal fires, and in came North Sea Gas with central heating and a gas fire in the kitchen. The scullery was enlarged by moving the downstairs bathroom to the small bedroom, so we gained a larger scullery at the expense of a third bedroom. The larger kitchen made little difference to how tidy it was kept, just a larger space to keep junk and clutter. The scullery was never tidy. I would do the dishes and bleach the new white Formica worktops to keep them clean, as I was sick of the mess. I suppose it was lucky that my brother David and I joined up, as it would have been difficult to stay in a two-bedroom house with my sister and us two.

I received my joining instructions in May 1972. I had to attend the RAF Careers office on the 4th of June 1972 to be attested into the RAF and to swear allegiance to Her Majesty the Queen. This was the day I joined the RAF. As part of the administration process, you had to sign the Official Secrets Act, at the time, you didn't fully understand the full implications of signing this Act. It is only later that the true magnitude is understood. The day finally came for me to leave home; this was the 5th of June 1972. I was to get to RAF Halton near Aylesbury, so I had to navigate London again. My mother could not bring herself to come to the station to see me off. She had not fully come to terms with me leaving home, as had my brother, who left home some three months before me. He was 15 years old when he joined the Navy. To be honest, it was the best thing he could have done, as he was a bit wayward and needed some structure and discipline in his life. Mam struggled with the two of us leaving home. If she had embraced this and taken a more positive approach, I am certain future events would not have occurred. Dad came with me to the station to see me off. As I remember, the parting was a handshake, no hugs those days, not in our family (something I would change with my children), and my next stop would be Kings Cross Station. Once I arrived at Kings Cross, I had to get to Marylebone Station, then take a train to Wendover. Eventually, I arrived at Wendover Station, which was a small station. On the platform were other people who were joining the RAF. What I did not know at that time was that all the other people were joining to train as nurses on course 53 State Enrolled Nursing course. A bus arrived, and a corporal jumped out of the cab and started to yell orders to get on the bus. I was not sure what I expected, but we all managed to get onto the bus. When we eventually arrived at RAF Halton, the men were ordered off, there were six of us. The girls were whisked away. Waiting for us was a small, rotund Corporal with a Welsh accent who was quite friendly. He took us to a large room full of beds, a wardrobe, and a locker. I had a small case with me, as I did not have many clothes, some toiletries, and towels—not much more. We chose a bed, dropped off our cases, and then went to get some bedding. We were given a bedding pack that consisted of two pillows, two pillowcases, two sheets, three blankets, and a counterpane.

Chapter Nine

DEATH

Mam lived in constant fear that Dad would die before her, as she would never have coped without him. Ironically, she died suddenly before Dad on the 13th of December 1998. I spoke to her on the 12th of December, which was a Saturday evening. She was in bed with various problems, she had aches and pains due to a broken ankle (some 10 years before), which became a major issue over many years. I told said to her 'that she must get up as people die in bed.' She died that night in her sleep.

Mam's death took me a long time to get over. Julie called me on Sunday morning to tell me that she had died. The police had to be called as it was a sudden death, and Mam would need a postmortem. To this day, I do not remember the car journey from Swindon to Seaton Delaval, North Tyneside. When I arrived, Dad was sitting in his chair, just staring into the room. He was still in shock. He had tried to wake Mam up, but when he could not rouse her, he called Julie, who at the time was doing her nurse training, so quickly worked out that Mam had died. The postmortem was done on Monday; she died of heart failure due to aortic stenosis (narrowing of the aorta due to calcium buildup). This meant we could get the death certificate.

It is funny what you remember, the day we went to register Mam's death was very strange. Julie and I went to the register office and were told that they had not received the coroner's report, so we had to walk about half a mile to the coroner's office to collect the report, then race back to register the death. We both felt that we were in a bubble, our only focus was to get the death registered. To us, the rest of the world was a blur.

It was the lead-up to Christmas, and everyone else was running about doing their Christmas shopping. All we could think of was getting back to the register office before it closed. When we arrived, the registrar was sitting behind a large wooden desk. There was a wicker basket on the side of the desk with a flowered plastic cover, it looked like she was ready to go.

She was wearing a tweed two-piece suit and was very prim and proper. We handed her the coroner's report, and she produced a fountain pen from her top pocket and started to write the death certificate, which seemed to take forever, almost like slow motion. Both Julie and I were very stressed at this point, so much so that I got Mam's birthday wrong. She was born on the 7th of April 1931. I told her it was 1932!

Mam's Death Certificate 1998

We left the register office gagging for a cup of tea, so we walked back up Blyth High Street to a large Coop store that had a café. Outside the main doors were two inflatable Father Christmases that were bobbing around in the wind, we wanted to punch them. It was very cold, so a warm drink was needed. It seemed unfair that everyone was preparing for Christmas, and here we were preparing to arrange a funeral for Mam.

We met the undertaker on Monday evening. Now that we had the death certificate, we could arrange the funeral, we were lucky as there was a space on Thursday. On Tuesday, we all went to see Mam at the Undertakers. I was not looking forward to this, but it had to be done for closure (I did not see Nana due to a bad experience when I was 15), so I was filled with trepidation and fear. When we arrived, we were shown to the Chapel of Rest, which was very quiet and serene. The coffin was in the centre of the room. I approached the coffin with a feeling of foreboding, as I was not sure what Mam would look like. I need not have worried the undertaker had done a good job. Mam looked at peace and looked like her old self; she was wearing her green silk blouse, and her hair and makeup were done to perfection. It was difficult, as this was the start of the process of saying goodbye. Mam and Dad were not particularly religious, but Dad wanted Mam to have a religious funeral. The Vicar came by on Tuesday, and we gave him a potted history of Mam's life. Dad wanted Abide with Me as the hymn. Mam was to be cremated. On the day of the funeral, it was very difficult for all of us. Dad was very distressed and needed to be supported while in the car. The service was appropriate, and the Vicar had captured Mam's life very well. The worst part of cremation is when the coffin disappears behind the curtains, as this is the final act of the person's life, now gone forever.

Up north, it was common to return to the deceased's house for a cup of tea and something to eat and remember the deceased. I can't remember having a wake as such, as is common practice today. As people drifted away, only the close family were left to grieve. Dad suddenly looked older. I had to get Mary, Andrew, and Matthew back to Swindon, and I had to get back to work. Before leaving, Dad, Julie, David (brother), and I asked the undertaker if he could split Mam's ashes into 4 caskets, as I needed a piece of her with me. It sounded like an unorthodox request, but the undertaker did a great job of getting four small caskets with a brass plate on top with Mam's details on them.

Mam's ashes

The ashes were placed on a shelf in my lounge and left there, as I was not in a good place to deal with them. It became obvious that I needed bereavement counselling as I was not coping; my emotions were all over the place, and I could not speak to my sister Julie without bursting into tears. Fortunately, the NHS Trust I worked for had access to staff support and provided six sessions of counselling. I contacted the service and booked an appointment. The first session was more of a triage service to establish the issues and then match you with the best counsellor. I remember that I spent most of this session in tears and became very distressed just talking about Mam.

I was sent an appointment for my first session, which I was dreading as I knew that it would be painful and difficult as I would have to open Pandora's Box and go into dark places. As I had anticipated, it was a very difficult hour. I spent most of the session crying and distressed, but as the saying goes, there is no gain without pain.

Over the subsequent 6 weeks, I was beginning to come to terms with Mam's death, and by the last session, I was able to talk without tears or distress.

Unfortunately, Dad died 3 months after Mam, which just compounded my grief, but it was different as I had been to see him in the hospital. He seemed resigned to his fate, and I think, to be honest, he had enough and wanted an end to his misery and pain. He missed Mam and never got over her death. While I was visiting him, he said a very odd thing. Several years before, Dad bought a large stamp collection from a guy who needed quick money. Dad never did anything with them but kept them in boxes and albums. He said to me and Julie, 'I don't want Charlie Ackers to get the stamps.' He was referring to David, our Brother. He said, 'I want Andrew to have them' (his Grandson). I put the stamps in the boot of my car for safekeeping.

Just as well as I did when David arrived with his wife and two daughters, they were ransacking Mam and Dad's bungalow looking for something, you guessed it, the stamps and a bottle of beer. The other thing that Dad had was a bottle of Task Force Special Ale, which was brewed by the Scottish and Newcastle Breweries for the troops returning from the Falklands War in 1982.

I managed to get hold of two bottles and gave Dad one. I felt that as I had given this to Dad, I should take it back, which I did, and I have this sitting alongside my bottle in my cabinet. David was looking for the bottle of beer but never found it. Apart from the stamps and the Task Force Special Ale, the only other thing I wanted was a

Task Force Special Ale 1992

video of the Titanic film that I had bought for Mam for Christmas, which she never got to see. One of David's daughters had a black plastic bag full of stuff. I asked her 'if she had the video'? She said 'no'. I did not believe her, so I took the bag and emptied it on the floor, and guess what? There it was. Why lie? I retrieved the video and put it in the car. David found a small box of stamps in the airing cupboard and thought he had found the "stamp collection," which he had not as they were in my car.

Again, Julie and I had to sort out all the arrangements, and David, our brother, did not come up till the day before the funeral. This was a less stressful experience than Mam's death, as Dad died peacefully of natural causes with Julie by his side. There was no postmortem to worry about, the death registration was straightforward, and I got his birthday correct.

We used the same undertaker as with Mam and requested that his ashes be split three ways this time.

Dad's Ashes 1999

Again, we would be coming back to the house for a cup of tea. This is where I fell out with Uncle Fred and Aunty Muriel, as they often did not come back to the house (I always felt this was disrespectful), so I said to Uncle Fred on the morning of the funeral, 'I want you to come back to

the house. If Muriel does not want to come back, then we are finished'
Looking back, I was very stressed, and on reflection, I could have handled this better.

When I first joined the RAF in 1972, I bought a made-to-measure 3-piece brown suit. Over the years, Dad would badger me to give him the suit, which I eventually did, and he would be cremated wearing this suit. When we went to visit him in the chapel of rest, he looked peaceful and very smart in my old suit, so he got his wish.

Mam and Dad had very little in the way of belongings or cash assets; they lived in a council bungalow. They had very little money, but Dad was a proud man and had saved up enough money to pay for the funeral. With a small amount left over of £1000, I said to David and Julie, 'Julie should have the money as she was a single mother, and David and I did not need the money'. This did not go down well with David. The following day, David and his family left. We had a very acrimonious parting, and we did not speak for many years.

I stayed with Julie for another week as we had to sort out the bungalow. This was done with the help of a friend of Julie's called Tony; he was great and helped us clear the bungalow. Julie and I spent hours talking and reminiscing about Mam and Dad. She also disclosed to me very personal things that had happened to her, which I can't write about, but suffice to say this was the first time she had told anyone about her past experiences. I was glad she was able to tell me.

Mam and Dad's ashes sat on my shelf for nine months, then one afternoon on my day off, I was in the house by myself, and it felt

Remembrance Rose

like the right time to deal with the ashes. I popped over to the local garden centre and bought a rose bush called "Remembrance." I had a space in my existing rose bed for it. I dug a hole, placed Mam and Dad's ashes at the bottom of the hole, and planted the rose bush. This was the final act of saying goodbye, which gave me closure. The rose is pink-white, and it has blossomed every year since planting in 2000.

When your parents die so suddenly, it leaves a yawning gap in your life as the sudden realisation that I am now "it." I am at the top of the next generation, and as such, you start to think about your own mortality. I know this sounds completely irrational, but after losing both parents so quickly, I did not have time to adjust and process this rationally. It has been 25 years since Mam died and 24 years since Dad died, but it does feel like yesterday. Mary and I always buy flowers for their birthdays and Mother's and Father's Day, they are never forgotten.

Chapter Ten

NANA

Nana, as she was known, played a big part in my life. She was a great cook; she could cook anything, but the wartime mentality was always there in her behaviour; she never wasted anything (a trait that I have inherited).

She used to have lots of small cups scattered around the scullery with used fat. She would drain off any used fat into cups, and when it cooled, it would become hard fat, which she would reuse for cooking

She still had a copper boiler to do the washing in, this was a large copper bucket with a gas ring underneath. The copper would be filled with water, and then a large gas ring would be lit underneath the copper to boil the water. The washing would be done with various whitening

Nana in her Scullery

products, and something called a blue bag would be added to whiten the clothes. When the washing was boiling, she would use a washing dolly. This was used to agitate the clothes with a copper head with holes around the rim, which was attached to a wooden handle. The clothes were rinsed then put through a mangle or wringer; this was done by hand. The washing was fed between two rollers, and a handle would be turned to squeeze out the water from the washing. Monday was "wash day." I'm not sure why Monday is probably historical.

All I can remember is that it was utter carnage until it was all done, when all aspects of washing were done by hand and there were no tumble dryers either. The washing was hung on a clothesline that was attached to the back wall of the house and went the length of the garden before being attached to a pole. There was a prop, which was a length of timber with a V shape cut out of one end. This was used to prop up the clothesline so the wind could blow through the washing. If it was raining or in the winter, the washing had to be dried in the house on a contraption called a pulley Nana had one as well. This was a clothes airer suspended from the scullery ceiling. There were long wooden slats with a cast iron holder at each end. This was then held up by a rope tied to a cleat attached to the wall. This could then be lowered and heightened as needed. This contraption dates to the Victorian era.

In my Nana's front room, there was a cream-tiled fireplace and a range oven built into the fireplace, which was heated by coal. At Christmas, she would always cook the turkey in this oven, even though she had a gas oven. The turkey was always cooked to perfection and was the highlight of the year. Nana had a spooky ability for reading tea leaves that were left in your cup. She would hold readings on various days (she had to be in the mood) she would read several people's tea leaves at a time. There was a ritual that had to be done after you had finished your tea. You had to leave a small amount of tea at the bottom of the cup, then you had to swish the cup around 3 to 4 times, then turn the cup over face down on the saucer. She would then pick up the cup and start your reading. To this day, I do not know how she did it, but she was not often wrong in her predictions. I always had my cup read when I came home on leave. I can't read leaves, but I know when things are going to happen, it's like a sixth sense. I am not often wrong. The other thing Nana used to do was make tea wine. It was potent, and after a couple of glasses, you would be pissed.

As we moved into the 1960s, both Mam and Nana bought a Hoover Matic twin-tub washing machine, which consisted of a washing machine and a spin dryer sitting side by side. You had to connect hose pipes to the taps to fill the washing machine and to rinse the clothes when spinning. There was an outlet hose that went into the sink to drain the washing machine and when spinning the washing. This was revolutionary for washing clothes. The machine was basic, just as well as the pumps broke down on a regular basis. Luckily, I was able to learn how to replace them at a low cost. I was always good at repairing things and kept the washing machines going for years.

Uncle Fred (remember him? half-uncle, really) was in the Royal Air Force as an engineer. He would come home on leave and stay with Nana across the road. He had a 3-wheeler, a Robin Reliant, with which he would take me and my Brother David to the seaside. Whitley Bay and Tynemouth were only a few miles away. This was the highlight of the year for us, as we never went anywhere. It was great to get out somewhere different. Fred also used to take me to the pictures (cinema) on a Saturday morning at the Tatler Picture House (cinema) in Newcastle. He liked to watch the cartoons, mainly Tom and Jerry. I think he used me as an excuse so he could go see the cartoons. After the show, he would take me to a little café, and we would have shrimps in vinegar with salt and pepper. This was a great treat. Sadly, in later life, our relationship broke down due to his wife, Muriel, who was very judgmental and nasty. He married her in the 60s, and I would go and see them in their flat. This was quite a long bus journey from where I lived, they lived in the west end of Newcastle. I lived in the East End, and the only bus was number 34, which dropped me off a short walk away. I got along with Fred very well, and I think Muriel just tolerated me.

Fred and Muriel would visit Nana once a week, they would drop in and would never have a cup of tea at Nana's house. Muriel would not drink out of Nana's cups. This really annoyed me, as it was very disrespectful. What really started the decline was when Nana died in 1996. I had just left the RAF in June 1996, and she died in July 1996 at Morpeth Cottage Hospital. Nana lived in Monkchester Green, which was the forerunner of sheltered housing. It was basically one-bedroom terraced bungalows built in a quadrangle with support from an on-call response service. At the time, just before she became ill, Mam and Dad had moved to Seaton Delaval, near my Sister Julie, which was on the opposite side of Newcastle from Nana. Fred and Muriel lived in Gateshead again, miles away from Nana anyway, when Nana became ill with dementia and diabetes. Fred and Muriel were very clear that they would not take her in, so Julie, without hesitation, took Nana to live with her. She deteriorated and was admitted to Morpeth Cottage Hospital, which was a place to die for the elderly.

I visited Nana just before she died, it was quite funny. She obviously knew that I was a nurse, but due to her confusion and the morphine syringe pump that she had, she was pleasantly muddled. As I arrived by her bed, she sat up and said, 'Dr Sanderson is here, he will sort me out'.

Well, it was funny and reassuring that she was well looked after and not suffering.

We all came up for the funeral (apart from David, my Brother). One of my greatest regrets was that I did not view her body. This was due to a bad experience I had when my Grandad Pop (Dad's father) died in 1969. His coffin was upstairs in one of the bedrooms of his house. There were people queuing up the stairs to view the body. I was thrust upstairs to see him. It was quite a shock, as I had never seen a dead body before. When I went into the room, I can still recall it today. The coffin was lying on two plinths, with the lid leaning against the wall. When I looked into the coffin, it did not look like Grandad, as his face was twisted, and his colour was grey and mottled. This was a traumatic event that took a long time to understand. I only had the resolution to this once I became a nurse and understood how death affects people.

Recalling this event has allowed me to relive the funeral of my Grandfather. I remember being in the funeral car with Mam and Dad going to Newcastle Crematorium. On the way there, we passed two Police Officers, both wearing old-fashioned helmets. They stood to attention and saluted as the hearse passed. This would not happen today!

Anyway, back to Nana's funeral. After the cremation, we all went back to Julie's house. It transpired that Auntie Muriel had taken Nana's jewellery, which should have been given to Mam. It was a quick cup of tea with some sandwiches, after which Uncle Fred and Auntie Muriel left. Once they had gone, I told Mam that she needed to ask Muriel for Nana's jewellery, as Mam was Nana's daughter, and she should decide what happened to the jewellery. The weather was lovely that day, and to our utter dismay, Uncle Fred and Auntie Muriel came over to Julie's house on the evening of the funeral in shorts, T-shirts and caps with a bottle of wine, like they were on holiday. I took the initiative and asked about the jewellery, and Mam was able to say her piece. I hate funerals because they bring out the worst in people. Suffice to say that the jewellery was returned to Mam, who kept it and did wear Nana's rings, justice was done that day.

Chapter Eleven

DAVID

It was no surprise that David joined the Royal Navy (RN) at 15 years of age as he was in the Sea Cadets. I think it was his saving grace, and it was my mother's, as he was always getting up to something dodgy. One of his more memorable escapades was when we had moved back to Wigmore Avenue when the lead overflow pipes coming out of the back walls of the houses were cut off. One morning it was noticed that all the pipes had been cut off, so the police were called, and they came out and said that the lead could be sold. That was that, or so we thought. Several years later, the truth came out. David had cut off the lead pipes to make fishing weights. My brother David was 4 years younger than me; he was born at 76 West Farm Avenue on January 30, 1957. This was the new flat that we had moved into. He was always a bit wayward as a child, more so in his teenage years. He would go away fishing with some of his friends to a place called North Shields, where you could fish off the pier.

David had no fear. Going to HMS Ganges was the right place for him to get some direction and discipline. HMS Ganges had a full ship's mast set up at one end of the parade square, and all the boys had to climb up the mast to a certain point. David was the button boy. This is the person who stands on the very top of the mast. He must have been mad.

He went in as a boy entrant, so life must have been hard. To be honest, we did not talk much as we were not that close. When he came home on leave, he generally had a different girl on his arm. When I joined the RAF, we sort of went our separate ways, only meeting up at weddings and funerals. He has been married to Jeanette for 49 years and has two daughters.

Mam, me, and David

The last time we met was at our dad's funeral, where we had a major fallout. That was in 1999. When I reached 60 years of age in 2013, I decided that life was too short to let things fester. I know the funeral was incredibly stressful, and certain things happened that upset me. So, I called him unexpectedly. He was surprised to hear from me. I told him why I had called and said, 'Can we reset our relationship'? Initially, he went back to the funeral. I said, 'Look, we can go back over this, but a lot of years have passed, and we can't change the past, but we can change the future'. So, we agreed to draw a line under the past, and since then, we have spoken on the phone at regular intervals until recently, when he has not called for several months. He sent me a text on May 24 saying he was having medical problems and would call when he felt able. We have a sort of normalised relationship by sending birthday, Christmas, and anniversary cards, which I guess is as good as it gets. We did meet up about 6 years ago while we were on holiday in Cornwall. He lives in Plymouth, so that was a plus.

Chapter Twelve

JULIE

As previously stated, my sister was born in 1964 when I was 11 years old. In those days, most births took place at home with the Midwife. I remember the day well when Julie was born. Mam was upstairs with Nana, presumably in labour. The Midwife was called, and she duly arrived. She was an older woman in her late fifties, portly and small in stature. She was wearing a grey and blue hat with a heavy grey overcoat. Once she removed her coat, she was in a blue dress with white frilly cuffs that wrapped around her sleeves, which were rolled up to her elbows, and a white starched apron. The hat never came off. She never asked for hot water!

Dad was sent downstairs to wait. Fathers were not allowed to be present at the delivery in those days. Several hours passed, and then suddenly, we could hear crying coming from upstairs. Nana came down and said it was a girl. Dad was now allowed upstairs first, and then me and my brother went up to see our baby Sister. When we entered

Nana me David and Julie

the bedroom, Mam was sitting up in bed. She was wearing a yellow bed jacket and holding Julie. This was the start of what I would call chaos.

Mam was not that organised. There was stuff everywhere (it was like a scene from the Royal Family television series, as I mentioned before). I used to make up the bottles for Julie when Dad was at work. Unlike today, the bottles were made of glass, not plastic, which had to be sterilised in boiling water along with the teats, which had to be pulled over the top of the bottle.

There was only one choice of baby milk called National Dried Milk, which was available free from the local clinic, along with cod liver oil and concentrated orange juice. The milk was available in 1940 and was fortified with vitamin D. It was the only option for mothers who could not breastfeed. My brother and I used to play for hours with the empty tins. It was my job to go and collect the milk from the local clinic. Fortunately, it was only a 5-minute walk from our house. Mam had a book of milk coupons, which allowed her to get the milk for free on the NHS

National dried milk

There were no disposable nappies in the 1960s. Nappies were made from terry towelling (a white, fluffy material). They were put on the baby by folding the square nappy to form a triangular shape. The baby was laid on the nappy, and the pointed end was pulled up between the legs. The other two sides were pulled over the tummy. All three parts were secured by a large safety pin. A pair of rubber pants with elastic around the legs and the waist were put over the nappy to prevent any leakage of urine and faeces. The dirty nappies had to be rinsed of any faeces first, and then we had a large white enamel bucket that was used to boil the nappies on the gas ring of the cooker. Once this had been done, they were then put into the washing machine, rinsed, and spun dry. If the weather was fine, the nappies would be hung on the line in the back garden. As the line stretched the full length of the back garden, a wooden prop was used to raise the line higher to catch more of the wind and stop larger items from getting caught on the ground. In bad weather, the nappies would be placed on a wooden clothes horse in front of the coal fire, which caused large amounts of steam to emanate from the nappies. The house was never the same again, a large pram blocked the hall, there were nappies everywhere, and the scullery was always in a mess, which I was constantly clearing up.

Julie and I are very close. We can talk about anything. I have supported her over the years financially, as she was a single Mam and at times needed this support. I am glad to say that she also trained as a Nurse, as have both of my nieces. Sarah is a Tissue Viability Nurse, and Rachel is a Mental Health Nurse. Julie is now a Health Visitor, which is an incredibly challenging job. She is not well these days as she has a chronic health condition which does impact her life. She has had a lot to contend with during her life, and I would like to think that I have been there for her over the years. We plan to go on a cruise this year, 2024, as Julie is 60, so we have booked 14 nights to the Southern Mediterranean in September. I can't wait.

Chapter Thirteen

ESME

In the 1960s, Mam shopped daily, or rather, Nana and I went to the shops daily. We used the local corner shop called Peggy Gairs, which was run by Peggy and her older sister, Rene. You could get most of the staples that you needed. Butter was sold from a large slab and cut to the weight you wanted; sugar was sold in blue bags. There was a hand-driven bacon slicer on the counter. All the bacon and other meats were sliced while you waited. We used to get bacon (which was delicious) and chopped pork for sandwiches. Tea came as leaves. There were no tea bags then. We used to drink Stewarts Tea, which came in ¼ of a pound packs. I used to be sent to Peggy's with a note from Mam with the instructions not to open the note but to give it straight to Peggy. She would then put something in a brown paper bag with the instructions, 'Don't look inside the bag. Give the bag straight to your mother.' This went on for several years until one day, I looked at the note, which said 1 packet of STs. Then I looked in the brown paper bag and it was sanitary towels!! How times have changed today, feminine products are commonplace in all supermarkets and shops. Even men buy them!

It was not long before the first local supermarket opened. The first one was opened further down the road from Peggy Gairs. It was called a Mini Mart. Customers went around the shop choosing the products that they wanted, then took the goods to the cash desk to pay. This was the start of a change in the way we shopped. About 5 miles away, there was a new housing development with a larger supermarket called Fine Fare. You needed a car (which we did not have), but fortunately, we had a family friend who did have a car. She was called Esme Charlton. She was a SEN working as a District Nurse. She would always pop in during the week for a cup of tea and a cigarette. Esme was a small lady, a staunch Welsh Catholic, an extrovert, and very funny with some of her stories. She was married to an ex-nursing assistant named Charles. He was quiet but a lazy man. He just sat in his chair. I used to get his cigarettes for him from the corner shop, as Esme would not get them.

I liked Esme, she was a breath of fresh air and brought some normality to my life. I would have to do the shopping with Esme, as Mam would not go to the shops, she would give me a shopping list and the money, and Esme and I would nip off to the supermarket. We always had a good laugh when driving to the shops.

I remember a rather frightening event when I was about 13 years old. I was going shopping with Esme, but she had to stop off at a patient's house to do a dressing. I waited in the car, and in front of Esme's car was another car. I must have been waiting for about 10 minutes when a woman walked past Esme's car and stopped at the car in front. Then she took out a metal bar from under her coat and started to smash all the windows in the car. I was terrified in case she was going to trash all the cars in the street. I was frantically knocking on the front door of the patient's house, but no one came down, so I just kept banging on the door till, eventually, the door opened, and I ran in and told Esme what had happened. When we went out, there was a large group of locals gathering around the car. The woman was screaming, obviously out of control, and there were lots of four-letter words. The police were called, and she was duly arrested. It turned out that she was an alcoholic, and the car belonged to her ex. I was in a state of shock, as I had never seen anything like this before. We still went shopping, and afterwards, Esme took me in for a cup of tea and a chat, which helped.

Esme had two children, Marilyn and Anthony. Anthony became a Catholic priest. He was the most unlikely person to be a priest, which will become clear later. He took me to a church event, some sort of Catholic Church Trade Fair, which was held in the Exhibition Park, which is a large open green space to the north of Newcastle City Centre. The event was held in large marquee-type tents with stalls and guest speakers. As the afternoon went on, the weather took a turn for the worst. It became very windy with driving rain, and everyone gathered in the main tent, where, at this point, the large wooden posts were starting to creek under the extreme wind. They started to move; it looked like the tent would collapse. Instead of evacuating the tent (which would have happened today), all the priests started to pray to God to stop the wind. Then suddenly, the wind and rain stopped. I cannot explain this, as it was a very spiritual moment. Following this event, I started to wonder about the presence of God, as this event was so dramatic that it made me question whether there was a higher power at play. This had a lasting effect on me during my teenage years. Several years later, Anthony left the priesthood, married, had two children, and ended up being the governor of Barlinnie Prison in Glasgow. See what I mean?

During the years between 15 and 17 years of age, I became quite close to Esme's husband, Charles. I found him a fascinating chap, but there were obviously issues with the marriage. He also enjoyed a drink. Maybe that was the problem. Anyway, I went around one evening, and we started to drink neat whisky. I had never done this before. Needless to say, I became drunk but had to get home. Esme's house was about a 5-minute walk from my house, so she put on my coat and pointed me in the right direction. All I had to do was walk straight down the road, then turn right into my street somehow. I managed to get home, then crawled up the stairs straight into bed.

Esme and Charles were leading separate lives. Esme had a little yappy dog called Sacha; it was a Papillon. Charles hated it and would do all he could to annoy it. Esme had a caravan at St Bees in Cumbria. She would go for long weekends and take me, Julie, Mam, and Dad. This was as close to a holiday as I got. When I left home, my sister Julie would go with Esme. It was great fun, and just to get away from the house, as every day was the same, it was a great treat for us.

The caravan had no TV, just a radio. We would get out to the beach and go walking and doing normal things that children should be doing. In the evenings, we would play cards and board games under a gas light. Esme was great fun and brought some normality to our lives, and I will always be grateful to her for this. Several years ago, I drove myself and my sister back to the St. Bees caravan site to do some reminiscing. It brought back lots of happy memories for both of us.

I spent a lot of time with Esme. She was great fun; we could talk about anything, and she was my inspiration to become a nurse, as I had been out with her on her rounds and talking about some of the conditions that she was dealing with. Esme was a SEN, and I trained to be a SEN in the Royal Air Force.

One last thing about Esme and Charles: one night, he had been drinking. He went to turn off the TV but could not reach it. Esme had been out, and when she came in, Charles was lying on his front with his right index finger pointing towards the off button on the TV. Esme saw the whisky bottle and assumed he was drunk and asleep, so she turned off the TV, put a blanket over him and went to bed. The following morning, he was still lying in the same place. It turned out he had had a stroke, which she was not aware of. He was then admitted to the hospital. He died several years later. Esme still lived in the same house and lived her life to the fullest until she died. She was a hilarious and genuine lady with whom I have many fond memories, and I owe her a debt of gratitude for bringing some normality to my life in my younger days.

Esme and me 1971

Chapter Fourteen

RAF YEARS

Basic Training

I was 19 years old when I started my Pupil Nurse Training. I was on State Enrolled Course 53 (same as my birth year, spooky). I had to spend 5 weeks at RAF Halton for initial training, including marching. I am not sure how I missed RAF Swinderby, which was the RAF Basic Training Centre for male entrants. I must have led a charmed life, as Halton was by far a better place for basic training.

The initial training consisted of marching every day. It was difficult as we were a mixed flight (this is the term used in the RAF for a group of personnel) of men and women. We had to learn basic first aid, the rank structure of the RAF, and understand nuclear, biological, and chemical (NBC) warfare and the training to support our survival. Remember, this was 1972, the height of the Cold War. One of the main things was getting the correct size and fitting of your respirator. Once fitted, we had to attend the gas chamber to check that there were no leaks around your respirator.

It was a lovely sunny afternoon, and we were told to meet on the grass outside this small old building, which looked like something that would not be out of place in the Second World War. We went in six at a time. The object of the exercise was to test that the respirator was fitted correctly and to let you

R.A.F. Institute of Health and Medical Training, Halton

No. 53 State Enrolled Nurse Course, (Basic) June 1972

Group photo SEN course 53 1972

experience the effects of CS gas. I have often wondered why it was called CS gas, and with a bit of research, I uncovered the following, "*CS gas is generally accepted as being non-lethal. It was first synthesised by two Americans, Ben Corson and Roger Stoughton, at Middlebury College in 1928, and the chemical's name is derived from the first letters of the scientists' surnames.* "Simple!

The instructing staff were already inside the chamber. They had some CS gas pellets that they lit on the floor, which filled the chamber with gas. The respirators did their job, and no ill effects were experienced, or so we thought! The next bit was the worst. We had to remove our respirator and say our name, rank, and number. I said my name before the effects of the gas overwhelmed me. We were then ushered outside into the fresh air. All of us were coughing our guts up. Our eyes were stinging and watering. We were then told to go outside with our arms at 90 degrees to our bodies to let the wind blow off any residual gas. Copious amounts of water were used to irrigate our eyes, an interesting experience that I would not care to repeat.

Every Friday was a pay parade, and we were paid in cash (very original, no cards then). The Flight Lieutenant and a Corporal from accounts sat behind a wooden table with a tray of money. We had to go up and say number, rank, and name. It was my turn, 'S8030222 AC Sanderson Sir' and salute. He would then give you your weekly wage. Eventually, we came to the midpoint of the training, and we were allowed a 48-hour pass, which allowed us to visit home.

I travelled to Newcastle with another girl called Katie, and both of us wore our number one uniform as there was no risk in those days of wearing a uniform in public places. I did not tell anyone I was coming home, so when I knocked on the door, my mother was overcome with emotion. In her own way, she was proud of me and my brother, but it did get more complex with her demands on us.

Mam and me

Nana lived across the road when I knocked on her door. She was pleased to see me when she opened the door.

Nana and me

I was paraded around all the neighbours so they could see me in uniform.

Back to Halton on Sunday, 48 hours went by very quickly. It was nice to see everyone, but I knew that I had made the right decision. As I had nothing in common with my parents and neighbours, I knew my life would be better. This did not mean that I did not care or love them any less. I just felt different.

Saturday nights at RAF Halton NAAFI (Navy Army Air Force Institute) (which is the junior ranks social club) were disco nights. The first night that we all went down, "Metal Guru" by T Rex was playing. This was the first piece of music that I heard in the RAF, which has stayed with me all those years ago. If I hear this music, I am transported back to RAF Halton in 1972. It was at RAF Halton I met a girl called Linda from Dundee and we sort of hit it off and started going out with each other. She was mad about sex; some may say great, but it was difficult to keep up with her. I took her home and we slept together on the bed settee in the lounge. We had sex as soon as the lights went out. That's what it was: pure sex, not making love! As the months went by, we got engaged. Don't ask. It just sort of happened. I then went to her parents' house in Dundee. We slept in separate rooms. I can't recall meeting her Father, but once her Mother left for work, we were at it again. It was never meant to last, as I soon found out she was seeing someone else as well. That's when I ended the engagement, I had a lucky escape.

Chapter Fifteen
RAF Hospital, Nocton Hall

Nurse Training

We were told we would be posted to RAF Hospital Nocton Hall, near Lincoln. I did not know what to expect, but after several hours in a military coach, we arrived at Nocton Village, which, in essence, was a single road with a row of houses, a church, and a village hall. We arrived at a sign that said RAF Hospital Nocton Hall. The Coach drove along a tree-lined drive. It seemed to go on forever. On the left side of the drive was a beautiful old stately house (this was used as the Nursing Officers Mess)

Nocton Hall Lincoln

We passed the hall and entered what were more familiar-looking surroundings. There was a road with signs and single-story buildings that looked like WW2 Nissan Huts. The coach then turned right, passed the hospital entrance, and drove along the road towards the accommodation blocks. The coach stopped, and all the men were ordered off with our cases. The coach then drove a little further to the female accommodation, where there was a very large Women's RAF (WRAF) Flight Sergeant who ushered the girls out of the coach and into their accommodation blocks.

We were just standing there, wondering what to do, as no one was meeting us. Then, out of the opening to the accommodation, this little man appeared with receding grey hair. He was wearing a brown dust coat. He introduced himself as Jock. He had a broad Scottish accent with a raucous laugh. He was the caretaker and would look after us in the early days until we settled in. We were taken into the block, which was a long corridor with other corridors coming off the main corridor. We were shown to our rooms. All the rooms were four-man rooms, and there were already two other people in the room I went to. Jock then came around with our bedding, two pillows, two sheets, two pillowcases, two blankets, and a counterpane. For most of us, this was the first time we had been away from home, and the stark reality was sinking in that we were on our own.

You felt completely isolated. You did not know anyone. It was a bit depressing, to be honest. We arrived on a Friday afternoon, so we had all weekend to get our bearings. What you learn is that being in the military, you are thrown together with people from all walks of life.

My bedspace at RAF Hospital Nocton Hall

And from different parts of the country, most of whom you will get along with, but there are some who you will never get along with.

— In my group, there were,

— Harry from Carlisle

— Dave from Swindon

— Tony (Taff) from Wales

— Andy from London

— Pete from Wales

— Mick from Northern Ireland

— Me from Newcastle

Harry was in my room, so at least we had each other for support. There was a Senior Aircraftman (SAC) named Paul who worked in the General Office. He was a nice guy, very supportive, and understood how we felt, but he did say give it a week, and you will be fine, and he was right. Once we unpacked and made the bed, the first place to find was the Airman's Mess to get something to eat. Again, everyone was very friendly, the food was amazing, and the rest of the course was also there, so it gave us a chance to catch up and see how everyone was getting along.

We quickly established where the NAAFI was, this was called The Winged Serpent Club, which was at the other end of the camp. The winged serpent is a symbol of the medical branch. We wore a small brass version on each lapel of our number 1 and 2 uniforms. They are also called Caduceus.

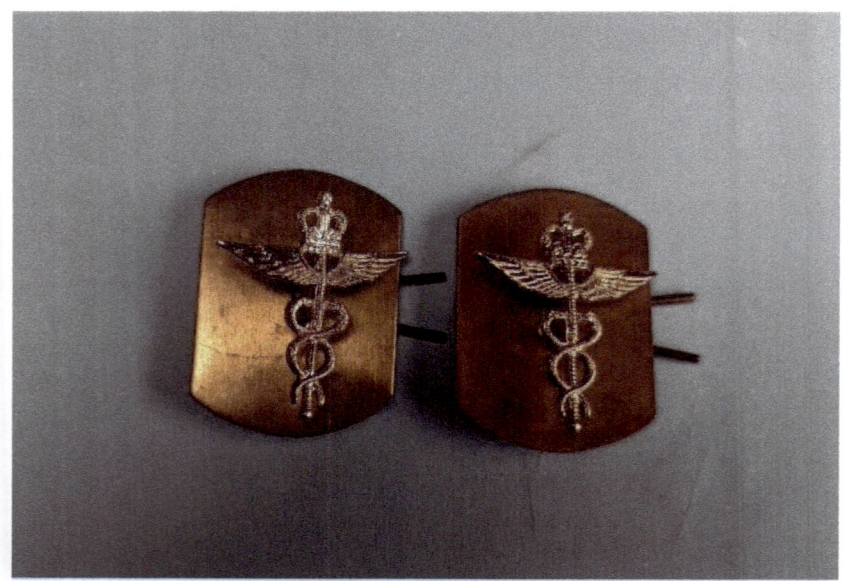

Medical caduceus

This identified us as medical staff. It was quite hard to understand how big the hospital was, but it seemed to cover a large area of land. I would explore the hospital more over the weekend. The wards started at number 3 and finished at number 12.

Saturday night at the NAAFI was disco night, which was run by volunteers. Remember, this was 1972, this was the height of disco, and we all watched Top of the Pops and listened to Alan Freeman on a Sunday evening with Pick of the Pops.

The NAAFI had a Manageress called Miss Gill. She was small in stature, her grey hair was always in a tight bun, and she wore a flowered pink nylon overall. She was polite but very strict and did not tolerate any bad behaviour. To be honest, the camp was very well-behaved. The main problem came when we had male visitors from surrounding bases chasing the nurses.

The facilities were basic. When you entered, there was a snooker room on the right with two snooker tables, which were always in use. To the left was a small room with a dart board. The main area consisted of a seating area, a dance floor, and the bar, of course, which we made use of over the weekend.

Course photo at RAF Nocton Hall 1972 in ward uniform

We had to report to the School of Nursing at 08:00 on Monday. We had to wear this awful blue serge number two uniform, very similar to that they would have worn in WW2. Fortunately, this was for a short time, as we were issued with white uniforms, a tunic, and trousers. This would be our ward uniform and what we would wear in the school of nursing. The white uniform was sent to the hospital laundry and came back heavily starched. It was a major job getting your legs into the trousers, and when they were new, you looked very smart. The School of Nursing was only a few minutes' walk from our accommodation block.

We were at the start of our nursing career with six weeks in the school of nursing. There were three nurse tutors: Chief Technician (CT) Noble, CT Hennel, and CT Snuggs. This was interesting as all the tutors were Senior Non-Commissioned Officers (SNCOs). The 6 weeks were called Preliminary Training School (PTS) for nurses, which was to give you theoretical and pre-clinical training. There was a lot of anatomy and physiology to learn. We had to learn everything including taking a basic set of observations, temperature, pulse, respiration, and blood pressure. The worst thing we had to do was pass a nasogastric tube (Ryles tube) on each other. This was a plastic tube that was inserted through the nose and into the stomach. It was not a pleasant experience, but it was beneficial to understand what a patient would be going through when passing this type of tube. Then there was a weird event: one of the girls was pregnant (she got through her medical examination and basic training without the pregnancy being detected), she had the baby in the toilets in the girl's accommodation, she said, 'she did not know she was pregnant'!

The SEN was called the bedside nurse (now replaced by Assistant Practitioners), who would look after all the patients' "basic needs." There were lots of lectures and film shows. At the time, they used 16mm film via a projector, which covered all aspects of nursing care and anatomy and physiology. There was lots of practicing with each other. The other thing we had to learn was all the medical forms that started with the prefix F Med followed by a number. Examples of this are as follows,

F Med 4 Your personal medical record

F Med 13 Observations chart

FF Med 100 Fluid balance chart

F Med 12 Laboratory request

F Med 12a Blood transfusion request

F Med 10 In patient record sheet

F Med 11 In patient continuation sheet

F Med 152 Drug record

F Med 289 X-ray request

These took some learning, but the more you used them, the easier it got.

During the 6 weeks in school, I had several days on the wards to see what goes on and to get some familiarisation before I started my ward placement. I was also given my ward allocation; my first ward was male medical Ward 12. Each ward allocation was for 12 weeks, with regular days back in the nursing school to consolidate our learning. I remember going to Ward 12 for the day. I was clueless and very nervous, but the other nurses were helpful and gave me a true insight as to how it was. The first thing I learned to do was make a bed. It sounds simple, but not as simple as you think. I had to master hospital corners, a skill that would become second nature over time.

The ward was managed by Chief Technician Cliff Hallows, who was a very funny and nice man and very supportive of the pupil nurses. There were several of us on the ward that day, so we were introduced to the sluice room. This was the starting point for most pupil nurses. The first thing we were shown was how to test urine, which was rather a faff as compared to today. We had to use test tubes and tablets to check urine glucose. This entailed pouring urine into a long glass beaker, then into the test tube about halfway up, as when you added the tablet, it fizzed up and changed colour, which you compared to a chart that gave you the percentage of glucose in the urine. Today we have dip sticks for testing everything that could be in the urine.

The other thing I was taught was how to clean urine bottles and bedpans. The urinals were made of glass and had to be rinsed and cleaned with a large bottle brush. Then, they were put into the bedpan washer and steriliser. You could sterilise only two bottles at a time, so it was a laborious task. Once they had been through the steriliser, the bottles were put in a paper bag and stored on a rack. The bedpans, which were made of stainless steel, were a little more complicated, as any faecal waste had to be put down the sluice first by rinsing the waste down the sluice (this was a heavy-duty toilet) before they were put into the steriliser once they had been through the steriliser, any marks on the inside or outside had to be cleaned by hand, then put through the steriliser again.

Again, the bedpans were put into a paper bag and stored on a shelf. Thankfully, we have moved on to Papier Mâché urinals and bedpans, which are disposed of in a macerator.

Being a Military Hospital, everything was regimented, and cleanliness and tidiness were the order of the day. The linen cupboard had to be kept scrupulously clean and tidy. When the clean linen arrived from the laundry, it was the responsibility of the pupil nurses to put it away. Sheets had to be rolled and stacked in neat piles, blankets had to be refolded so they were all looking the same, draw sheets had to be folded (these were smaller sheets that were used on top of the sheet for protection), and were part of the operation packs, which had to be made up with a green blanket, and canvas (to lift the patient from the bed using two poles) and two draw sheets. Once these were made up, they had to be stacked in a neat way. Looking back on this now, it seems rather futile, but it gave you a good grounding in the basics of nursing, and if the ward was kept clean and tidy, the patients were looked after in the same way.

The Matron would visit all the wards daily, doing her rounds. As a Pupil Nurse, I had to take the Matron around the ward, where you had to know everything about your patients. The wards had to be spotless even down to having all the wheels of the beds facing in the same direction and lined up in a straight line. Once a week, the Commanding Officer, Matron, and Station Warrant Officer (SWO) would visit the wards, which had to be extremely spotless for this visit as the SWO would check all the toilets and annexes during the inspection.

When I started in 1972, the wards were well-staffed, mainly because of the trainee nurses. We had year 1 and year 2 trainees, who were differentiated by the wearing of an armband with a green stripe, one stripe for the first year and two stripes for the second year. Staff arrived on the ward at 07:20 hours for handover by the night nurse (only one nurse on nights, generally a second-year pupil nurse). Staff were allowed to smoke in the ward office, not the trainees, only the trained staff. Patients were also allowed to smoke. If mobile, they would go to the day room. If bedbound, e.g., orthopaedic patients, they would smoke in bed.

On one occasion, when we were on the ward for a day, one of the pupil nurses was asked to draw up penicillin for injection. Basically, penicillin comes in a vial in powder form, and water has to be added to make a solution so it can be drawn up into the syringe and then injected into the patient. Unfortunately, this was not fully explained to the pupil nurse, as she did draw up the penicillin, but she drew up all the powder into the syringe and forgot to add the water. We did laugh, but it does show that effective communication is needed and don't assume that the person understands what is being asked.

Suddenly, the first year had flown by, and I was now a second-year pupil nurse with two green stripes on my arm, and I was promoted to Senior Air Craftsman (SAC).

It was Christmas 1973 when we did something stupid. We had been to midnight mass at the local church, and when we returned to the barrack block, someone said, 'Let's have a séance. So, we made an Ouija board. This is what happened.

Chapter Sixteen
THE SÉANCE CHRISTMAS EVE 1973

My recollection of the night was that several of us went to midnight mass at the local village church. When we returned to the barrack block, one of the group members suggested making an Ouija board and having a séance. One of the main protagonists was a guy named Dennis. He was a lot older than the rest of us. So, there was me, Harry, Lee, and Dennis. Once it started, Dennis seemed to be the worst affected. He was acting like he was possessed, speaking in an indescribable language. He was holding onto the glass with both hands. The rest of us had just one finger on the glass as it moved across the table, hitting separate letters. The first word it spelt out was Pop. This was very unnerving, as my Grandad was known as Pop. A cold shiver went down my spine, but before I could get a message from him, the glass started moving so quickly that I could not write down what the letters were. By this time, the other 3 of us had let go of the glass, just leaving Dennis holding onto the glass.

It was at this point that we were aware that the room was freezing. Eventually, the glass flew from Dennis's hands and smashed onto the floor. This whole event was very distressing for us, which hit us all very hard, especially Lee, who had a psychotic episode the following day and had to be admitted to the hospital for sedation. He was so bad that he had a nurse with him 24 hours a day. Overnight, Lee became worse and needed specialised care. Lee was transferred to RAF Hospital Wroughton, where they had a specialised Psychiatric Unit.

As I had worked the Christmas period, I was on leave over the New Year period. When I got home, Mam sensed that something was not right as I was not sleeping and was very unsettled. I told her what had happened, and she said, 'a very strange thing that she had been woken up by the smell of pipe smoke' as no one smoked a pipe at the time, it seemed strange. She then said, 'It was like Grandad Sanderson's (Pop) pipe as he smoked a pipe all the time.' she then said, 'It was not a frightening feeling, more of a comfort and reassurance' I thought bloody hell this just gets spookier by the day. I suppose that Mam felt it was a comforting experience. I felt that Grandad would not wish to do me any harm, which gave me some comfort. I arrived back on camp following the New Year break, and the next thing that happened was that all the lads in the block were called for an interview by the Special Investigation Branch of the RAF Police (SIB), who seemed very interested in Lee and what he got up to when he went on leave. We were called individually into a room with a small table in the centre, two chairs on one side, and a single chair on the other side. We were not offered any support or legal representation, which, looking back, was outrageous.

I was aggressively interviewed about Lee, who his friends were, and did I take drugs. Then they asked if I knew about "Lee's sexual habits". I suddenly thought they thought he was gay (at this time, gay was not a term that was used). They used the term homosexual and other derogatory terms (queer, puff. Homo). These hateful terms have thankfully been confined to history, but at this time, it was like the police were enjoying trying to get us to say Lee was gay. What I do know now, looking back, is that Lee was a caring, happy, and helpful young man. He was effeminate yes, but no one bothered about this as this was Lee, and we accepted him for who he was. In the end, the SIB got nothing from any of us. The police searched all of our rooms, not sure what they were looking for, but they did not find anything. Their behaviour was outrageous.

However, they weren't that clever, as they missed Lee's stash of gay magazines hidden at the back of his locker muppets!!! We found them and destroyed them.

Lee did return briefly to RAF Hospital Nocton Hall prior to his discharge. Still, sadly, one of the Neanderthals bumped into Lee outside of the barrack block and punched Lee in the mouth with the usual expletives that I mentioned previously. This was typical of how other men reacted to gay men at this time. God knows why, but for me, it shows their inadequacy.

Looking back at this event now, it was shocking how we were treated by the police with no legal representation or support officer during what was a very aggressive interview. Lee's treatment by the RAF was also disgraceful. Thankfully, now gay men and women can remain in the RAF and not have to live double lives. It's only taken 50 years, better late than never.

Following the séance at Christmas 1973, we were all aware of some sort of presence in the barrack block. I know it will be hard for others to understand, but parts of the corridor were colder than the rest of the corridor. I am sure this was worse for us than for those who were not involved. The room I was in did not feel right either, it was hard to get to sleep, and I was always aware of another presence, which I could not

crucifix

see. I became more and more unsettled along with the others who were involved. It was around this time that we went to see the Padre and started going to church. I had a large wooden crucifix by my bed, which did give me some comfort.

It was very unnerving going into the barrack block at night, as when I passed a certain point in the corridor, the hairs on the back of my neck stood up and had a feeling of terror. The room where the séance took place became the focus for supernatural activity; items would be moved around the room, and at its worst, lockers were moved around. To outsiders, this may seem implausible, but to those of us living through it, it was very real.

The presence (I can't think of another name to describe it) was becoming worse and was influencing my mental health. Others were experiencing the same. After several weeks of seeing the Padre and going to church, things were worsening. It was at this point that the Padre called in a Church of England Exorcist (I thought these only existed in films). This may seem incredible now, but it was being taken very seriously by the Church and the RAF.

Chapter Seventeen
THE EXORCISM

The Padre arranged a date with the Exorcist to visit the hospital, and we had a good tidy-up of our rooms. I was in a four-person room, and we had arranged the wardrobes to divide the room to give us some privacy.

We met the Padre and the Exorcist in the Hospital Chapel. The Exorcist was an elderly man around 70 with thinning grey hair and of small stature with a slight bend to his back. He talked us through what would happen and told us not to get too distressed by what we would be witnessing. We started off with a service in the chapel. He had a small brown leather case with him, which he opened and put on the altar. There was a large metal crucifix, a bottle of holy water, a box of salt, and his vestments. During the service, he blessed these items. Then he changed into his vestments. We started to walk to the barrack block, which was a fair walk from the hospital chapel. On the way, the Exorcist said, 'It knows I am coming'. We arrived at the block and walked to the corridor where our room was located. The whole corridor was freezing. As we approached the room, banging and the movement of furniture could be heard.

The Exorcist grabbed the door handle, opened the door, and went in first. The room was a complete mess; lockers had been overturned, and all our personal stuff was thrown all over the floor. We were told that we had to be part of the exorcism as we were all affected. By this time, the room was icy cold. The Exorcist opened his case and laid the items on top of one of the lockers. He kept looking at the ceiling and asked if we could open the windows before he started. The exorcism started with a joint service with us all. He came around and held each of our heads in his hands and said, 'Begone'. He then took the holy water and salt and started saying what was presumably the exorcism service. He kept repeating this over and over again. At the same time, he was throwing holy water and salt around the room while holding the crucifix. Then, suddenly, it was like he had cornered a rabid dog. All his energy was directed to the top left corner of the room. He kept shouting Begone Demon. This went on for about 15 minutes. It looked like a battle of wills who would succumb first. I am pleased to say that the exorcist triumphed. When it was over, the old man was exhausted. He was sweating profusely and needed several minutes to regain his composure. Immediately, the room felt different, as did the corridor. Whatever happened that afternoon (to this day, I can't explain it), it worked. He said that we had unleashed a disturbed spirit that was now gone.

We held a short service, thanking God for the peace and return to normality. What was clear in my mind was that I would never get involved with an Ouija Board again, and if I heard of anyone contemplating its use, I would move heaven and earth to stop them, as I know how destructive this can be.

Since this event, it has been clear that there is an evil presence. I don't know what or where it comes from, but no one should dabble in the occult as it never ends well. One of the long-lasting implications of this is that I can't sleep in silence. I need a radio on at night. This started soon after the problems in the barrack block, and I suppose it was a sort of comfort and reassurance that you were not alone.

Some 50 years on, I still have the radio on at night. I suppose I have gotten used to it. Even when I go away, I take a small portable radio. Luckily, it now serves another purpose as I have quite bad tinnitus, so having the radio on helps with this. My wife has also got used to this, just as well, as I was not a good sleeper. It has taken years to get the GP to prescribe the right sleeping tablets, which they have now done, and I sleep all night for the first time in years.

Chapter Eighteen
SECOND YEAR

It was in our second year that we had our geriatric placement (now called care of the elderly) at St. George's Hospital Lincoln. This was hard work as the ward was full of high-dependency patients, many of whom had been in for years. The ward was of nightingale design (beds down each side of the ward), with a total of 30 beds. Sister Chapman was in charge of the ward. She was lovely and very supportive of the RAF Pupil Nurses.

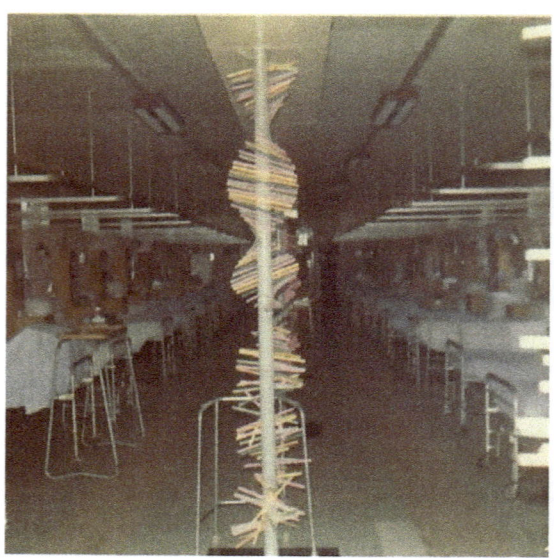

Geriatric Ward St George's Hospital Lincon 1974

Sister Chapman St George's Hospital Lincon 1974

We would be working over Christmas 1974, which would be a challenge but also fun.

We had to get transport there and back, which was a 5-tonne truck (a very large truck), which we had to climb into the back and then sit on wooden benches for our trip to Lincoln. It was not a very comfortable ride. Looking after 30 elderly patients was hard but rewarding work. There were several long-standing patients that had been on the ward for years. There was one particular chap who needed a manual evacuation of his bowels. This was a daily job left to the "male" pupil nurses. This entailed removing faecal matter with your fingers. Not a pleasant job, but it was the only way he could evacuate his bowels. There was another chap you had to keep a close eye on. He had an indwelling catheter to drain urine from the bladder, but he had a habit of getting an erection and masturbating mainly during visiting time, so you had to quickly pull the curtains around his bed. Looking back at my time in the geriatric ward, the patients were well cared for, even though some of the nursing practices were a little archaic. As we had been working Christmas Day, when we returned to camp, the Airman's Mess served us up with a Christmas Dinner which was great.

Me and Sister Chapman Christmas 1974

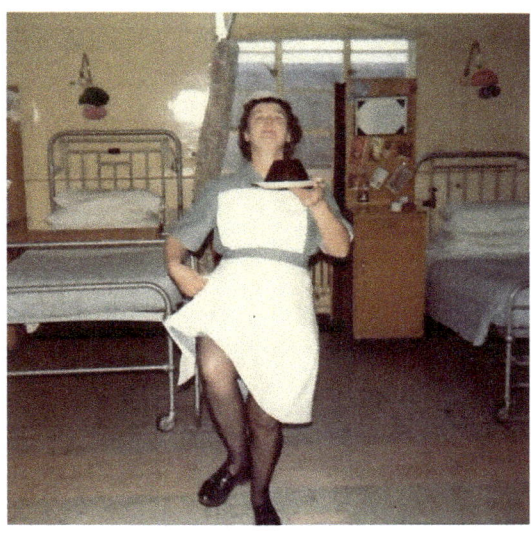

SEN St George's Hospital Christmas 1974

Christmas dinner after shift at St George's Hospital 1974

February 1974 was my 21st birthday. I was on a set of night duty for my birthday. Sister Fournier was the Senior Night Sister who was also an Aquarian. She gave me a birthday card which laid out all the qualities of an Aquarian which I still have. She wrote a lovely piece inside the card telling me to train to be a State Registered Nurse.

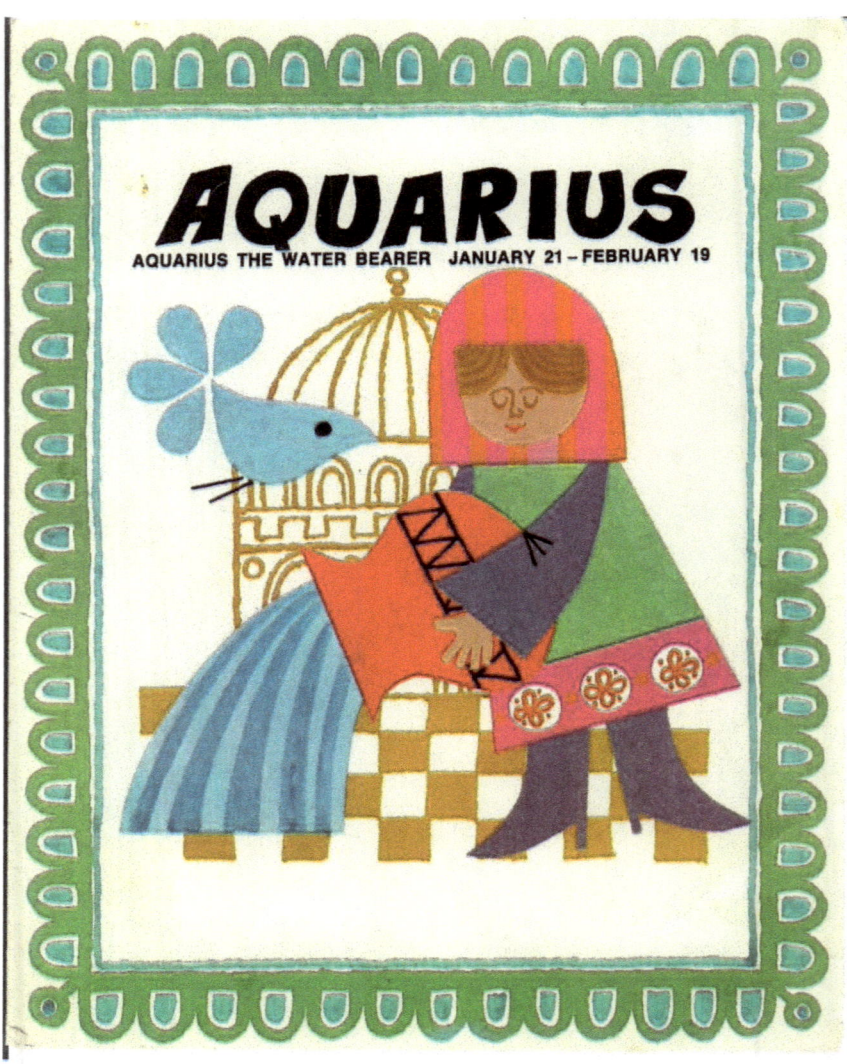

21st birthday card 1974

This was realised in 1989, some 15 years later. I was coming to the end of my training, and I was then looking forward to my final exams and assessments. An external examiner assessed you, and I had to demonstrate an aseptic dressing technique using forceps, which was a tricky skill to master, unlike today when sterile gloves are available, which makes life a lot easier. After this was finished, there was the drug round of all the patients on the ward, so I had to know all the patients' names, diagnoses and drugs being administered and what they were used for, which is no mean feat when you have 30 patients.

My last placement was in Male Surgical Ward 3. I was in my second year now and had done a spell of nights, which was quite scary as I was on the ward by myself. It was a lot of responsibility, but there was an on-call Senior Night Nurse who would come to the ward to help with the drug round and anything else that you needed help with. This experience was a great learning opportunity as you were responsible for your patients overnight. There were two ward domestics to look after the ward. One had a habit of grabbing your crotch (an instant flashback to when I was an apprentice) and would give a running commentary on the size of your tackle. The other domestic was called Lyn. She had rather large breasts, and when she was doing the teas, she would engage in smutty barter with the young lads on the ward and squeeze her breasts together. The lads lapped it up!! There was one occasion when a member of our course was being admitted for a circumcision. He was a little bit frightened of Lyn, who was threatening to go into his room and pull back the sheets. As a member of staff, he was in a side room with a bathroom. He had his premedication and was somewhat drowsy, at which point Lyn burst into his room. He immediately jumped out of bed and locked himself in the bathroom. Although it was amusing at the time but not a great way to be prepared for surgery, Lyn was spoken to by the charge nurse and told to pack it in, which she did.

I am pleased to say that I passed the written paper and assessment, and I qualified in July 1974. Once qualified as a SEN, you had to apply to go on the General Nursing Council's Register, which cost £10, which the RAF paid. This was a lot of money in 1974. Once I was qualified, I would

Registration certificate with General Nursing Council 1974

be posted to my first unit, which was RAF Hospital Cosford near Wolverhampton.

Graduation group photo course 53 1974

Chapter Nineteen

NURSING IN THE 1970S

I qualified as a SEN in 1974 and went on to become a Registered Nurse (RN) in 1987. I retired from the Royal Air Force in 1996 as a Warrant Officer (this was the highest non-commissioned rank in the RAF). I continued to work as a nurse till 2017 when I came off the nursing register. During COVID-19, I went back on the COVID-19 Register till 2020. I have been nursing for 48 years. I was an Advanced Nurse Practitioner and Independent Prescriber for the last 10 years of my nursing career. During this time, there have been many changes to the nursing profession. The stark contrast from 1972 to modern-day nursing is unbelievable, I had a degree and was working at a very high level with no medical support. Florence Nightingale said, *'Let us never consider ourselves finished nurses.... we must be learning all of our lives'* (Nightingale, 1859). This is true today as it was when she said this. I am an example of this.

Nursing has evolved since I started in 1972. Back then, nurses were generally subservient to doctors and were very much the "handmaiden." I remember the Consultant ward rounds with trepidation. There was one Consultant Orthopaedic Surgeon in particular who insisted that all the male patients wear paper knickers, as back then, most of the young lads who were on traction did not wear any underwear or pyjamas in bed. The genitals needed to be covered for his ward rounds. It was priceless to watch. If he pulled back the bed covers to see that the patient was not wearing paper knickers, he would storm out of the ward and tell the Sister he would come back when the ward was ready for his rounds.

Most consultants in the RAF were Wing Commanders or Group Captains. All the different specialities would come onto the ward to see their patients, generally with an entourage of Junior Doctors, the Sister or Charge Nurse, followed by the Pupil Nurses, hoping you would not be asked a question. In those days, the patients were seen as a collective, all receiving the same nursing care. A Kardex system was used to hold the patient's nursing record, which sat on the Sister's/Charge Nurses' desk, and only they could write in the notes, except for the night staff.

At the start of each shift, the Sister/Charge Nurse would give a report on all the patients. As a pupil nurse, you had to know all the patients as you would be looking after them all, unlike today, where the nurse is responsible for a group of patients. You had to know the name, rank, and diagnosis of all the patients on the ward. The wards were known as Nightingale Wards as they were long, with beds on two sides only separated by curtains. Nursing was a series of tasks that happened, like clockwork observations such as temperature, pulse, and respirations, which were done every 4 hours. At this time, we were using mercury thermometers, which were kept in a glass container with a solution of Hibatain in spirit (alcohol). Before use, they were wiped with a gauze swab and shaken down so the mercury was at the bottom of the thermometer, then put under the patient's tongue for 2 minutes. During this time, you took the pulse and respiration rate. The thermometer was wiped and shaken to move the mercury back to the bottom of the thermometer, and the used thermometer was put into a separate container for cleaning. The wards had 30 beds, so it would take some time to get around all the patients for their observations. Only the Doctor could change the frequency of the observations.

During the ward round, the Sister or Charge Nurse would accompany the Consultant, writing down their instructions in an A4 book so nothing was missed. All this information was written in the Kardex at the end of the ward round. Work was allocated at the start of each shift by the Sister or Charge Nurse. At the start of the day, breakfasts would arrive on the ward in a large silver heated trolley. The Sister or Charge Nurse would command the trolley and pull out the trays with the patient's names on them. The trays were given to the Nurses to take to the patients. Those patients who were not bedbound would sit around a large table in the day room.

Once breakfast was done, all the mobile patients were confined to the day room, and all the beds were pulled out one side at a time. The ward domestic would hoover the floor, and the "male nurses" would mop the floor. This was done by 2 nurses standing side by side and mopping the floor. The mops were moved in tandem left and right. Once you got the rhythm, it was good fun. Once one side was dry, the other side was done. All hard surfaces were damp, dusted window ledges back of the beds and lockers. When both sides were mopped, the centre of the ward was mopped. While this was drying, other things had to be done: the sluice had to be cleaned, and the linen cupboard had to be tidied. This ritual was done every day the wards were spotless, and infection rates were very low. "I wonder why.".

All bed-bound patients had 2-hour pressure area care. This entailed the nurse having a pressure care trolley that had clean linen, a plastic bowl, surgical spirit, and talcum powder. All patients, regardless of age, who were in bed had pressure area care. The patient's back was washed and rubbed, as were the buttocks and heels. Depending on the patient, either surgical spirit or talcum powder was applied to the patient's skin. There was no evidence-based nursing at this time. It was just handed down from one nurse to the next. There was some theory for rubbing the patient's skin, which was to stimulate circulation in the underlying tissue. This would be seen as madness by modern-day nurses. All I know is that we never had pressure sores!

Occasionally, patients would be admitted with pressure sores. What I am about to say will seem completely insane to modern-day nurses. We treated pressure sores with a combination of egg white and oxygen. There was some sort of logic to this: egg white, being protein, would aid healing by blowing oxygen onto the wound. This would help with the circulation, so you had to get an egg to break it, separate the yoke from the white, apply the white to the pressure sore, and then get an oxygen bottle with some tubing attached to blow oxygen onto the wound to dry the egg white. I know what you're thinking completely bonkers, but at the time, this is what we did. There were lots of other things we had to do that were not done today, for example, preoperative shaves. Any patient having surgery on their abdominal region would have a nipple-to-knee shave. If you were on night duty and had several patients to shave, you had to start around 5 a.m. to get them all finished before the day staff came on. If the patient were unfortunate to be having bowel surgery, they would have to have a rectal washout. This was done by inserting a rubber tube (with a stainless-steel funnel attached to the end of the tube) into the rectum, and warm water was poured into the funnel. The patient would be lying on their left side, and the funnel was held higher than the patient to allow the water to run into the rectum. Once the water had gone in, the funnel was lowered into a bucket to drain out the water and any faecal matter. This process could take up to an hour as the water had to drain back clear. If there was any faecal matter found in the bowel at surgery, the Surgeon would come to the ward to see the Sister or Charge Nurse to complain. Thank goodness for oral bowel cleansers that are used today.

All patients for surgery were made nil by mouth from 10 p.m. the night before, regardless of when their operation was. All patients had a premedication injection of Omnopon and Scopolamine again, regardless of the type of surgery. Omnopon is an opioid, and scopolamine is a drying agent, unlike today when patients turn up on the day of surgery to the theatre with no premedication. Once the patient had the premedication, they were drowsy and had to be lifted from the bed to the theatre trolley. This was done by using a theatre pack consisting of a canvas with two slots for two wooden poles to go through two draw sheets and a green blanket. This was a manual handling nightmare as the patient had to be lifted four times, once from the bed to the trolley and then in the theatre from the trolley to the theatre table then the same on return from the theatre. Prior to the premedication, all patients had a Hibitain bath, then were placed in gowns and paper knickers before lying in the theatre pack.

Chapter Twenty
WEEKEND CLEANING

In the RAF everything was structured, and everything was carried out by rote. A good example of this was what was called weekend cleaning. Generally, there were fewer patients at weekends, so the ward was cleaned from top to bottom as there was no shortage of labour, i.e., loads of trainee nurses. There was a weekend cleaning book that had to be completed and signed as being done, which the Sister or Charge Nurse would check.

There were three main areas to clean: the sluice, the linen cupboard, and the treatment room. The sluice was the worst job, this was generally assigned to the most junior of trainee nurses. Yes, even then, there was a pecking order. All the urinals (which were made of glass) had to be cleaned by hand with a large bottle brush before being put into the bedpan washer/sterilizer. Then the stainless-steel bedpans had to be scrubbed and put through the washer. Once cleaned, the urinals and bedpans were put into paper bags. All the plastic bowls used for washing patients had to be scrubbed and dried.

The urine testing cupboard had to be cleaned out and checked. Urine testing strips were just being developed. We had a basic strip for blood/protein, glucose in the urine was tested by putting urine in a test tube, and a tablet was added to the urine. The urine would fizz and change colour, and this would give a % amount of glucose in the urine depending on the colour of the urine. Specific gravity was also a manual process;

urine was placed in a tall glass container, and a specific gravity device (a hydrometer) was placed into the urine. The specific gravity was taken from the scale on the side of the measure.

The linen cupboard was one of those jobs that no one wanted to do. All the linen had to be removed, the cupboard cleaned and dusted. The linen had to be folded in a set way, sheets one way and blankets another. There was also a linen trolly, which had to be restocked.

The treatment room was a nightmare as all the bottles had to be removed from the cupboards, which had to be wiped clean, and all the lotions had to be checked, wiped, and put back in the cupboard. As most of the lotions were in bottles that were dispensed from the pharmacy, there was no way of knowing how long they had been in the cupboard and no expiry dates. There were some lethal concoctions, such as mercurochrome (basically mercury in a bottle) and EUSOL (Edinburgh University Solution of Lime), which were put into patients' wounds. Hibitane in spirit (alcohol) for soaking thermometers aqueous (water-based) Hibitain is used for cleaning wounds. To modern-day nurses, this may seem pointless, but it instilled discipline and pride in your ward, and in the end, you were doing your best for all your patients'.

Chapter Twenty-One
RAF HOSPITAL COSFORD, 1974–1975

Arriving at a new posting was always very daunting, as you did not know anyone or what the place was like. You had to go through an arrival procedure where you had to visit all the departments with a blue card and get signatures in all the boxes, then return this to the general office. I suppose in some ways it was useful in some respects, as you got to know where the departments were and who was the main contact.

The base was split into two sites: the main camp, which was a training unit, and the hospital site. All the hospital staff were accommodated on the main campsite, and we had to be transported to the hospital. I suppose RAF Cosford was the next piece of fate to unfold as I met my wife Mary there, and we were married on the 13th of March 1975 at the Wellington Registry Office near Shrewsbury. Before we could get married, we had to submit a *"General Application"* for permission to get married to the Station Commander, which, looking back, was very arcane as the last line said, "I, Sir, remain your obedient servant." This was then signed and passed to the Station Commander, who approved it or not! Thankfully, he approved the application. We had just finished a set of seven nights and got married on the morning of our last night shift, March 13, 1975.

Wedding day 13 March 1975

This was another blow to Mam, as she was not there for the wedding, but in another twist of fate, my Dad was able to attend. It's a bit of a long story, which I won't go into. He was waiting for an epidural (an injection of local anaesthetic for back pain). He had been waiting for several months, so I spoke to the Consultant Orthopaedic Surgeon at RAF Cosford, who said if he could get to Cosford, he would arrange the epidural.

As it happened, he had the epidural a few days before our wedding, so he was able to attend. There were only 9 people present at the register office, and it cost us just the registrar fees, from memory, around £6

Wedding day with Dad 1975

Wedding day group photo

We then took the train up to Newcastle as Dad had to get back home, so it killed two birds with one stone, so to speak. This went some way to placate Mam, as she was able to see us on the day of the wedding. Considering we only spent the cost of a marriage licence, we have been married for 49 years, and our golden wedding is in March 2025.

It was at RAF Hospital Cosford that I met my best friend, Ray Lennon. We hit it off straight away, and I shared the same room with Ray while I was at RAF Cosford. He also knew Mary, as she was at Cosford before I arrived doing her nurse training.

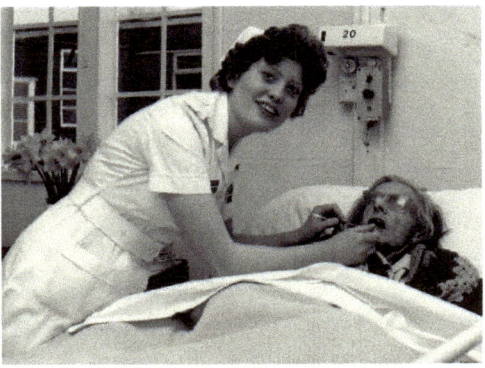

Mary doing mouth care 1975

I was only at Cosford for a short time, but I packed a lot in terms of learning new skills. As RAF nurses, we were all generalists, as we did not have specialist nurses as there are now, e.g., emergency medicine, intensive care unit (ICU) paediatric nurses, and many more.

There were two notable events (apart from getting married) that happened while I was at Cosford. On the main camp, there was an old airfield where there was a gliding club. One afternoon, there was a glider crash with two people inside. Both were seriously injured and brought straight to Cosford Hospital. Both had to be put on ventilators, and they needed emergency surgery to sort out the numerous fractures. As Cosford only had a single-bed ICU, space was cleared in one of the wards to nurse both patients together. It was about 15:00 hours when I was called to the Matrons Office to be told to go back to the accommodation block and get some sleep (easier said than done) as I would be one of two nurses to look after the two patients on night duty. This was a typical scenario in the RAF. I spent several weeks looking after these two patients, who, I am pleased to say, both survived.

Several years later, I came across one of the guys at RAF Hospital Nocton Hall while he was attending outpatients. It was funny, I recognised him straight away. I did ask him to check first if he was in the glider crash, which he was. We had a long chat about the accident and his recovery, and I am pleased to say he made a full recovery from the accident.

The other event was somewhat more bizarre. Ray and I were both summoned to Matron's office. The first thought in your mind was that I was in trouble.

This time, we were told that premature twins had been born in maternity and that they needed to be looked after 24 hours a day. Ray and I were put on permanent night duty, 7 nights on and 7 nights off. We were sent to the maternity ward to be shown how to tube-feed a premature baby (this would not be allowed now and is not for the fainthearted). It's a scary thing to do, I can assure you. Anyway, the Sister collected all the items needed to tube-feed: milk, a 20-ml syringe, and the tiny tube that had to be passed into the babies' stomachs through their mouths.

She assured us that the tube could only go into the stomach (something to do with premature babies' anatomy), as I had visions of pouring milk into the baby's lungs. So, we watched her do two, then she watched us do two, and that was it (experts!!). We were sent off to come back at 19:30 hours to start the night shift.

This was more ground-breaking in many ways in that never had "male nurses" in the RAF worked on a maternity ward, let alone looked after premature babies. It was also a novel experience for the mothers, in fact, it worked very well. In the mornings, one of us would go around with the tea trolley if the midwife was busy in the labour ward, and we built up a good rapport with the ladies. Ray and I worked for 3 months on permanent nights in the maternity ward.

After returning to work after our last set of nights, we were told that both babies had been discharged home (shame that we missed this), and we would like to think that we played our part in their recovery. Mind you, if any neonatal or paediatric nurse reads this, their heads would blow off, but at the time, you did what you were told and looked after your patients to the best of your ability.

That was our claim to fame in 1975. Ray and I often spoke about this and wondered what happened to the twins as they had grown up. We will never know. That's nursing.

RAF Hospital Cosford Nurse Training School was due to close in July 1975, which meant Mary had to move to another training hospital.

She was posted to RAF Hospital Nocton Hall. As we were now married, I was also posted to RAF Hospital Nocton Hall with her.

Ray and I went back to Cosford in 2018 for a visit organised by Princess Mary's Royal Air Force Nursing Association. We had a group photo of all those people who had served at Cosford over the years. Sadly, many of those in the photo have died, including Ray.

Cosford Veterans 2018 RAF Cosford

Chapter Twenty-Two
RAF Hospital Nocton Hall, 1975–1978

As there were no married quarters available, we had to live in the male and female accommodation blocks, which was not a great start to married life. Then, I found a bungalow for rent in the village of Metheringham, which was about 3 miles from the hospital. As I could not drive and could not afford a car, I bought a Honda 50 motorbike, which was great to get back and forth to work. As service pay was very low, I applied to the local council for a rent rebate, which, looking at the guidelines, I was entitled to claim. However, I received a letter back that said, "As you are in the RAF, you have to claim a rent rebate through the RAF." I went to the general office and asked for the forms to apply, but I did not qualify for this.

I was pissed off about this, as it should not have made any difference if I was in the RAF or not, so I wrote to my MP, who at the time was Ted Short, MP for Newcastle East. About 3 weeks after writing, a married quarter suddenly became available, and I found later that on my record was the letters PE, which had been added and translated into Parliamentary Enquiry. As it turned out, Mary was pregnant and was discharged from the RAF within the week. Once pregnant, you were discharged from the service, unlike today, when women can have a career and children and stay in the services. It was lucky that we had been allocated a married quarter.

So, our first married quarter was at 7 Akrotiri Square, Nocton, Lincoln. As we had nothing, we had to rely on having all RAF furnishings and fittings, even pots and pans. This was all fine and dandy until you had to move out, as everything had to be spotless, otherwise, there was a financial penalty. The worst thing was the cooker, as it was closely inspected, and any bit of crease or dirt meant you were in trouble. The process of taking over and handing back a married quarter was called "marching in" and "marching out". This consisted of the Station Warden (who was a civilian) and the Families Officer, who could be a Warrant Officer or Flight Lieutenant. They would go into every nook and cranny looking for dust and any damage to the fabric of the married quarter. This was quite a degrading process. Today, married quarters get cleaned by a cleaning company.

Andrew, our first son, was born on the 29th of February 1976 at RAF Hospital Nocton Hall. I was not present at the birth, as in those days, men were chucked out of the labour ward. Mary could not breastfeed, so when she came home, it was bottle and bath duty.

Unfortunately, Mary developed a breast abscess, was very unwell, and had to be admitted to the hospital, where she had surgery to drain the breast abscess. So, there I was with a 6-week-old baby to look after, which, from my perspective, was not a problem (I had looked after premature babies, after all), but Matron had other ideas. I went to see her, asking for time off to look after Andrew, and was told, and I

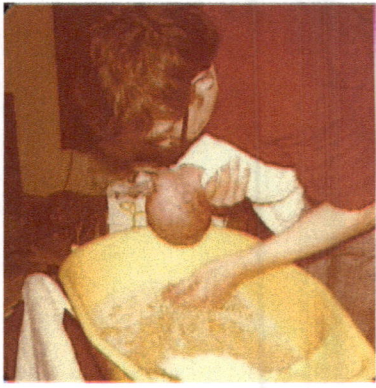

Me bathing Andrew 1976

quote, "Can't you send the child to a relative?" Obviously, this was not an option. I was given some annual leave as compassionate leave was not considered, and this was long before paternity leave.

It was my Nana to the rescue once again at the age of 67 years old. She came down from Newcastle and looked after Andrew while Mary was in the hospital and stayed on when she was discharged home, which meant I could go to work. She was a lifesaver. 1976 was the year of the heat wave, which went on for weeks. It was so hot that the Matron allowed the female nurses to remove their tights for work this was unheard of. There was no green grass anywhere, and water became a problem as we had no rain for months.

This bloody Matron was single and had no compassion or understanding about family issues. Thankfully, things are much better these days, but back then, it was a nightmare.

While at RAF Hospital Nocton Hall, I became involved in various clubs, including the drama club. My claim to fame was playing Widow Twankey in Aladin, which I thoroughly enjoyed. I did not know I had this in me to play in front of an audience and be funny.

Me playing Widow Twankey 1976

Me on stage playing Widow Twankey 1976

I became a qualified projectionist and would run the station cinema at weekends. We would request two films a week which were delivered to the unit. I was also involved with local charities. It was 1977, the year of the Queen's Silver Jubilee. I was very proud to be awarded the Queen's Silver Jubilee Medal.

BUCKINGHAM PALACE
7th June 1977

By Command of

HER MAJESTY THE QUEEN

the accompanying Medal is forwarded to

SENIOR AIRCRAFTMAN ROBERT F SANDERSON RAF

to be worn in commemoration of

Her Majesty's Silver Jubilee

6th February 1952 : 6th February 1977

Silver Jubilee Medal Certificate 1977

Only 30000 were issued to nominated individuals, making this one of the rarest Coronation and Jubilee medals awarded. It was while at RAF Hospital Nocton Hall, working in the medical ward, that I started working with a Consultant Physician, Wing Commander Bill Larkworthy, who introduced fibre optic gastrointestinal endoscopy into the RAF. I was present when he removed the first coin from the stomach of a seventy-six-year-old retired member of the Royal Flying Corps (forerunner of the Royal Air Force) using grasping forceps that were specially made by the manufacturer of the endoscopes. It turned out to be a 1953 sixpence, which saved him from having open abdominal surgery. Shortly after this, a chance comment was made by Wing Commander

Larkworthy to a Consultant Surgeon, where he was telling him that he had removed a coin using the endoscope. The Surgeon then said, 'He had a soldier on the surgical ward who had swallowed a 2-shilling piece (alcohol was involved) and was scheduled for surgery the following day to remove it. He said, 'Why don't you have a go at removing it?' which he did, saving the soldier from having to have abdominal surgery.

I was present at the first and second removals of coins from the stomach using an endoscope with grasping forceps. I was also involved in early clinical trials of Cimetidine (an H2 receptor blocker), which reduced the amount of gastric acid. I remember one patient in particular who had Zollinger-Ellison syndrome. He was a watchmaker from Lincoln and had severe ulceration of the oesophagus and stomach. Following treatment with Cimetidine, the appearance of his oesophagus and stomach ulceration improved dramatically (Reference, ***Cimetidine in the Management of Zollinger-Ellison Syndrome, W. Larkworthy & H. L. Davies Postgraduate Medical Journal (December 1977) 53, 749–750).*** Although this was groundbreaking medicine, we had a rudimentary system for cleaning the endoscopes. Two lengths of plastic drainage pipes were filled with cidex, an awful green liquid, which was Glutaraldehyde, used as a cold sterilant to disinfect and clean heat-sensitive equipment such as dialysis instruments, surgical instruments, suction bottles, bronchoscopes, and endoscopes. We had to soak the scopes for around 10 minutes, then rinse with deionized water. It was a race to get the scopes cleaned between patients, as we only had two endoscopes. Today there are purpose-built endoscope washers, and the awful green cidex has gone. The patient was sat up on a bed with the head of the bed in an upright position. My role was to stand behind the head of the bed and push the endoscope in and out, depending on what the Consultant said. The biggest risk was the patient biting the scope, so we had bite guards that were placed between the teeth with a hole in the middle of the scope to go through. It was the nurse's responsibility to make sure that the patient did not bite the scope. At times, this could be a challenge, as the scopes were a lot bigger than they are today.

One other memory relating to endoscopy was that one evening, I was working a late shift in the medical ward where patients were recovering from an endoscopy that they had in the morning. I was attending to the evening meals when a patient said that there was water coming from under the bathroom door. There were only two of us on duty: me and a Sergeant State Registered Nurse (SRN) called Arthur. He was very introverted and quiet. The door was locked. Arthur went out of the office window to see if he could gain entry into the bathroom via a window. I went to the bathroom and opened the lock with a 2 pence coin, as the locks had slits on the outside in case of emergency, which this was. When I opened the door, there was a patient submerged underwater with the hot tap running, and he looked like a lobster, very red. I turned off the taps, pulled out the plug, and started mouth-to-mouth resuscitation. Fortunately, after several breaths, he started to cough and breathe by himself. Luckily, he did not sustain any significant burns to the skin, just a little red. The duty doctor saw him, and I was praised for my quick action, which undoubtedly saved his life. The following morning, Wing Commander Larkworthy was informed of what had happened, and a review took place. In those days, patients were brought into the hospital the day before the procedure, they were made nil by mouth at 22:00 hours, and on the day of the procedure, they were given a premedication of 100mg of pethidine. Just before the endoscopy, an anaesthetic throat spray was administered to the back of the throat, and an intravenous injection of 10 mg of diazepam was given. So, the patient was heavily sedated. Diazepam has a long half-life between 30 and 56 hours. This means that the drug takes a long time to clear the body, so sitting in a hot bath was not a good idea after having intravenous diazepam in the morning. It was agreed that patients could not have a bath on the day of endoscopy. We had no showers.

My time at RAF Hospital Nocton Hall was coming to an end as I was posted to RAF Lyneham Station Medical Centre (SMC) in Wiltshire on the 4th of January 1978, on promotion to Corporal (Cpl). This was my first and last Medical Centre. You could not live in the married quarter and clean it, especially if there were children around, so you had to send your family to a relative. Mary and Andrew went to my mother's while I sorted out the house. This has been recorded in an earlier chapter.

Chapter Twenty-Three
RAF LYNEHAM 1978 TILL 1979

I was posted to RAF Lyneham in 1978 to work in the SMC. Up until this point, I had always worked in hospitals so this would be a new experience for me. Again, there were no married quarters available, so I had to live in the barrack block for 4 weeks which was a pain in the arse as it was right at the end of the runway.

RAF Lyneham was a massive base and was home to the Hercules fleet of transport aircraft, a very busy station as all the aeromedical evacuation flights came through RAF Lyneham. Sadly, RAF Lyneham has been closed and is now an Army Training Unit. All transport aircraft now fly out of RAF Brize Norton in Oxfordshire.

RAF Lyneham was my first posting as a Junior Non-Commissioned Officer (JNCO). I arrived at the SMC to be greeted by Warrant Officer (WO) Jimmy Pringle. He was what was known as Medical Admin. He was in charge of the SMC with a Sgt (who was a right git as he hated nurses) who was his deputy. I was told that I would oversee the treatment room. This was essentially where all the nursing interventions were carried out. There were two other nurses, one a Senior Aircraft Woman (SACW) SEN and a civilian SRN who just happened to be the wife of the Wing Commander in Charge of Administration (known as OC Admin, a very important position) for the station. This would be a challenge as it is never easy when the Wife of a senior officer is working alongside service personnel.

There were several doctors who were General Practitioners led by a Senior Medical Officer (SMO) Wing Commander with 5 Flight Lieutenants. To be honest I did not warm to this type of nursing as I was a hospital nurse at heart. However, I had to get on with the job, which was varied with treatment room activities, these were mainly preliminary observations prior to medicals. All aircrew must have these done on a regular basis, dressings, taking blood and inoculations. We also had to respond to any emergencies on the base. I delivered one baby and sadly had to deal with a stillbirth on the way to the hospital with a lady in the back of an ambulance.

There were 3 ambulances available: 2 Land Rover vehicles appley, named Red Cross 1 and 2, and a normal road ambulance for transporting patients to the local military hospital at RAF Hospital Wroughton.

I had been there about a week when WO Pringle called me to his office. He had my medical record file (F Med 4) on his desk. He said he had read through and noted that I had a mental health issue in the past and said 'he did not want any repetition of this' to say I was gobsmacked was an understatement. This was wrong on several levels. He should not have read through my medical notes, and secondly, he should not have referred to my mental health. This was 1979 and things were so different to today that he would have been in serious trouble should I have reported this, but I did not want any trouble.

The other place you were expected to work in was the dispensary again; all the staff were expected to work here, and none of us were trained to dispense medicines. Having said that, most of the drugs were simple, e.g. if you had a sore throat, cough or cold-like symptoms, the standard treatment was soluble aspirin, which you had to dissolve two tablets in water then gargle and swallow, for the cough, you were either given Benilyn or Pholcodeine both were supplied as a linctus. For nasal congestion, the standard treatment was karvol capsules, which came in a small capsule. The top had to be cut off, and the liquid was put onto a handkerchief, which you inhaled.

The SMC also looked after all the families of the service personnel on the base. Again, most of the drugs were either the contraceptive pill or antibiotics for the children. More complex drugs were also dispensed. Again, looking back, there was only one person working in the dispensary, no checking by another person to ensure that you had dispensed the correct medication. Anything more complicated was referred to the local Military Hospital at RAF Hospital Wroughton.

I had to take my turn as Duty Medic. This was a 24-hour duty, so after a full day's work, you remained at the SMC with a driver for any emergencies that may occur. I was able to sleep, but I was always on high alert in case anything happened. We also had to cover the airfield when a Hercules carrying medical evacuation patients was landing, or an aircraft was in trouble. We had several that landed on one engine.

I hated this as it was invariably at night, and the airfield was just a mass of lights. Let's be clear there was no training given you had to learn on the job and were heavily reliant on the drivers who knew the airfield well. This was all fine and dandy until you got lost, which happened to me on my first venture. There was a map of the airfield in the vehicle with grid references. The Air Traffic Controller would send you to a certain location we got lost, or rather, I got lost as I was navigating, so the air traffic controller took great delight in sending us to various grid references around the airfield until we got it right. I had to master the radio as well and all that radio speak, using the phonetic alphabet (Alfa/Bravo/Charlie, etc.) I kept thinking about getting back to a hospital.

I took over my second married quarter at 10 Melsome Road Lyneham Chippenham Wiltshire, which was about a 15-minute walk to the main camp, as I still did not have a car as I had not passed my driving test. Luckily, I managed to get a test through the RAF at Lyneham and passed which was a great relief as we could now get a car. My first car was a white Vauxhall Viva. Mary and Andrew arrived from Newcastle and were pregnant with our second child, Matthew. The second pregnancy was not straightforward as Matthew was breach (feet first) all the way through the pregnancy. During the antenatal appointments, a caesarean section was never discussed. This would be common practice today. Mary went into labour. I drove her to RAF Hospital Wroughton with Andrew in the back of the car, where Matthew was born via a vaginal delivery on the 10th of January 1979. There were some problems encountered during the birth, and there was some question of him being starved of oxygen. All in all, it was a difficult birth. This did have consequences for Matthew and the whole family as he grew up, as he was diagnosed with Autism Spectrum Disorder (ASD) and Asperger's later in life.

I had been at RAF Lyneham for around 8 months when I was told I was being posted back to a hospital, RAF Hospital Ely in Cambridgeshire. I had never been to RAF Hospital Ely before, so I spoke to the WO and said, 'Is there any way I could go back to RAF Hospital Nocton Hall' he said 'he would speak to the postings officer who he knew' and as if by magic with one phone call my posting to RAF Hospital Ely was changed to RAF Hospital Nocton Hall.

Chapter Twenty-Four
RAF HOSPITAL NOCTON HALL 1979 TILL 1981

We went back to RAF Hospital Nocton Hall again for the third time and our third married quarter at 15 Khormasker Drive Nocton Lincoln. It was during this time that Prince Charles married Lady Dianna Spencer I, along with others, and arranged a street party for all the children at the camp, which was a great day. All the children were given a commemorative tankard for the occasion.

Royal Wedding Street party 29 July 1981

Street party for Royal Wedding 29 July 1981

Street party for Royal Wedding 29 July 1981

I spent most of my tour on Ward 5 male orthopaedics. The Charge Nurse was a chain smoker and would buy 60 Sovereign cigarettes from the newspaper trolley that came around the wards in the morning. He would smoke all day in the ward office. I was a bit of a Jack the Lad during this time as I was an agent for Littlewoods Football Pools. I collected the coupons on a Thursday night around the local village and cycled into Metheringham, which was about 3 miles away from RAF Hospital Nocton Hall, I used a fold up bike which I bought second hand which did the job. The only issue was the dark nights and the bad weather. On Friday, I would nip off the ward to collect the football pools around the camp, which took about an hour. This gave us some extra money as I was paid a commission from the takings.

I had a friend called Ian, and we did all sorts of money-saving schemes. The biggest one was a tree that had broken in strong winds and was just lying on the ground, so we hired a chainsaw and were able to cut enough logs to last us through the winter as we still had open fires. We also did painting and decorating around the local village. One job we did turned into a complete disaster. There was a ward domestic on ward 5 called Joyce who wanted her parlour redecorated. She was very house-proud. The houses in the village were mainly cottages, and most of the time was spent in the back kitchen, which had a black range coal fire. Joyce had numerous brass ornaments, which she polished weekly, and the back kitchen was immaculate. So, Ian and I turned up to start. We removed all the old wallpaper and began to paint the ceiling with white emulsion, unfortunately, the ceiling had distemper *(Distemper is an early form of whitewash, also used as a medium for artistic painting, usually made from powdered chalk or lime and size a gelatinous substance)* on it so as we applied the emulsion paint the distemper caused the paint to peel off the ceiling and to drop on to the floor. What we did not know is that you can't paint over distemper! Anyway, Joyce came home and walked in on this complete carnage, and she went berserk despite us telling her we would sort it, which we did. After this experience, the painting and decorating came to an end.

Following a short spell in the Ear Nose and Throat Ward, which was tedious, the remaining time at RAF Hospital Nocton Hall was uneventful.

I was posted again in 1981 to RAF Hospital Wroughton in Wiltshire, this was to be an interesting and long posting.

FROM BOILER SUIT TO BLUE SUIT

Chapter Twenty-Five
RAF HOSPITAL WROUGHTON, 1981–1995

On this occasion, we had a married quarter already assigned and ready to move into. Our furniture, which had arrived the day before, was waiting for us to unpack. This was to be our last married quarter at 105 Thorney Park, Wroughton, Swindon. The hospital was situated on top of a hill with the village of Wroughton in a valley below. It was a great place for the boys to grow up in a very safe and fun place to play. As we were on top of the hill, the weather was extreme. We had hot summers and lots of snow in the winters

Typical winter at RAF Hospital Wroughton

Summer with the boys in the paddling pool at RAF Hospital Wroughton

Boys on hay bales RAF Hospital Wroughton

My first ward was Ward 4 Male Orthopaedics, which was run by an Army Major called Gruber. His nickname was Herr Gruber. He was a right misery. I stayed on Male Orthopaedics for about 9 months, then was moved to Male Medical, which I enjoyed very much as you had to think about and understand the disease process of your patients.

In early 1982, I was promoted to Sergeant (Sgt). I had to go on a course called General Service Training 2 (GST 2) at the Airman's Command School, RAF Hereford. It was a Senior Non-Commissioned Officer (SNCO) training school to ensure that you had the knowledge and skills for the rank of Sgt. This was a gruelling three weeks, which happened to coincide with the Falklands War. The course cumulated in a 72-hour outside exercise where we all had to take the lead. It was knackering and had bugger all to do with my job, but it was essentially a test of leadership.

Airman's Command School 1982

I passed the course and went back to RAF Hospital Wroughton and was moved again to SNCO in charge of the Casualty Department. This was a tiny department with just two staff members, me and one other. We were covered by the Civilian Medical Officer (CMO), who was a civilian GP who was clueless about emergency medicine. If we needed specialist input, we would call the on-call registrar. I arrived back at RAF Hospital Wroughton just as the Falklands casualties were being transported back to the United Kingdom (UK). There were lots of families attending the hospital, so all of us living in married quarters were asked if we could put up some of the families. We were able to accommodate the parents of one of the servicemen coming back.

All the casualties arrived by coach and were brought into the hospital via the Aeromed Department. The casualties were triaged and sent to the most appropriate ward. The vast majority had severe burns, especially on the hands. This was an opportunity to look at how burns to the hands could be treated in a different way. Any burn will cause contractions to the skin, especially in the hands, so all causalities with burns to the hands were put in what was called "flamazine bags," which was a cream called flamazine applied to the hands (which is a topical antibacterial cream with an active ingredient which belongs to the group of antibiotic medicines called sulphonamides. Flamazine is used to prevent infection in severe burns) and then the hands were placed into a plastic bag, which allowed the casualty to move the fingers. This prevented contractions in the fingers and infection. The other condition that was prevalent in the infantry and Para's was trench foot. This was last seen in the Great War, as troops spent long hours with their feet in damp, cold conditions or immersed in water. It was the same scenario as in the Falklands, where wet and damp conditions prevailed, and the boots were wholly inadequate. The boot only came up to the ankle, and then putties were wrapped around the lower leg to the top of the boot. Following the Falklands, a new design of boot was introduced. During this time, it was very demanding for the staff to look after all these casualties. I did a spell of Senior Nights (in charge of 5 wards), and then the screams started once the lights went out. Some of the stories (I don't feel able to write about this as I can't verify if this or what was being said happened) the troops told were difficult for us to understand because we were not there. Still, these were men who had been involved in hand-to-hand combat using bayonets. It was kill or be killed.

Several years later, I was on night duty in the Male Orthopaedic ward at RAF Hospital Wroughton when an Army Warrant Officer came into the office. He was in a wheelchair as he had recently had surgery on his knee. He asked, 'if he could talk to me'. He started to cry, and I soon established that he was talking about his experiences during the Falklands War, lots of unresolved issues now known as Post-Traumatic Stress Disorder (PTSD). I referred him to the Psychiatric Centre, which was leading the way in managing patients with PTSD. One of the Consultant Psychiatrists who became a leading expert in PTSD, John McCarthy and Terry Waite (hostages in Lebanon) were debriefed at the hospital by the Consultant.

There are numerous ex-servicemen and women still suffering from PTSD from subsequent conflicts that have never been addressed. We mistreat our veterans in this country, unlike in the United States, which has Veterans' Hospitals. Since the demise of the UK military hospitals, most Veterans have been at the behest of local NHS services, which have sadly failed many. A new scheme has just started where your medical record at your GP is flagged as a Veteran. There is also a nominated GP for Veterans.

Chapter Twenty-Six
HOLIDAYS

As I previously stated, I never went on holiday when I was a child. This was something I was determined to change with my children. It was when we were posted to RAF Hospital Wroughton, which is in Wiltshire, that we started going on holiday. We found this lovely place in Cornwall called Holywell Bay. It is on the Atlantic side of Cornwall, South of Newquay. We started off camping. I bought a large frame tent with two bedrooms and a kitchen area.

Holywell Bay has a campsite and a caravan park with a short walk to the beach. Holywell Bay has been used for several TV series Poldark was the latest. It has a distinctive view out to sea with 2 large rocks poking out of the sea.

Andrew and Matthew at Holywell Bay

Sunset at Holywell Bay

We had some great holidays when Andrew and Matthew were young. The site had a club which provided evening entertainment for adults and children. We would stay until 9 pm and then make our way back to the tent. Camping is great when the weather is good, but it can be quite miserable when it is raining. After 5 years of camping, we stared to rent a caravan for 2 weeks. At least there was a TV if it was raining, and it was much more comfortable than sleeping on air beds. We continued holidaying at Holywell Bay until the boys were grown up.

Mary and I still had our holiday in Cornwall until we caught the cruising bug. We are very fortunate to live in Wiltshire as Avebury, with its Stone Circle, is 15 minutes away. Barbury Castle, a Hillfort along the Ridgeway Route first occupied some 2500 years ago, is only 10 minutes away, and Stonehenge is 45 minutes away with some beautiful countryside.

We did have a very special holiday to celebrate our 40th wedding anniversary. In 2015, we went to Venice on the Orient Express. This holiday was a once-in-a-lifetime event as it was very expensive as we took the train there and back. We booked the Cipriani Hotel, which was fabulous.

Hotel Cipriani Venice 2015

We stayed at the Union Jack Club in Waterloo on the 19th of September 2015 as we had to be at a London hotel early the next day. We arrived at the hotel, and the whole process was very slick. Our luggage was taken, and we were given our boarding passes. We were departing from Victoria to Folkstone on the British Pullman. The hotel was just across the road from the station, so it was a short walk to the station. We had a VIP lounge while we waited, then were taken to the train, which was very plush. We departed Victoria at 10:45 hours on the 20th of September 2015. On the way to Folkstone, we had a lovely lunch on the train with a Bellini, which is made with Prosecco and peach puree. Once we arrived at Folkstone there was a brass band playing as we left the train. Just a short walk from the station several luxury coaches were waiting to take us to Calis via the Channel Tunnel. The coaches were the ones used for Premier League football teams, and they were very luxurious. Again, there was food and drink available from the holiday representative. Once we reached Calis, the coaches pulled up next to the Orient Express. The train staff were all standing in line in front of the train.

Train staff in front of Orient Express

We were then shown to our cabin by the Steward, who was called Rupert. Interestingly, he looked after David Suchet when he did a documentary on the Orient Express as part of the Agatha Christies murder mystery "Murder on the Orient Express" This train was opulence on a stick. Our cabin was beautifully made with two large seats and a very clever washing facility (no shower), but it was only one day and one night) Our suitcases were already in our cabin, ready for dinner. We were going to second sitting around 8:30 pm.

Restaurant Orient Express 2015

We had lunch in the cabin brought in by Rupert then just sat back and enjoyed the scenery. We changed for dinner and had the choice of one of three dining cars, all very different. As we were traveling back on the train, we would sample all three. When we were having dinner, Rupert would transform our cabin into bunk beds for sleeping. I would take the top bunk. In the morning, Rupert would transform the cabin back for sitting and breakfast. As we travelled across Europe, the scenery was spectacular. At the borders, we would have to change engines, which again was very slick.

We arrived at Venice on Monday, the 21st of September 2015, at 17:56 hours and were met by the holiday representative and taken to a small launch. We were taken to our hotel by the launch and dropped off at a small pier at the hotel where we were met by hotel staff. We were booked in and taken to our room, which took our breath away. It was just fabulous.

Hotel room Cipriani Hotel 2015

our suitcases were already in the room waiting for us. Once unpacked, we went exploring Venice. The hotel had a shuttle launch which ran every

10 minutes night and day. Once back on the mainland, we started in St Mark's Square and then found a restaurant for something to eat as the prices in the hotel were exorbitant. Luckily, breakfast was included in the cost. We found a great local restaurant which served authentic local food, which was delicious. This is where we were introduced to Limoncello as they gave us a shot at the end of our meal. It's morish; I still drink it now. We stayed at this restaurant for our time in Venice. We also had to have a trip in a gondola at a cost of €70.

Me and Mary on condoler Venice 2015

Breakfast arrived on a trolly with a large, shiny, domed cover. When we removed the cover, the breakfast was delicious.

We had a walking tour booked for mid-morning on the 22nd of September 2015 called the Hidden Venice walking tour. The guide took us to parts of Venice which tourists often missed. After the tour, we spent the rest of the day exploring. Oddly, you take a turn and you end up in a different place. You cannot get lost as you just need to get back to the Rialto Bridge. Then, it is a short walk to St Mark's Square. This was an expensive trip, but as I said, once in a lifetime. The total cost was £10850; we arrived in Venice on Monday, 21st of September 2015, and arrived back in London on the 27th of September 2015, at 17:40 hours. It was worth every penny.

Breakfast hotel Cipriani Venice 2015

We have been back to Venice on a further two occasions while on a Mediterranean cruise we walked into the centre of Venice and got the launch back to the ship. We know our way around Venice now, so I'm quite happy wondering about it. On the last cruise the ship did a transit of the Grand Canal at midnight. This was fabulous to see Venice at night from the ship

FROM BOILER SUIT TO BLUE SUIT

Transit of Grand Canal Venice midnight

Chapter Twenty-Seven
RAF HOSPITAL WROUGHTON CONTINUES.

Detachment to RAF Molesworth, February 1985

In early February 1985, I was called to the Matron's office to be told I had been detached to RAF Brampton in Cambridgeshire. I had to be there on the 4th of February 1985 with my full combat kit. I was told I would be fully briefed when I was at RAF Brampton. I arrived late in the afternoon and was shown to the Sergeant Mess to be booked in and get my room sorted out. In the evening, I was sitting in the bar when WO Bill Bell walked in. The last time I saw him was when I was training at RAF Hospital Nocton Hall in 1972. We greeted each other, shook hands, and ordered a couple of beers. He did not know why he was there, either. Then Sgt John Neild walked in again, the last time I had seen John was at RAF Hospital Nocton Hall in 1978.

We all sat down and had a catch-up. Being in the dark about why we were there was very unnerving. We were called in for a briefing on the afternoon of February 5, 1985. Joining us were two Senior Aircraftmen (SAC) Medics. So, the team was one WO SRN, two Sgt SENs, and two SAC Medics. We were told we would be the medical support for a night operation to take back RAF Molesworth from the peace protesters. This would include troops and police. We would be part of a large convoy of vehicles leaving around 01:00 hours on the 6th of February 1985, and we would be dropped off at a hangar to set up a medical centre. We met at the Station Medical Centre to sort out the kit and vehicle that we would be using later that night. We had a wide range of equipment and drugs to take with us so we could treat most injuries and illnesses.

At 01:00 hours on February 6, 1985, 1,500 troops and police were deployed to secure the seven-mile station perimeter for the Ministry of Defence. The operation has been described as "perhaps the most dramatic occurrence in all the peace and anti-nuclear campaigns of the 1980s in the UK.' The troops had been training for weeks in the rapid deployment of a three-metre-high (9.8 ft), six-roll Dannert wire fence (which is a type of barbed or razor wire that is formed in large coils that can be expanded like a concertina) behind which a 5-metre-wide (16 ft) no-man's-land concrete roadway would be constructed along the line of the fence. A 10-foot-high (3.0 metre) Weldmesh steel fence (which is an electric fusion welded prefabricated joined grid consisting of a series of parallel longitudinal wires with accurate spacing welded to cross wires at the required spacing) was erected beyond that. Floodlights were installed every 100 yards, and the Ministry of Defence Police and armed guards were patrolling the fence 24 hours a day. The Secretary of State for Defence, Michael Heseltine, arrived by RAF helicopter, wearing a camouflage jacket over his suit. The roads around the station were blocked by trucks carrying construction materials and fencing. The cost of the operation to clear and fence RAF Molesworth was in the order of £6.5 million.

We were dropped off near a disused hanger. The temperature was minus 15 degrees Celsius, bloody freezing. We approached the hanger in total darkness with just torches of light. Guess what? The door was locked, so we had to call for someone to either bring a key or bolt cutters. After about an hour, a chap arrived with bolt cutters to remove the padlock. Once in, we set up a basic medical centre. When daylight came, we could see what had happened overnight: a perimeter fence had been put up. There were portable toilets but no shower facilities. This would come later. All of us were frozen to the core as we were in a cold hanger. The good news came later in the day when we were told that our portacabin would be installed the following day. This would hopefully give us heat and running water. Once we had the portacabin, we could set up more functioning medical facilities, which we did. We were put on a rota of two weeks on one week off. As the weeks went on, we had to run the gauntlet of the peace protesters to get back onto the base. Once the warmer weather came, life was more bearable. This detachment lasted for 3 months in total, then returned to RAF Hospital Wroughton Casualty Department.

Outside Medical Centre RAF Molesworth 1985

Bob and Clive with ambulance RAF Molesworth 1985

During my time in Casualty, one memorable event came to mind. It was summer, and we were advised that three Army personnel were being sent to RAF Hospital Wroughton with heat stroke. On arrival, one of the patients, a big chap over 6 feet and very muscular, had completely lost it. He had ripped off his clothes (he looked like the Incredible Hulk) and was stark naked. He started to become aggressive and then ran out of the department down the main corridor with myself and a Doctor in hot pursuit. It was obvious that we were not going to stop him on our own, so we gathered another three Male Nurses and an injection of midazolam (this is a sedative). We had the patient

Visit by Sir John Stanley Minister for Armed Forces RAF Molesworth 1895

cornered, so we took our chance to get him on the floor so that we could give him an intravenous injection of midazolam, which had the desired effect. He was then put on a trolley and taken to the medical ward for treatment. When he recovered, he had no recollection of this event, just as well.

I also started running around this time and would go for an hour's run at lunchtime. Several of us would run from the hospital to Barbury Castle and back, around 6 miles. I was very fit and thin due to the running; I did one marathon in Berlin in 1987 and numerous Great North Runs. I ran my last with my sister Julie. I still have the T-shirts to prove it!

Me and Julie after the 1992 Great North Run

In 1984, the rules of the game were about to change. The SEN was being phased out, and all nurses would now become Registered Nurses (RN). The RAF had joined up with civilian hospitals to jointly run what was called conversion courses from SEN to RN. The only snag is that you needed 5 GCE O levels to be able to apply for the course (*remember that*

I left school with no qualifications; now it gets interesting). How could I get 5 O levels in such a short time? The first conversion course was to start in 1985, but I could not make that or the second course, so I was looking at the third course.

I looked at what was on offer at Swindon College. I could do human biology, sociology, English language, and economics all on a Monday, so I went to the Matron to ask for a day release to do the O levels. To my surprise, I got a Monday off, and in September of 1984, I started my road to the conversion course. It was difficult at the start as the classes were full of 16+ youths who did not want to be there. I had to get this done and dusted, so I had to bite the bullet and get on with it.

I was diligent in doing all the homework, and to my astonishment, the Human Biology Lecturer held up my homework as an example of how this should be done. It was very embarrassing!!

The RAF Education Department also ran weekend GCE O-level courses. It was sitting back and taking in all the salient points, and then soon afterwards, I would take the exam. I enrolled in commerce and economics and decided to have a go at the English language paper. You never know. I thought I might be lucky. I sat the exams in June of 1984, and to my astonishment, I passed all three with a grade of A in English and Bs in commerce and economics. So, with three down and two to go, I pulled out of the English and economics glasses at Swindon College, as I had just passed the exams so that I could concentrate on human biology and sociology. I took the exams in 1985 and got a grade of As for Human Biology and Sociology, all in all, 3 As and 2 Bs, not bad for a lad who left school with no qualifications.

While waiting to hear about the conversion course, I was told that I was being posted to RAF Hospital Wegberg in Germany. Again, the Gods were looking down on me as there was a Sgt SEN in Wegberg called Graham who did not want to come to Wroughton and wanted to stay in Germany, so we did an exchange posting, which was accepted, thankfully.

The next thing was to apply for the conversion course. I applied and was accepted for the 1988 course at the Princess Margaret Hospital in Swindon. There was no need to move. The conversion course from SEN to RN was 12 months long. We spent all our clinical placements at The Princess Margaret Hospital in Swindon. We had some good tutors, George Chun and Jan Oakman, and a useless one who did not last long. Essentially, we spent time in the School of Nursing looking at evidence-based nursing and research. We spent hours in the library finding research papers to support the assignments that we were submitting. This was before the computer. There were 12 on the course, a mixture of civilian and service nurses.

Group Photo Conversion Course 1988

We had to choose a topic for our final examination. I chose HIV and AIDS. I had to remember and use the right research to support what I was quoting in the essay. I practiced this every night at home. I even recorded the whole essay on a tape cassette so I could play it in the car. Following the exam, we waited for the results, which was very stressful. After about a week, we were all called to the School of Nursing to collect our envelope containing the letter with the results I passed, which was a relief. I was now a registered nurse at last, this was something that I had aspired to since starting my nursing career. We were all then waiting to see where we would be posted. Again, I was left in situ at RAF Hospital Wroughton. What a relief.

I was assigned to Male Orthopaedics. The ward was run by an Army Captain and a Flight Lieutenant Nursing Sister, both living in the dark ages. I had come back into the military system full of new knowledge and was using evidence-based nursing care rather than just doing what we always did. This resulted in some tension and conflicts as to what should be best practice. It ended up being a battle of wills, but I was not going to compromise the care of my patients. As luck would have it, the Army Captain was posted, and we had a new boss who was much more receptive to modern nursing. I had decided that I would like to specialise in Orthopaedic Nursing, which would require another 6-month course at the Royal United Hospital Bath.

This was just as well, as Matthew was having problems at school with learning and behavioural problems. In those days, autism, dyslexia, and attention deficit hyperactivity disorder (ADHD) were not understood by teachers, children were classified as naughty, he gradually fell behind and was essentially abandoned.

We had to fight to get him assessed by an Educational Psychologist. Eventually, we had a statement of special needs awarded, which meant that he would get more help at school, or so we thought. This did not materialise, so when Matthew went to senior school, it was a complete disaster. What he needed was a specialised school that dealt with both psychosocial and educational issues. We found such a school called Ravenscroft just outside of Bath, but it was private and would have to be funded. The RAF had what was called a Special Educational Needs Allowance (SENA), which would partially fund the school. All we had to do was see if Wiltshire County Council would stump up the rest. After numerous meetings and endless forms, they agreed to jointly fund the placement. Ravenscroft was residential during term time, which gave us some respite. Matthew was a nightmare at times and would get into all sorts of trouble. He had bright red hair, and I lost count of how many times there would be a knock at the door with being asked, 'Are you Matthews Dad'?

Which meant there was an issue somewhere. He had no fear. I can recall several incidents that he was involved in. Where we lived in married quarters, there was a 100-foot water tower. He had climbed up to the top and had to be coaxed down without falling off, which he thankfully did.

He ended up in the hospital several times after going down a very steep hill on his bike and hitting a wall. Another time, he broke both his arms by falling off a tree. On one occasion, Matthew and his friend found a JCB excavator with the keys left in. You guessed it, they started the engine and somehow removed the keys, leaving the JCB abandoned and the engine running. Someone was coming over to my house, and before they could open their mouths, I said, 'Yes, I am Matthew's dad, I will sort it'. The only way I could stop the engine was by bending the fuel pipe to cut off the petrol. Thankfully, it stopped.

Matthew went to Ravenscroft School from the age of 12 to 16 years of age, and they helped him a lot, especially an Educational Psychologist called Ged Lombard, who worked with Matthew during his time at Ravenscroft. Ged was to be a great help several years later, as he put us in touch with a specialist in assessing people with possible autism. We paid privately to have Matthew assessed. He was 39 years old at the time. It cost £1000, but it was money well spent. Matthew was diagnosed with Autism Spectrum Disorder (ASD) and Asperger. This opened various doors, and he was able to claim Personal Independence Payment (PIP) and get a free bus pass.

Now, I was a Sgt. I had to do a set of senior nights, which meant I was responsible for all the male wards from 19:30 hours until 07:30 hours for 7 nights. One patient has always stayed with me. The other night, I was watching one of the many fly-on-the-wall medical programmes, this one was called Critical Care from the Royal Stoke Hospital Emergency Department (ED). They follow critically ill patients through their treatments. During this episode, one of the nurses said, 'Certain patients stick in your mind'. As she was talking, it brought back memories of a patient I looked after and got to know well on the medical ward at RAF Hospital Wroughton. The patient was a Sergeant called Brian, who had been in and out of the medical ward at RAF Hospital Wroughton for many months. I enjoyed medical nursing as you had to think about the condition and the aetiology (cause) of the disease, as sometimes there are more complex medical problems for the patient.

Brian first came into the medical ward with a heart attack. Over the months, he went into heart failure. This would have been around the 1980s. At the time, treatment was limited. Brian needed a heart transplant, was referred to Papworth Hospital, and was put on the waiting list. I got to know Brian and his wife very well over the months that he was coming in. He was from South Shields, which is in the Northeast, so we had something in common.

I was on night duty when Brian came into Ward 9 at RAF Hospital Wroughton, primarily for rest and further medical treatment and stabilisation. Brian had been in Ward 9 for a week and was due to go home on Sunday this was Saturday night. I visited all my wards to speak to all the patients and see the staff checking for any concerns they may have had about their patients.

Ward 9, at the time, was my normal ward when I was not on nights. It was staffed that night by an Army SEN and a Pupil Nurse. I tended to have my break on Ward 9 at about 03:00 hours. I spoke to Brian that evening, who seemed in good spirits and was looking forward to going home in the morning. He was also acutely aware that he needed a heart transplant.

I went to Ward 9 for my break and was sitting in the ward office, which was close to the first 4 beds on the ward. Brian was in the second-to-last bed on the right side of the ward, close to the ward office. I was sitting, having a cup of tea, and had a sudden urge to go into the ward. I can't explain this. I took the torch and went straight to Brian's bed. He was in obvious pain, and his hand was clutching the top rail of the bed. I shouted for help just as Brian went into cardiac arrest. The crash call was put out, and I started cardiopulmonary resuscitation (CPR). One of the other nurses brought the crash trolley with the defibrillator, and the Duty Medical Officer and Duty Physician arrived on the ward. At this time, it was only Doctors that could provide advanced life support.

We had put a heart monitor on, and Brian was in ventricular fibrillation and needed a shock. I gave the first shock of 360 joules (under the direction of the Doctor) with no response. We battled hard to save Brian but to no avail. Sadly, Brian died on the 24th of July 1984, age 44 years. I had to contact the Orderly Officer from his base unit so they could contact Brian's wife to tell her this sad news. It is funny how particular patients stay with you for life, as I can recall this event as if it was yesterday.

I am content that we did all we could to save Brian, but sadly, we were unable to save him.

Chapter Twenty-Eight
Gulf War 1

In November 1990, I was teaching a group of nursing officers drug calculations at RAF Hospital Wroughton. Believe it or not, some of them could not work out a simple drug calculation. This was in preparation for Gulf War 1.

It was quite bizarre for me, as maths (if you recall from my school days) was not my strongest subject, but I had put in a lot of effort to learn what was required for this session. The Senior Nurse Tutor said she had been advised that I had not been earmarked to go to the Middle East (kiss of death). Three days later, I was called to the Deputy Matrons office to be told I was being deployed to Bahrain as part of RAF War Hospital Muharraq. Staff from RAF Hospitals Halton and Ely would make up the bulk of the contingent. It was now early December 1990, not great timing, but we all know that when we join the military, we may be called upon to serve our country in conflict and be prepared to give the ultimate sacrifice of our lives.

The first thing that I had to do was complete a mountain of paperwork, including dog tags (these were two metal plates with your name, rank, number and blood group on a metal chain,

FROM BOILER SUIT TO BLUE SUIT

My dog tags 1990

just in case you were killed, they could take one of the plates for identification purposes) and the Geneva Convention card. As medical staff, we were governed by the Geneva Convention. *The Geneva Conventions and their Additional Protocols form the basis of modern international humanitarian law, setting out how soldiers and civilians should be treated during war.*

Although they were adopted in 1949 to take account of the experiences of the Second World War, the four Geneva Conventions continue to apply to armed conflicts today. Two more protocols were adopted in 1977, which expanded the rules. Then, a third protocol was agreed upon in 2005, which recognised an added emblem, the red crystal.

What are the four Geneva Conventions?

1. Protect the sick, wounded, medical, and religious personnel during the conflict.

2. Care for the wounded, sick, and shipwrecked during war at sea.

3. Treat prisoners of war with humanity.

4. Protect all civilians, including those in occupied territory.

We had to wear red cross armbands to show we were medical staff.

I was then told there was pre-deployment training at a place called Saighton Camp near Cheshire. This was well named as it was pronounced (Satan) Camp. Believe me, after we had finished, the devil himself could have been training us. We arrived around mid-December 1990. It was an old-style army barracks, think Black Adder Goes Forth, and that is what it was like. We were there to undergo Nuclear, Biological, and Chemical (NBC) training, the focus being on biological and chemical, as the thought was that Saddam Hussain had large stockpiles of weapons of mass destruction (WMD), including chemical and biological agents.

We had all been kitted out in combat uniforms. Some of us had desert-style combats. Others had the normal green combats. We were all issued with NBC kits, we already had our own respirators.

It was very intense, with lots of running about in full NBC kit, including respirators. There were also classroom sessions going through some of the likely scenarios and weapons that Saddam had and could potentially use. There was a major concern about the use of anthrax, plague, and nerve agents. We had to go through full decontamination procedures and the bloody gas chamber again (last done in 1972). I did not mind this time as this could save my life. On the second day, I picked up a vomiting virus with a high fever. Guess what? The one thing no one had thought about was the medical cover for the staff. This was ironic, as the whole detachment was made up of Doctors and Nurses. The Commanding Officer came to see me (he was a Doctor) and recommended that I spend 24 hours in bed and was given an anti-sickness jab and paracetamol. The other lads in the room looked after me as well. The following morning, a medical centre was set up (better late than never), with a Duty Doctor rostered for the day!

I was feeling much better after 24 hours in bed, but not 100%. We all had to pass a test called NBC degradation. This was a test of endurance (not ideal when I have been in bed with vomiting). Essentially, you had to work in pairs with a full NBC kit and respirator. You had to run 100 yards carrying a stretcher with a 70 kg casualty. This was a killer. Most of us were physically exhausted, vomiting, and felt like death warmed up. We all passed no surprises there.

After this, we were back in the classroom again, looking at a map of the Gulf with Iraq, Saudi Arabia, and Kuwait shown with Iraq at the centre. There were several coloured rings drawn on the map, showing the range of Saddam's missiles. We were assured that they could not reach Bahrain (this was not strictly true), as we later found out when we arrived in Bahrain. The Commanding Officer called the whole detachment together and said he had managed to delay the flight to Bahrain by one day (whoopie). We would be flying out in the early hours of Boxing Day 1990, so at least we could have Christmas Day with our families. Personally, I had always believed the flight was on Boxing Day, but as a morale booster, he made it look like he had delayed the flight.

It was midnight when we left RAF Hospital Wroughton in Wiltshire. We were on our way to RAF Brize Norton in Oxfordshire to meet up with the rest of the detachment. We arrived around 01:00 hours and met up with the rest of the team, most of us knew each other from previous tours.

We were due to leave at 03:00 hours on a Kuwaiti Airways 747, which seemed a little spooky as we thought we would be going on a military plane.

Several machine guns (minus any bullets) were handed out to random personnel to look after until we reached Bahrain. We all boarded the plane with high spirits. I think it was part excitement and part nervous tension. Once in the air, the onboard map came on, which was still programmed for Kuwait City. Fortunately, the pilot disregarded this. The cabin crew handed out free Kuwait badges to all on board.

Free Kuwait badge 26 December 1990

As the sun started to rise, looking out of the window, all I could see was desert sand. This was all we would see for three months.

We landed in Bahrain around 09:30 hours, and although it was December, it was still mild. Once we cleared customs, several coaches were waiting to take us to our accommodation in Arad, which was about a 20-minute drive from the airport. We arrived at the accommodation site, which was an old contractor accommodation site. The Army's 22 Field Hospital was already there, waiting for us to relieve them so they could move up closer to the Iraqi-Saudi border. There were so many of us there that the bunk beds were set up three high. This only lasted a few days as they were off to their new deployment.

One of the initiatives the Army had set up was sending two staff to the Bahrain Defence Force Hospital. From a cast of thousands, a young Flying Officer and I were sent to replace the Army personnel. We were told that transport would be laid on to drop us off and collect us at around 17:00 hours. The transport was there to take us at 08:00 hours (we had no clue where we were going). We were dropped off, and I said to the driver, 'Don't forget to come back and get us tonight at 17:00 hours'. 'Yes, Sergeant, not a problem,' he said as he drove off. I had a bad feeling about this!

I was allocated to the Intensive Care Unit (ICU), and my colleague was sent to Accident and Emergency (A&E). What became apparent very quickly as I was a man in a Muslim country, I was not expected to do any of the menial tasks (that I would do in the UK) that were left to the Asian nurses and Health Care Assistants. To be honest, I did not want to be there as I wanted to be back at my own hospital to help to get it set up. Lunchtime arrived, and I met up with my colleague, she was having a fun-packed time as well. We were shown into the canteen, so we proceeded to see what was available. First, there were no glasses or cups, only stainless-steel beakers and plates. Most of the dishes were something and rice, which all the staff ate using their hands. I eventually found a couple of forks. The other thing that you need to know is that we were dressed in full combat gear, including a respirator tied around our waist and a red cross-arm band around our left arm, so we stood out like a sore thumb! 17:00 hours could not come quickly enough for me, as I had had enough. I could not even empty a bin. What was the point of this?

At long last, we had finished. I met up with my colleague at the main entrance, expecting to see our transport waiting for us. You guessed it, they were not there. We waited for 30 minutes to see if they would turn up, there was no bloody chance we were abandoned. The major issue was that there were no communications set up yet at the hospital, and we had no way of making contact, no mobile phones. We both started to become anxious at this point, as firstly, they had obviously forgotten about us, and secondly, our personal safety could be at risk.

I found a Bahraini Defence Force Major who said, 'They had no transport they could offer' (great), but she said 'there was a bus that went to Manama', which is close to Muharraq. This was our only option, bearing in mind that we had no clue where we were or where this bus was going. We boarded the bus, and both of us were now on a heightened alert for any suspicious passengers. Most were women dressed in the full Burka. All you could see were their eyes. The bus seemed to be stopping at every village. At one stop, a couple of men got on and gave us the once-over. By this time, my head was in overdrive. What if we were shot? No one would realise until the next day, then where would they look? We both just sat in silence, watching where we were going. We did say this to the driver, 'Muharraq', in the hope he understood. It was getting on to 19:00 hours when what looked like civilization started to appear in front of our eyes. The bus crossed over the bridge and then stopped about 200 yards from the end of the bridge. We looked out of the left-hand window, and there was the main gate of RAF War Hospital Muharraq. We thanked the driver as we got off.

I was steaming by now and went looking for one of the Deputy Matrons. I spotted one not too far away, so I made a beeline to her. I said,

'Ma'am,' I need a word with you, at which point she started to laugh and joke. This was like a red rag to a bull, so I dispensed with any further niceties and gave it to her straight from the hip. When I had finished telling her of the experiences that we had endured, I told her, 'I was not going back' and walked away. I thought, bugger it, what's the worst that can happen—a firing squad unlikely, charged with insubordination possible—but I have been under extreme stress, so that would not stick, and we had a psychiatrist with us, so I would go and report sick to see him.

About 30 minutes passed, and I was asked to go and see the Commanding Officer. I thought I was in the shit! I went into his office, and he asked me 'to sit down'. I had calmed down by this time. He was a reasonable guy, so I thought, "Let's hear what he has to say". I went through what had happened, and he apologised and said, 'This should not have happened, and he agreed that we were isolated and potentially at risk'. He said, 'I fully understand why you don't want to go back, but would you go back tomorrow, and I will replace you after that?' I said, 'Yes, as long as I have a guarantee that transport will collect us at the arranged time'. He said, 'He would guarantee that would happen'. So, I went back for one further day (and he was as good as his word. I was replaced), which was a complete waste of my time. This whole exercise was politically motivated.

Now that I was back, I could see what we were supposed to be doing. The first thing that happened was that we were split into two shifts, day shift and night shift. This would start when the war begins. I was on the night shift.

The Army had done a good job in setting up the hospital, however, as always happens, the RAF had to put their mark on it and made several changes, mainly in the resuscitation room and ward area. The hospital is comprised of two distinct areas. There was a tented area on the periphery, which needed to be covered in white paint

RAF War Hospital Muharraq 1991

with the main hospital being in a chemical protection enclosure (COLPRO) with air locks and high internal air pressure to maintain a chemical-free environment. There were small internal pods that could be sealed for greater security during a chemical attack. The thinking was that Saddam had both chemical and biological weapons. The days leading up to the conflict starting were taken up by further NBC training and getting familiar with the kit we had and how to use it.

Looking at some of my photographs, the medical equipment was very basic.

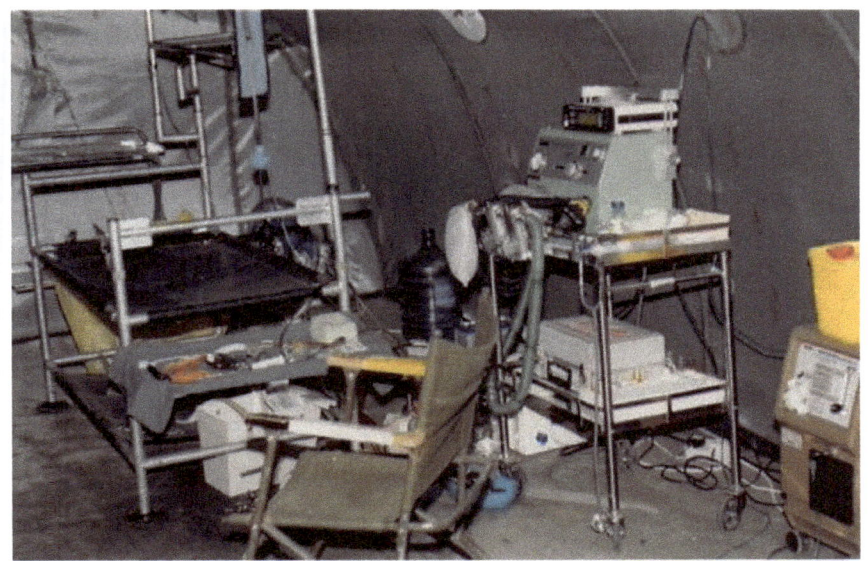

Resuscitation room RAF War Hospital Muharraq 1991

On the same site as us was an American Field Hospital Chemical Unit. It was brilliant, all the mod cons put our effort to shame. We made sure we had good relations with the Americans. They were a great bunch. We also had Australians and New Zealanders who were an equally great bunch of guys. We all worked together with the aim of treating any casualties that came our way.

The nursing hierarchy, as ever, was worrying about non-nursing issues, believe it or not. They were faffing about getting cushions and other non-essential equipment, which was totally irrelevant to the current situation. Remember, this is the Princess Mary's Royal Air Force Nursing Service (PMRAFNS), and some of the senior officers can be ineffectual. The Matron and the Commanding Officer had their own cars! Not bad in a war zone!

We were all brought together to discuss the various possible outcomes. It was more about preparing for the worst and hoping for the best. During the briefing, it was made clear that all the rules of nursing, i.e., what a nurse could or could not do in peacetime now, did not apply. If a patient needed a chest drain (we had been shown how to do this) and there were no doctors, you had to get on with it. We also did night cover as there were a few patients with normal surgical issues. We had an appendicectomy (removal of the appendix) to look after, and we could prescribe drugs without a doctor as we were in a war zone. I remember someone asking, 'What about the UKCC'? This was the United Kingdom Central Council for Nursing, Midwifery, and Health Visiting (UKCC), and we were told that the normal rules don't apply in a war zone.

We steadily moved through January 1991, getting everything set up and having exercises to make sure we could get our NBC suits on quickly and learn how to drink from our water bottles without taking off our respirators. I have to say the boffins who came up with this kit have my greatest respect, as the kit we have is the best in the world.

Due to the perceived danger of chemical and biological attacks, we were all vaccinated against anthrax and the plague. The anthrax vaccine was given in combination with the whooping cough (pertussis) vaccine to boost the immune response. The Ministry of Defence (MoD) later explained that the boost was required due to the short time available between administering the vaccine and the expected start of hostilities.

For protection from chemical and biological attacks, British troops were asked to take a Pre-treatment Set of tablets (NAPS during the conflict) containing pyridostigmine bromide (PB), a drug used during the Gulf War as a pre-treatment to protect troops from the harmful effects of nerve agents. I was also issued with 2 atropine auto-injectors this was to combat the effects of nerve agents. Some scientists now believe that taking the NAPS tablets may have been a contributing cause of neurological problems in veterans. After the war, numerous personnel, including myself, became ill, which would later be called Gulf War Syndrome. The government has never accepted that this condition exists. I will discuss this later.

It was becoming increasingly clear from the news reports that we were edging to war with Iraq due to their invasion of Kuwait in August 1990. The hospital was directly opposite the airfield, and we could see large trucks with bombs and other munitions moving onto the airfield. There were numerous Tornado multi-role combat aircraft on the flight line. On January 14, 1991, we were invited onto the flight line to perform what I believe is a ritual that goes back to WW2, that is, to paint a message on the bombs. "F*** you, Saddam" springs to mind, which was a bit of light relief.

On the night of January 17, 1991, we were on the night shift. In the early hours of the morning, we could see and hear the jets taking off in waves. As it was dark, you could clearly see the afterburners in the dark sky.

Tornado in Flight 1991

After about an hour, we were all called into the briefing tent for an update from the Commanding Officer. His words were quite chilling. He said, 'the largest air campaign since WW2 was underway, we had to expect some reprisals'. The Padre said, 'Some words of comfort and a prayer'. It's amazing how many people turn to God at times like this. It was the right thing to do as we had a lot of youngsters with us and inexperienced Nursing Sisters. You could see the fear in their faces, as no one knew what would happen. It was now up to the Senior Non-Commissioned Officers (SNCOs) to step up to help support and give guidance to the younger and inexperienced personnel.

We were all told to put our NBC kit on, including our respirators, and then we were allocated pods within the COLPRO (Collective Protection System). There were 8 personnel per pod. I had 7 very young nurses and medics in my pod. Just before the pods were sealed, one of the female anaesthetists had a panic attack, which was quickly ended by one of the Flight Sergeants slapping her across the face, followed by 'pull yourself together, ma'am'. It did the trick. Not long after, we were all sealed in our pods, then the air raid sirens screeched along with a message over the Tannoy, "Missile attack red, missile attack red," which meant that there were incoming missiles. Obviously, this was a terrifying moment, as it sort of brought the reality of war right into our pod. I remember looking at all the staff to see if they were OK. All I could see was their eyes through the respirator. The saying eyes on stalks was a good description of what I saw. All their eyes were bulging with a look of fear. The air raid warnings were still being broadcast over the Tannoy system. We were waiting for the explosion (which never came). Still, we had no information apart from a small radio we had, so we were frantically trying to find an English-speaking radio station that was broadcasting news. We stumbled across one that gave very little information. After about 90 minutes, the all-clear was broadcast over the Tannoy.

We removed our respirators as we were sweating buckets and had been breathing through the respirator for about 2 hours. It was great to breathe fresh air without the respirator. There were several more air raid warnings during the first night, but nothing happened. By the morning, we were absolutely knackered. The aircraft were beginning to return to the airfield as dawn broke. No one knew what had gone on as we did not have access to a decent radio.

When we arrived back at the accommodation, we all made a beeline for the only television in the building. We found CNN, which gave us the full story of the first night of the air campaign. It became clear that the initial air campaign had taken out many scud missile launchers and most of the Iraqi command-and-control facilities.

Back at the accommodation, we were looking forward to some well-earned rest. However, this was short-lived as more air raid warnings were being broadcast, so we had to don our NBC kit, plus a respirator and go down to the basement. This pattern went on for several more days.

On the hospital site, there were several air raid shelters, unlike the shelters in WW2, which were underground. Our shelters were constructed at ground level out of numerous 50-gallon oil drums, which were then filled with concrete.

RAF War Hospital Muharraq air raid shelter 1991

These were used as supports for a 1-inch steel plate that formed the roof, and then the whole structure was covered in hundreds of sandbags. There was some science as to why this type of air raid shelter was used. It was all about chemical and biological weapons. If they were delivered in a gas form, they would sink to the ground, so being underground was not a good idea. The only thing you had to remember when entering the shelter (as the entrance was quite narrow) was to watch your head as the steel plate was uncovered, and if your head met the steel, you would remove a large part of your scalp. It was advisable to wear your helmet before entering.

RAF War Hospital Muharraq inside air raid shelter 1991

Each shelter had a person called a Shelter Marshal who was responsible for accounting for those personnel who were in the shelter and maintaining order while the shelter was being used. These shelters were enormous and went far back. The only light was something called a pickup cable, which was a single strand of cable to which light sockets could be attached, and then a bulb was added. Looking at this in the shelter, it was quite eerie as the further the lights went in, the bleaker it looked. The shelter was very claustrophobic, and the message was to move to the back of the shelter, which no one wanted to do, so most of us stayed near the entrance as the thought of being buried beneath tons of steel did not appeal to most of us.

As the air war progressed, we started to get daily DVDs (set to music) sent over from the aircrews as they were using smart munitions. They had a camera on the nose of the missile or bomb, which could be followed right up to the point of impact. These videos showed the devastating effects of modern warfare. I still remember when the TV news caught a cruise missile skimming along a street.

Although we did not get any casualties, there were ups and downs over the coming weeks. There was the scud missile attack on Israel. This was aimed at pulling the Israelis into the war with the potential of fracturing the coalition. Fortunately, the Israelis did not retaliate. This was due to the Americans supplying them with the Patriot Missile System, which would be able to intercept any incoming scuds.

Then we heard the news that a Tornado had been shot down. This was the plane of John Nichol and John Peters, who had been captured by the Iraqis, and we all saw the pictures of the two of them on our TV screens after they had been beaten up. This brought home the reality of war.

The air raid warnings kept coming, but it was apparent nothing was going to happen as this had gone on for weeks, so we all got a little complacent until one night, at about 04:00 hours, there was a loud boom. A scud fell into the sea and exploded. This was a wake-up call to take the air raid warnings more seriously. We later found out that when a scud was launched, there was a Gulf-wide alert sent out. That's why we had so many alerts that were not specifically related to our area.

One evening, I was asked to see the Commanding Officer again! I had been on my best behaviour since my last outburst. What could I have done? I entered his office, and he said, 'I have a job I would like you to do'. 'There has been a stabbing on one of the Royal Fleet auxiliary ships, and the person has died'. 'They will be flying the body in to be stored in our mortuary fridges,' I said, 'OK,' so the plan was I would be in an ambulance, one of the Land Rover types with the two rear doors. The helicopter was to rendezvous with us on a piece of wasteland near our base so I could transfer the body to our ambulance with minimal fuss.

I have no idea what happened to the plan, but the helicopter landed right in the middle of a sports field, which was about 500 yards from where we were parked. This was supposed to be a low-key operation, but unfortunately, due to the location of the landing, all the locals came swarming out of the woodwork, and they were everywhere. The driver drove as fast as he could to get to the aircraft. We managed to navigate ourselves through the crowds, opened the back doors, and reversed to the door of the helicopter, using the back doors as a screen as I did not know how the body was packaged. Fortunately, the body was wrapped up in numerous thick black plastic bags and tied with duct tape. We managed to pull the body into the back of the ambulance, closed the doors, and then we were off. The helicopter took off once we were clear. I delivered the body to the mortuary as instructed and left it to the others to sort out the rest of it.

Chapter Twenty-Nine
Post-Traumatic Stress Disorder (PTSD) and other things

When we were deployed, we took with us a Padre, a Consultant Psychiatrist, and two Registered Mental Health Nurses (RMNs). They had their own tent, which seemed to attract a lot of personnel for a chat and support. There was some new research about how to deal with PTSD and the lessons that they learned from the Falklands conflict.

The idea was that "we" would talk about our feelings in small groups, a sort of hot debrief while in theatre (a term for war zone). We were all broken down into smaller groups and sent to discuss any issues. Not surprisingly, no one wanted to talk, so this great idea never worked.

The war ended on the 28th of February 1991. I had my birthday on the 16th of February 1991 and was presented with a cake, which was a kind thought. We spent a further two weeks clearing up and

RAF War Hospital Muharraq 1991 birthday cake

waiting for our flight home. During this time, we had some great entertainment from the musicians from the various RAF bands who were assigned to us as stretcher-bearers and general support. These guys were great, and they could turn their hand to anything. One of their highlights was something called the plate dance, which entailed those taking part in removing all their clothes (completely naked) apart from two paper dinner plates, one covering the genital area and the other on the chest, so dancing to music, they would swiftly keep swapping the plates.

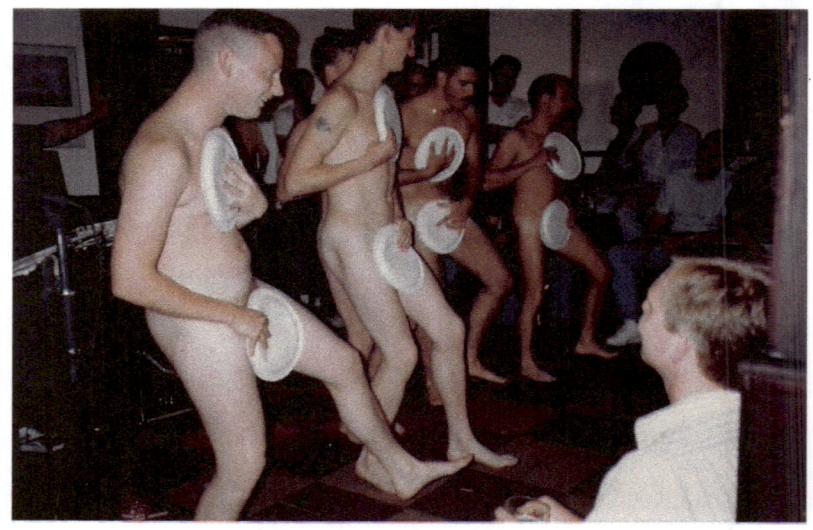

RAF War Hospital Muharraq plate dance 1991

They were so good at it that no one saw anything. Brilliant entertainment. One of the most obscure events was when we were invited to a visit to the Princess of Bahrain's residence two of the girls bumped into her when they were out one day. Then we had this invitation to attend her residence. We set off with a series of coaches on the way. One of the Senior Nursing Officers said, 'We

RAF War Hospital Muharraq plaque 1991

should give the Princess a gift,' so what do you give a Princess? What else but a RAF War Hospital Muharraq plaque!

When we arrived there was a large marquee with several round tables for us to sit. The food was out of this world we were well looked after and had a fabulous feast. When we finished, we had a tour of her farm there was an English vet who was permanently residing at the farm. There was a herd of Jersey Cows, horses, and various other farm animals. This was a very surreal experience, given what we had been through.

Lunch with the Princess of Bahrain 1991

Chapter Thirty
HOME SWEET HOME

Then, the day came to go home, which was around mid-March. We were given 24 hours' notice to get our kit together and be ready to go.

The British Military are generally a force for good, and we were no exception. We had an Indian cleaner for our accommodation called Jamil. He was terrified of his boss and told us not to make our beds as he had to do them. He was saving up from his meagre salary to buy his plane ticket back to India. The day before we left, we asked all the personnel in the accommodation if they would like to donate any spare dinars (Bahrain currency) that they had so we could give them to Jamil. Everyone pitched in, and we managed to get him his flight back to his family.

Bob and Jamil 1991

Jamil being given his airfare in 1991

Our flight back was on a RAF VC 10 March 1991, which stopped off in Cyprus, Germany, and Brize Norton. The most amazing site on our return was seeing the green fields and trees when we flew into the UK. It was the most pleasing view ever "England's green and pleasant land"

sprung to mind. Once back, we had a period of leave, then back to reality. It is an odd feeling when you must go back to normal, as those with whom you are working have no idea what your experiences were like. It felt like it never happened because there was no one around to talk about the shared experience.

I can imagine this is what a lot of Sailors, Soldiers, and Airmen must have felt like after World War II. We all have short memories, and moving on is easier said than done.

Chapter Thirty-One
BACK TO NORMALITY

Following my return from Gulf War I in March 1991, I returned to Male Orthopaedics. Shortly afterwards, I was promoted to the rank of Flight Sergeant (FS). A few months after returning, I was presented with my Gulf War Medal with Bar by the Station Commander.

Again, I expected a posting, but I was left at Wroughton. The Gods were looking after me again. This meant Matthew could stay at Ravenscroft, which was too important to lose. We decided to buy our first and only house in Wroughton Village in April 1992, as my 22 years of service were complete,

Being presented with Gulf War Medal 1991

which meant if I left, I would get my RAF pension. At this point, I had no immediate thoughts of leaving the military. However, things can change very quickly, as I soon found out. I applied to undertake the English National Board (ENB) 219 Orthopaedic Nursing course, which was approved, so this was another 6 months in a civilian hospital, primarily Princess Margaret Hospital Swindon and a 2-week secondment to RAF Headley Court Rehabilitation Unit, where I followed patients through their treatment program. I made a video, which was part of my assignment, which achieved a grade A pass, which I was very pleased about. As I was coming to the end of the course in 1993, I was promoted to Warrant Officer (WO). Again, I was not moved, which is leading a very charmed life it was unheard of not being moved on promotion.

Chapter Thirty-Two
DEPRESSION!!!

Then, during 1994, I was aware of becoming low in mood with intrusive thoughts and started to become paranoid. I did not know what was going on. I went to see the Station Medical Officer, a GP called Robin Davey. He was a retired Group Captain. I spoke to him, and he sent me immediately across to the Psychiatric Centre to be seen by a Psychiatrist. That's what I call a quick referral! This was my worst nightmare as you had to wait in public with staff whom you knew would be walking past, which in my head was very embarrassing and made me feel very vulnerable.

I was seen by a Consultant Psychiatrist, and after an assessment, he said, 'You have clinical depression'. This was like a lightning bolt. How did this happen? Was it due to my time in the Gulf, or was it something else? To be honest, I was glad to have a diagnosis, as I thought I was going mad (pardon the pun). He started me on an antidepressant called (I was signed off work for initially 6 weeks, and I went to see my boss, who was sympathetic, but that's as far as it went) Seroxat, which was the first antidepressant I was put on, but this did not agree with me and made me feel worse. I was then put on 150 mg of Amitriptyline at night. This is an old drug that has many side effects but was effective in treating my depression. Bearing in mind that I held the rank of Warrant Officer, which is the highest non-commissioned rank in the RAF, you would at least expect to be contacted by your boss, the Deputy Matron, or even the Matron, but I had no contact with any senior officer during my illness.

It was left to the other ranks to offer me the support that I needed. In the military, we have a black humour that we all understand. The guys and girls on the ward had got me a get-well card inside it said, "The Warrant has gone mad" with a Polaroid photograph of them all in the ward office smoking, drinking, and watching television, all done in the best possible taste. Adrian Evans, one of the Sgts, came to see me and brought the card. It was great just knowing that someone cared.

During my time seeing the Consultant Psychiatrist, I remember one appointment in particular. It had just been announced that RAF Hospital Wroughton was facing closure. He had been working on a new super duper Psychiatric Centre. During my appointment, he started ranting about this and threw all his files in the bin. I was still a bit flaky, so I let him know that I was not happy with the way the appointment was going and stormed out. The SMO asked to see me and said that I would have to see him again as he was treating me, so reluctantly, I went back to see him. When I went into his room, he was very apologetic for his behaviour at my last appointment, so we kissed and made up!

All in all, I was off work for 9 weeks. I was feeling better, or so I thought, so I arrived on the ward after 9 weeks off, not to a fanfare of trumpets or even an interview with the Matron to see how I was.

So, there I was, walking along the corridor to the ward. As I walked onto the ward, I started to feel anxious. How would people react? How would I be spoken to, too? What if it became too much for me? As luck would have it, standing by the ward office was one of the Orthopaedic Consultants, Wing Commander Peter Schranz. On seeing me walking towards him, he said, 'Welcome back, Mr. Sanderson, shall we get on with the ward round' completely normalised the situation. It did not matter that I did not know the patients; I just tagged along, but within a couple of hours, I was back on the horse, so to speak! I still never saw the Matron!!

The next event showed me how perilous depression can be. All can seem well with life ticking over. Then, suddenly, the walls come crashing down. I soon realised that my time in the RAF was coming to an end as the depression had taken something away from me. I was resentful at the way I had been treated by the nursing management, so was there a way out?

Yet another review of military hospitals was undertaken by the government, with some facing closure, including Wroughton. They were asking for people to apply for redundancy, so I put in the forms in early 1995 and started looking for potential jobs. Probably not the best plan, but in my head, I was out and needed a job. A position for a Ward Manager of the elective Orthopaedic Ward at the Princess Margaret Hospital in Swindon came up. I applied, interviewed and was offered the job on the proviso of getting made redundant from the RAF. The date given was September 1995, when we would know who was getting redundancy. The day came, and Matron was calling staff, mainly Sgts, down to her office, telling them that they had been made redundant. I was never called, so I had to assume that I was not successful.

Again, why could she not call me down to tell me this to my face rather than me just working it out for myself? This event showed me how you live on a knife edge with depression. As I fell off the edge that day, I felt like all the stuffing had been knocked out of me, so I went home to gather my thoughts and said, 'fuck them' and to come back fighting.

The only option was to apply for premature voluntary release (PVR). I applied and explained to the manager at the local hospital the situation. She said she would give it 4 weeks if I could not take up the post by then, and she would withdraw the offer. I tried every way to get out but to no avail. I was given a discharge date of September 13, 1996, which was 12 months away.

To rub salt into what seemed like enormous gashes on my back, one of the Sgts (who I did not get on with) had been made redundant and was offered my job as Ward Manager at the local hospital. This was a devastating blow.

The decision was made soon after that RAF Hospital Wroughton would be closing and that Royal Naval Hospital Hasler in Gosport would remain open. Which meant I would have to go to Haslar for 6 months! My claim to fame on the day RAF Hospital Wroughton was told that it was closing was that I did an interview on Sky News to give my opinion on the closure.

On the afternoon of the 23rd of December 1995, I was in the ward 3 office helping to clear the ward when the phone rang, and it was for me. I took the phone and said, 'WO Sanderson' then the other person said, 'This is the Matron from Royal Naval Hospital Haslar' 'Afternoon, ma'am,' I said, and I was thinking, what does she want, as it was odd to take a call from a Matron before you arrived at your new unit? I was soon to find out. She said, 'Mr. Sanderson, I am calling to see where you would like to work'. This was a surprise, as, in the RAF, you were told where you would be working, which is what I told her. She then said, 'But you are a WO, a senior rank, in the navy this counts for something' I thought, fair enough, let's see where this goes. Before I could say anything else, she said, 'I have a proposal for you. I need a Senior Nurse to manage orthopaedic outpatients. I know that you will be leaving in 6 months, and you are living in a mess away from your family' 'Yes', I said. Next, she said, 'The job is Monday to Friday, and you can have a half day on a Friday to travel home. How does that sound'? In my head, I was thinking, this sounds great. I said, 'I would be happy to take this on' My starting date was the 3rd of January 1996.

Chapter Thirty-Three
ROYAL NAVAL HOSPITAL HASLAR, FROM JANUARY 3RD, 1996, TO JUNE 5TH, 1996

Over the weekend, prior to starting at Haslar, I started to get my bits and pieces together to make the next six months as comfortable as possible. I had an old camping fridge in the loft, and I thought this would be ideal for keeping my drinks (alcoholic) and milk cold. I also had a spare VHS video tape recorder, which was a little bit of a luxury that would help me plan for my evenings. Lastly, I had my trusted kettle, which I had taken to the first Gulf War in 1990.

The drive from Wroughton to Haslar in Gosport was straightforward. It took around 3 hours. I arrived and was shown to the Senior Rates Mess. In RAF terms, this would be the Sgts Mess. I had a massive room, which was great so that I could get all my stuff in. A large contingent of RAF nurses also arrived at the same time; however, they were in for a shock as they were allocated cabins, not rooms, which were considerably smaller than they were used to. Some had various kitchen appliances that would not fit into the room. There were two RAF WO Nurses at Haslar, myself and WO Jackie Jones, and the RAF Commanding Officer Nursing was my old friend who was at Wroughton and did not manage my mental health illness or the redundancy particularly well! As far as I was concerned, she could go and swivel. Funny old thing, though, the Junior Ranks were not happy at Haslar, so who did she turn to, you guessed it, the two WOs to sort out the issues as she was bloody incapable of organising a piss-up in a brewery?

On my first morning, I walked into the department. I was early to see the place before any of the staff arrived. My first impressions, it looked shabby, with notes everywhere. The phone was already ringing, which went to answerphone there were loads of calls to be answered.

As the staff began to arrive, I started to introduce myself. Most of the RAF orthopaedic surgeons had come from Wroughton, so I knew all of them. There was a Group Captain, two Wing Commanders, and two Squadron Leaders. The naval surgeons consisted of a Surgeon Commander (equivalent to a Group Captain) and two Commander Surgeons (equivalent to a Wing Commander). There was a Petty Officer (PO) RAF equivalent Sgt and a Leading Hand this is still a mystery to me! The PO was called Sean, who was not managing the department effectively. A good example of this was when I found a pile of F Med 4s (personal medical records) in a room; there were hundreds of them. When I asked him what they were, he said, 'These are referrals for the Tidworth Clinic'. These were all Army personnel who needed to be seen by an Orthopaedic Surgeon. The PO had done nothing about it. This was to be my challenge over the next 6 months. I got access to the Patient Administration System (PAS) so I could set up clinics. What I did was work till 17:00 hours, then go to the Senior Rates Mess at Haslar for dinner, then return to the department at 17:30 hours and work till 21:00 hours. I worked setting up the clinics and allocating an orthopaedic surgeon to attend the clinic. I cleared the backlog in 4 months. This is where my video recorder could be used. I am an avid fan of Coronation Street, never missed an episode. So, I was able to record the episodes while I was at work. I know it's sad!!

The next thing I did was move the phone from the back office to the reception desk. It just took a screwdriver to do the job. All staff were instructed to answer the phone and only use the answerphone at lunchtime because all calls had to be answered on the day. This did not go down well with the existing staff, but the system they were running was wholly inadequate. I think they forgot that we were there to provide a service to the units that depended on the hospital.

I had a good civilian secretary who was behind the changes. We worked together on the Tidworth Clinics, and she would make up the notes for the clinics. We had so many notes that I had to get more shelving put up in our office. I would like to think that I made a difference during my short time at Haslar. I think having something to focus on made the time go quicker and gave me a sense of achievement.

Chapter Thirty-Four
LAST 6 MONTHS IN THE RAF

During my last six months at the RAF, I started looking for jobs. I had been on several resettlement days looking at how to produce a good curriculum vitae (CV) and interview techniques. It was all in preparation for looking for jobs. There were some do's and don'ts, which were useful tips as I had not had an interview for some 25 years, with the exception of the Charge Nurse post at Swindon in 1995.

It must have been around April or May 1996. I was flicking through the Nursing Times, and two jobs near where I was living caught my eye. One was a Charge Nurse post in a Community Hospital Minor Injury Unit in Malmesbury, Wiltshire, about 30 minutes from where I lived, and the other was a Care Home Manager in Farringdon, again about 40 minutes from my home. The care home job was with a private company, and the Charge Nurse post was with the NHS. I applied for both jobs at the same time and was invited for an interview at the care home. Then, I received a letter inviting me to interview for the Charge Nurse post. I wanted the Charge Nurse post as it was with the NHS, and the pension was better. I attended the interview at the care home. The interview went well, as I had a lot of transferable skills to offer a prospective employer. The next day, I went to Chippenham Community Hospital for the interview for the Charge Nurse post. I was interviewed by the current Charge Nurse of Chippenham Community Hospital Casualty Department, David Sharp.

Chippenham was the largest Community Hospital in Wiltshire Health Care NHS Trust. Again, the interview went well. I thought I had done enough but did not know if there were any other candidates.

I went back to Haslar Hospital to carry on managing the Orthopaedic Outpatient Department. The months were going fast, and I realised that I would be leaving Haslar in June but would still be paid by the RAF until September 13th. As it turned out, I was offered the job of Care Home Manager, which I accepted as I had not heard from the NHS Trust. However, the following week, I received a letter offering me the post of Charge Nurse, which I accepted and then withdrew from the care home job. I had to give two references. I asked the Surgeon Commander, who was the Senior Surgeon at Haslar, who gave me a cracking reference, and the other was my old boss while at RAF Hospital Wroughton Geoff, who sadly died suddenly several years ago.

Mrs Marlene Hitchcock
Personnel Manager
Wiltshire Health Care NHS Trust
St John's Hospital
Bradley Road
Trowbridge
Wiltshire   BA14 0QU

2 7 JUN 1996

Dear Mrs Hitchcock

Re: Robert Sanderson
      Charge Nurse - Applicant
      Interview Date - 27 June 1996

I am able to commend, without reservation, the above named as being both professionally and personally an ideal choice for the post.

I have known Mr Sanderson since July 1994 when I assumed the post of Orthopaedic Unit Manager at Princess Alexandra Hospital and became his immediate line manager. He had been a member of the Orthopaedic Unit staff for considerably longer.

This is a man who is widely experienced across nursing and with specific commitment to, and formalised knowledge of, orthopaedics and trauma. His practice is innovative and dynamic, with excellence in patient care his focus. Intelligent and articulate, he is very orientated to developing nursing care on a firm research base.

Since its implementation he was a stalwart supporter and change agent in our implementation of a Primary Nursing System across the Unit. Indeed, I have been fortunate in being able to draw on his contributions and leadership skills. So much so that I was, without regret, able to appoint him as the Senior Primary Nurse on one of the wards, effectively giving him complete day to day control in a role which would equate with a 'G' grade in the National Health Service. In this role he was superb, leading his team with firm, yet fair, example. He remained in this role until March 1996 when our hospital was closed.

He is an excellent and loyal manager able to support and achieve established goals and in doing so enabling all individual members of staff to feel ownership. In support of individual staff members who have had any difficulties, either professionally or personally, he is particularly adept and appropriately supportive. Without doubt he has single handedly uplifted the practice of several of his staff, thereby contributing greatly to enhanced performance across the Unit.

His attendance record is exemplary and chronic sickness has never been an issue.

In conclusion, this is an honest, dependable family man held in high esteem professionally and in his local community. Wiltshire Health Care NHS Trust would indeed be fortunate to secure his services, his full potential is yet unexploited.

Yours sincerely

Geoff Holliday

Reference from Geoff Holliday 1996

Mr Robert F. SANDERSON

Mr Sanderson worked for me as departmental manager of the Orthopaedic Department for a period of some months, prior to his leaving the Royal Air Force. Despite the fact that he knew that he was leaving the Air Force, that he was working at a distance from home, and that he was only going to be doing the job for a few months, he threw himself wholeheartedly into running and reorganising the department in the hospital following major expansion of the department.

He showed himself to be an outstandingly loyal, highly committed organiser, who achieved results by example (working many hours into the evenings to get things done). Put together with his tactful and sensitive handling of people, both subordinate and senior to him, he was a major asset to the Orthopaedic Department and is already sorely missed.

I am sorry that he has left the Air Force at the end of his engagement, I would gladly and willingly re-employ him at any time and strongly recommend him to you.

M A FARQUHARSON-ROBERTS
Surgeon Captain Royal Navy
Head of Orthopaedic Department

26 June 1996

Reference from Surgeon Captain Farquharson-Roberts 1996

I had to submit a health declaration in which I disclosed that I had a depressive disorder. No surprise, I was called into occupational health. This all went well, and I was given health clearance. By this time, it was coming up to June 1996, and I was due to leave on the 5th of June 96. Before leaving Haslar, I had to see the RAF Matron, who was a Group Captain. I told him what I thought of the RAF Senior Nursing Management and swiftly left. My car was already packed so I jumped in and drove away and never looked back.

I received a formal job offer with the NHS with a start date in early July 1996, which worked out well. I had a month off before starting and was being paid twice. I had to go through the Trust's induction training, uniform, pay (started as F Grade), and pension, you bet, as this was very important some 18 years later when I retired

Job offer letter

Chapter Thirty-Five

MALMESBURY COMMUNITY HOSPITAL, JULY 1996–MARCH 2000

On my first day, as the new charge nurse came, I arrived at 8:00 a.m. The unit had 4 staff nurses plus me. One of them looked after the Treatment Suite, which was an old barn which had been converted into a clinical area where the GPs did minor surgery. This was paid for by the League of Friends (LOF). There was an endoscopy service and once a month, a visiting surgeon would perform sigmoidoscopies. I was responsible for the Minor Injury Unit, Outpatients, and the Treatment Suite.

The Casualty Department was covered by two nurses from 08:00 till 20:00 one on the early and one on the late shift. The local GPs provided medical cover for the unit. They would do a clinic late in the morning, so generally, those patients who could wait would come back to see the GP. The staff nurses made no decisions. It was all left to the GPs. This was something I was keen to change, but I was dealing with outdated thinking. The nurses felt they were there to run after the doctors. A classic example of this was the Out-Patients Department, which Jane covered. She was very old-school and a Farmer's Wife. She was a robust lady. She ran around after this one consultant, making him a cup of tea in a China cup and saucer with biscuits. This was crazy. I was not used to this way of working. The other shock was staff would just call in sick. In the military, you had to go to work first (unless you were dying) and then attend a sick parade.

Something to which I had to adapt too. The other was that the work ethic was totally different from that of the military. Again, I needed to adjust to this as I was now a civilian and life was very different in the civilian world.

The local GPs were very nice and easy to work with, apart from one who was a lazy bugger who could be difficult to get hold of at weekends and did all he could to avoid coming in to see patients. Sadly, he was killed in a plane crash a few years later.

The hospital covered Malmesbury, Sherston and the surrounding villages mainly because both GP surgeries covered the unit. The GPs at Sherston were difficult to get hold of, especially one, the Senior Partner. There was local politics at play here, as Malmesbury GPs would not see Sherston patients and vice versa, which made it difficult to get patients seen.

Going back to the Treatment Suite, this was run by a rather pompous staff nurse who had been allowed to rule the roost. She did not like the fact that I needed to know what was going on in the Treatment Suite as I was ultimately responsible for the whole of the 3 departments. I also needed to be able to do all the procedures in case she was off sick and to cover holidays. Just as well I did this as she found her husband dead one day when she arrived home from work, and she was subsequently off work.

This was the time of GP fundholding so that the Malmesbury GPs could purchase services for their patients. The Treatment Suite was already performing upper gastrointestinal endoscopy (examination of the oesophagus, stomach, and duodenum), sigmoidoscopy (examination of the bowel), injecting haemorrhoids, vasectomies, and minor surgery. There was an appetite to expand the services provided in the Treatment

Suite, which would include day-case local anaesthetic inguinal hernia repair.

This was a particular concern as this was operating inside a body cavity, and the air exchange system in the theatre had to meet a certain standard of air exchange per hour. It was decided that the air exchange unit was adequate to meet the standard, so plans were developed to start hernia repair. This will make you laugh. My manager told me I would have to learn to be a scrub nurse, bearing in mind that I had not worked in an operating theatre since my student days, but that did not seem to concern my manager. There was another Community Hospital in Westbury that had a theatre, and they had been doing hernia repairs for a while, so I went down to watch and learn, it was very much observe, assist, and good luck!

There were two visiting Surgeons from the Royal United Hospital in Bath, one a Consultant and the other a Senior Registrar. The Consultant was a prima donna who thought he was "God" and enjoyed being quite nasty to the nurses. The Senior Registrar was more reasonable but could have his moments.

Well, as luck would have it, I asked the Facilities Director to investigate the air exchange system in the treatment suite just to make sure that we were conforming to the correct standard. We did one hernia repair, and then I had confirmation that the air exchange did not meet the standard for operating inside a body cavity, so that stopped this service in its tracks as it was not safe. I was also concerned if something went wrong or if a patient collapsed, as there was no backup apart from calling 999.

So, I looked for something else we could do safely. One of the Consultant Urologists (specialist in all things to do with the urinary system) from Swindon did a clinic once a week at Malmesbury. I got to know him well; he was an easy man to work with, and he thought that if we could secure funding from the League of Friends, we could set up a cystoscopy service (looking into the bladder with a flexible camera). We worked on this together, much to the Staff Nurse's surprise that I could sort this out. We needed 3 cystoscopes, which were not cheap. This was discussed with the local GPs as they would have to refer patients. They were all happy to support this project.

All I needed was the funding, so I went back to the LOF. (Malmesbury is a very wealthy area, and the LOF had a lot of money). I needed £20,000, so I went to the LOF meeting and presented the case, which they were happy to support. I ordered the cystoscopes. We already had an endoscopy washing unit that would be able to take the cystoscopes. It was my view that diagnostics was the way forward. It was much safer than hernia repairs. It was fairly low risk, but you had to select the patients carefully. I became known within the trust and was soon upgraded to a G-Grade Charge Nurse. Within Wiltshire, there was a network of Community Hospitals in the following market towns,

- Malmesbury
- Chippenham
- Melksham
- Trowbridge
- Devizes
- Bradford on Avon
- Westbury
- Warminster

By the time I left, the axe was beginning to fall, and the hospitals started to close. In hindsight, this was not a bad thing, as most of them were old, dilapidated buildings not fit for modern healthcare. All the units were nurse-led and supported by local GPs which included the wards where there were community beds where patients could be transferred from the main hospital in Bath to complete their recovery.

Malmesbury was a lovely place, but it was in a time warp of bygone years. Nurses did not take on many responsibilities for patients as any decisions were put back to the GP. I don't think you can blame the nurses, as they were not being developed professionally and had not done any up-to-date training.

The defibrillator was ancient, still using paddles, not stick-on electrodes. I advised the Trust that this was a risk, so we were able to update the old defibrillator to an Automated External Defibrillator (AED). I also updated the crash trolley, and staff were given the appropriate training. I also gave some training to the ward staff, which paid off as we had two successful resuscitations on the ward.

One of the nurses who worked in casualty was Jane (remember her from Outpatients), who was well into her 60s. She was the Farmer's Wife, whom I referred to earlier as the sort of lady who would take most things in her stride. One day, some cows broke out of a field that backed onto the hospital, and there were cows coming into the car park. Jane was straight out there and ushered all the cows back into the field. Admittedly, she was covered in cow dung but still managed to laugh about it.

Jane was great to work with, as she just got on with the job and, with the extra training, started to show more confidence in her own abilities. Jane's finest hour was yet to come. She was working a late shift one weekend when one of her sons came in with central chest pain. There were no Doctors present at the time, so Jane did an electrocardiogram (ECG) and started to do some observations. The worst possible scenario happened; her son went into cardiac arrest. Jane then went straight into nurse mode. Thankfully, we had a modern AED and Jane had the training to use it.

(This was the first time the AED had been used.) Jane followed the prompts and had to shock him and carry out cardiopulmonary resuscitation (CPR) while waiting for an ambulance. I am pleased to say that he survived, thanks to Jane's swift actions. This event showed Jane's best attributes. I could have imagined her during the war organising the war effort. She was that type of lady. She was also a great supporter of Malmesbury Hospital and did many fundraising events to support the work of the LOFs.

Malmesbury was becoming less challenging as time went by. I needed more!

Chapter Thirty-six

PROJECT MANAGER, SWINDON WALK-IN CENTRE, 1999–2000

I was on a late shift at Malmesbury, and I was reading the Trusts newsletter and there was a job advertised for a Project Manager to open a new Walk-in Centre in Swindon. This was in 1999 and was part of New Labour's reforms to the NHS. It was two days a week at I grade and could be done as a secondment as we were the same trust following a merger a couple of years before. This looked interesting as it was nearer home and would give me more of a challenge (it certainly did that later). I called the manager who advertised the post and had a chat with her in which she outlined the job. To be honest, she did not have a clue about the magnitude of the job or what this would entail. I said I would think about it. I left it for a week, as I was not sure if I wanted the hassle, but it would only be for 6 months, from October 1999 to April 2000.

Just after a week, I got a call from the manager asking if I was still interested in the post. She offered me a 2-day secondment. I would be managing the whole project, and I agreed to meet her in Swindon to discuss this further.

Well, what a bloody shambles. The Primary Care Group (PCG) was asked by the Trust if they should put in a bid for funding for a Walk-in Centre in Swindon. They agreed to submit a bid. One of the outgoing managers completed the bid paperwork with a "tongue-in-cheek" approach. No one believed that they would be successful, so it came as a shock when the bid was approved. The only problem was that no one knew what to do. As mentioned previously, this was part of the Blair Government's plan to give more access to healthcare, especially to vulnerable groups. They were throwing money at this project. So, the Walk-in Centres, along with NHS Direct, were part of this increased access to services. Both NHS Direct and Walk-in Centres (WICs) were going to be predominantly Nurse-Led. There would be 40 WICs across the country. I was offered the job as there were no other applicants! And they were desperate. It was not long before I realised that I had taken on a poison chalice.

The WIC had to open on the 1st of April 2000. I had never done a Project Manager's job before, but my years in the RAF gave me the experience to organise and manage the project.

I was given all the relevant paperwork to read to give me background on the bid and what was asked for in terms of funding. I was also given a Microsoft Project Management disk, which I never used. It soon became apparent that this was going to be a complete nightmare to manage. The manager who submitted the bid had now left the Trust and knew nothing about this type of service. It transpired that the WIC was allocated two rooms within Swindon Health Centre, no waiting room, and no dedicated reception. They had forgotten these "minor points." Also, it soon became clear that the same GPs who had supported the bid did not want the WIC. The Accident and Emergency Consultant was also hostile to the bid, as were the other users of the Health Centre.

Swindon Health Centre was located on Carfax Street and was always known as Carfax Street. The building had three GP practices, Community Dental Service, Podiatry, and Sexual Health, all of which were hostile to the WIC being put into Carfax Street. The WIC was allocated two consulting rooms on the ground floor, which were previously used by Sexual Health. This caused animosity straight away, as Sexual Health had to vacate these rooms and did not want the WIC patients mixing with theirs as it would be a shared waiting room. Bizarrely, there were already fixed views on the types of patients that would be attending the WIC. There was a perception that we would attract alcoholics, drug users, homeless people, and sex workers to our service, so what if we did? This may be their only access to health care. Some of the clinical staff of the other services, including GPs, were very judgmental.

There were letters and statements pinned on notice boards by the GP practices stating their opposition to the WIC, bearing in mind that these were the same GPs that had supported the bid.

The users of the building wanted a meeting, which was arranged. It was like being thrown into the lion's den, all moaning and questioning why we had to have a WIC anyway. I reminded them that it was not me who asked for it but the PCG. All I was doing was setting up a service that the so-called clinical leadership had asked for. I had some heated discussions with the A&E Consultant, who said, 'Give me the money so that he could see more patients. They were all missing the point. All the detractors were signed up for the bid being put in, so they either did not understand what they were bidding for or did not want the bid to succeed.

I also had to do a presentation to a wider audience, including the Leader of Swindon Borough Council, who was very left-wing. I happened to say that we would help with the problem of asylum seekers and would be a service that prostitutes could use. The Trust's Public Relations Manager was present, and the Council Leader passed her a note which said, 'tell Bob that the asylum seekers are not a problem and there are no Prostitutes in Swindon,' which was not strictly true. We call them sex workers now.

What's odd as well about the A&E consultant's view is that, on the one hand, he was complaining about the number of minor illnesses and emergency contraception patients he was seeing, which is what the WICs could do. He eventually gave up his opposition as the decision had been made by the Department of Health to allocate funding for the Swindon WIC.

I had to set up a user group of all interested parties in the health centre so they could have their five pennies worth, just moaning and inventing problems. It soon became obvious that this job would be my greatest challenge in my nursing career, it felt like this was my destiny to end up here.

My first job was to recruit staff again. This was completely wrong. They bid for one H-grade Nurse and one Health Care Assistant (HCA) per shift, and the costs were all wrong. When I pointed out that we needed 2 Nurses per shift, it soon became clear that they had not asked for enough funding. They only had enough funding for 6 Nurses, including me, to cover a service from 07:00 to 22:00 hours 365 days a year. When I pointed out that the Nurses would need 2 days off, annual leave, and what about sickness? The nurses would have to work autonomously as there would be no Doctors. This would cause problems later.

The advertisement went out for G-grade nurses. No surprise, when we got applications from A&E and the community, we ended up employing three from A&E, one from a Community Hospital, and one District Nurse. If only I knew then what trouble this lot was going to cause me, I would have left there and then.

The first issue was off-duty. This is what a nursing rota is called. The Nurse from the district suddenly needed every other weekend off for childcare, in effect asking for a fixed rota. I told her that this would need

221

to be discussed with the others first to get agreement. We had a meeting and discussed this proposal of one of them doing a fixed rota. Well, they all agreed, but it would turn out to be the biggest thorn in my side.

In my head, the WIC was a Community Hospital Minor Injury Unit in an urban setting, so this was the model I used. The next issue was sorting out a Reception Area for the WIC and some sort of office for me. I met with the local Facilities Manager in Swindon, who was decidedly unhelpful. He was negative and said he could not change reception. The only office space available was to move the Health Centre Manager (this went down like a lead balloon) out of her office. I was getting to know who he was, so I went over his head to the Facilities Director for the Trust, as I knew him well from my job at Malmesbury. The next day, the Facilities Manager was back, and things started to happen. I don't think he was aware that I knew the Facilities Director, but it worked. The reception was altered to accommodate the WIC patients. Unfortunately, we had to use the existing reception staff (as they had not accounted for this in the bid), and again, none were supportive of the WIC. The next issue was some form of IT system to record the consultations (again, not thought of in the bid), so in conjunction with the very helpful IT Department, we developed a bespoke IT solution from their current District Nursing Service system.

I also needed a reporting system, as the Department of Health (DOH) wanted regular statistics. We eventually designed a system using the community IT software, which worked in the short term. The main concern from GPs now was that they wanted to know when their patients had been seen in the WIC, and it had to be an A5-size letter to fit in the Lloyd George (these were the historical methods of writing patient notes by a GP) notes, these have now been replaced by computerised systems.

Soon after we opened the WIC, the DOH mandated that all WICs use the same IT system as NHS Direct, which was primarily designed as a telephone triage system. Moving to a new IT system was going to cause mayhem as we had just managed to get the receptionists trained in the current system. I had unfortunately inherited the current receptionist team, who were not receptive to working with computers.

All staff had to attend training in Bristol at the main NHS Direct site. The system was based on algorithms. When a patient presented, you had to find the specific algorithm that fitted the presenting complaint, following the pathway depending on the patient's response. This was a complete change to our current system, which was a written record of the patient's presenting complaint, examination, diagnosis, and treatment. This new system was one of many decision-making programs. The company was called Clinical Solutions, their system was called Clinical Assessment System (CAS). They were based in Basingstoke and won the contract to supply NHS Direct and all WICs with the CAS system. One of the main drivers for using this system was its reporting functionality for the DOH, which needed monthly statistics on how many patients were using the services. The WICS and NHS Direct were flagship policies of the New Labour Government in 1999, which gave patients more choice and put Nurses at the front line in delivering these services.

At the time, money was no object. Millions of pounds were thrown into both services. To give an example of this, the National WIC Lead visited Swindon Health Centre, and when she arrived, she was not impressed as the building was old and drab with very heavy front doors that looked like a prison. When she came inside, the décor was shabby, not in keeping with this new service. I informed the National Project Manager that the initial bid was flawed as very little capital funding was asked for, and the staffing model was too tight. She authorised the front doors to be replaced by automatic doors and a new suspended ceiling right through the ground floor. This did improve the aesthetics of the front and inside of the building, but it did not distract from the sheer incompetence of the person submitting the initial bid document.

This was made more apparent when I visited Bristol, which had two WICs, one in the city centre and one in a deprived area of the city. Both were new premises and looked great. This made me angry that Swindon had only two rooms in a rundown Health Centre. The project management job was becoming more difficult as I was constantly battling with the local GPs, A&E consultants, and other users of the building. April 2000 was rapidly approaching, and I had to decide whether to walk away or take on the Lead Nurse role. I decided to take on the Lead Nurse role, as I had done all the hard work in setting up the WIC. This was the start of 18 years of managing the WIC.

Chapter Thirty-seven

LEAD NURSE OF SWINDON WALK-IN CENTRE 1ST APRIL 2000 TILL 2003

In the early days, we had to produce a list of services that we would provide, which was mainly minor illness and minor injury, along with providing emergency contraception, which was a problem as we had no protocols in place to provide this service.

We had to work with something called Patient Group Directions (PGDs), a way of supplying medicines to a specific group of patients, but none were available, another flaw in the system. The law around PGDs makes it clear that you need a group of professionals, including Pharmacists, Medical Practitioners, and Microbiologists, where antibiotics are involved. In my opinion, this should have been sorted out at a national level, but it was left to local WICs to sort out their local PGDs. This proved more difficult than I anticipated, so we set up a trust-wide PGD group to develop PGDs for the WIC and Community Hospitals. There was little understanding by Senior Management of the law and complexity of PGDs. They thought that Nurses could just give out emergency contraception. I was called in by the Chief Officer of the PCG, who told me, 'That we had to give out emergency contraception'. She had no idea of the process or the legal aspects of issuing drugs to patients.

Looking back at this just reinforced my thinking that those who submitted the initial bid were totally incompetent and did not have a clue about what they were bidding for, and there was no local support. It was like having to fight all the time. I was trawling the internet looking for sample PGDs that could be rewritten for the WIC, but I still needed a Pharmacist and Doctor to sign them off. As we were a standalone service, I had to go to the local Hospital Pharmacist for help. Unfortunately, he had no concept of Nurse-Led services, as the old model was led by Doctors.

The opening was rapidly approaching as we had to open on April 1, 2000. The staff were in place (such as it was), but again, the Finance Manager had no idea of the service. When I told them that we needed two nurses per shift, they were apoplectic, as it completely buggered up their "sums." You don't have to be a genius to figure out that six staff members, including me, was not enough to run a service from 07:00 to 22:00 hours 365 days a year. I had to rapidly start a nurse bank to cover the service when staff were on annual leave.

All the staff had issues. I have to say this was a very stressful time with all their individual wants and needs. Bearing in mind that these were G-grade nurses, they were behaving like D-grade nurses. It was like "herding cats." Cats would have been easier to manage!

Then, soon after we opened, one of the nurses told me that she was pregnant. She eventually left and returned to A&E, as she could not cope with the nurse-led bit. There were three A&E nurses employed in the WIC, and what they were doing (unknown to me) was phoning A&E and getting advice from one of the A&E Doctors to check their decisions. I knew this would have to change, but I was stuck with them for the foreseeable future.

There were constant moans and groans from one Nurse. This was not right. She needed more training, etc. Swindon WIC rapidly became very popular, and patient numbers were increasing. As the months passed, another issue came up from the Nurses, as we were open until 22:00 hours, which meant that there would be patients left to be seen after the doors closed. Some nights, the late staff were not getting off till 23:00 hours and would have to be back for an early shift the next day. In hindsight, it would have been better to close the doors at 21:00 hours, but the times were mandated by the DOH, and what I needed was more staff. In the end, I went to the National Project Lead to get more funding, bearing in mind that this was a flagship policy and could not fail.

I went to numerous meetings in Leeds and London and stayed at expensive hotels, all paid for by the DOH. They must have spent millions of pounds on the WIC project. Swindon was cheap compared to WICs in Soho, Nottingham, and Bristol, which all had purpose-built premises with loads of staff. However, in a bizarre twist, Swindon became the one WIC that was seeing the most patients, we were at 24000 patients in the first year. This is partly due to offering services that patients wanted, such as early morning blood tests, dressings, needle exchange, and emergency contraception, once we had the PGDs sorted out. The second Crown Report of 1999 outlined the expansion of independent non-medical prescribing. This would revolutionise nurse-led services but would not come into force for the WIC until 2004.

Due to the number of patients, it also became clear that we needed more clinical space. This became another nightmare as the only space available was a large room called the "Health Education Room," which was used occasionally by various health professionals but not all the time. I was able to get funding from the DOH for the work required, as funding was coming from the "centre," not locally. I just needed the agreement of the other users. I had to have numerous meetings with the other users and an intransigent Health Centre Manager to plead my case for taking a chunk of this underused room. Eventually, after weeks of discussion and compromise on my side, I got the agreement for my third consulting room.

So, a third room was established, and more staff as well, however, the staff issues continued, with two of them always whining about something and the third being extremely slow in seeing patients. I was also undertaking my Nurse Practitioner degree at Oxford Brookes University. I started in 2000, which meant one day away at university and self-study at home. The stress at the WIC finally got me, and I needed a break, so I took a Nurse Practitioner post with a local surgery, which was a complete disaster!

Chapter Thirty-eight
ABBEY MEADS/PENHILL SURGERY, 2003–2004

The job was primarily in their Branch Surgery within a deprived council estate. This was a chance to complete my degree in a less stressful environment, or so I thought. It took a while for me to become established, as the patients did not understand the role of the Nurse Practitioner. Again, prescribing was an issue, as this was before the role of nurse prescribing, and there were no PGDs written. What happened was that you would see a patient, then print out the script and get the GP to sign it, which was madness as they never saw the patient, but this was common practice at the time. Like all these ideas that GPs have, they don't think it through. What they wanted was to remove a GP from the Branch Surgery and replace them with a Nurse Practitioner.

The Branch Surgery was chaotic as there was not an appointment system in place; patients would queue up as soon as we opened and the doors would close at 11:00 hours, so all those patients who managed to get in would have to be seen. There was no triage system, so I was seeing patients that the GP should be seeing, and the GPs were seeing patients that I could see. It was a baptism of fire, but on the plus side, I learned loads of new stuff very quickly. It soon became apparent that I was seeing more patients than the GPs, who would leave the surgery at 11:30 hours, leaving me on my own for an hour in the morning. My afternoon clinic started at 15:00 hours. Again, GP support was variable. There was one good GP who would support me, but they used a locum GP on a regular basis who was a retired paediatrician whose practice was 20 years out of date. He would listen to patients' chests through their clothes. I reported this to the Senior Partner, who said, 'She would speak to him'. Working with him was a nightmare, and then the straw that broke the camel's back happened when a patient died due to his incompetence. I reported this again to the Senior Partner, and the outcome was that the patient was old and had had heart failure.

I suppose this was the start of my disillusionment with the surgery. I was coming to the end of my degree. I had a study day a week, which helped to prolong my sanity for a bit longer. It became increasingly obvious that this was not the job for me, and again, the depression came back as it always did with perpetual regularity. I needed some time off sick, and this really showed the caring side of one of the GPs. I was in bed very low, and the senior partner called me. He did not ask me how I was and did not offer any support. Not bloody likely. All he said was, 'Have you had anything like this before'? So, I lied and said no, as I could not take any further interrogation. I was off work for 3 weeks. I think the stress of the Branch Surgery and the lack of support combined with writing up my dissertation were probably the catalysts for this episode of depression.

I spoke to my Tutor at Oxford Brookes and told her about the depression. I was offered an extension but decided to finish it as I did not want to prolong the agony. My dissertation was an audit of hypertension management (management of patients with high blood pressure) within the branch surgery, as I had a feeling it was not that good, so I needed to prove it. I devised an audit tool and set about going through the patients' notes that were coded with hypertension. This was the easy bit. Analysing the data was a difficult bit.

I had to get my head around spreadsheets and data analysis software, which I borrowed from the University. I spent 3 weeks locked in the spare room, working day and night with books research papers, and using the internet (which was not that fast back in 2004) to get this finished. I did manage to get it done and handed it in on time, but I did not expect a great result. To my amazement, I achieved 90% for the dissertation, giving me a high second-class degree, a 2-1, not bad, as I had left school with no qualifications.

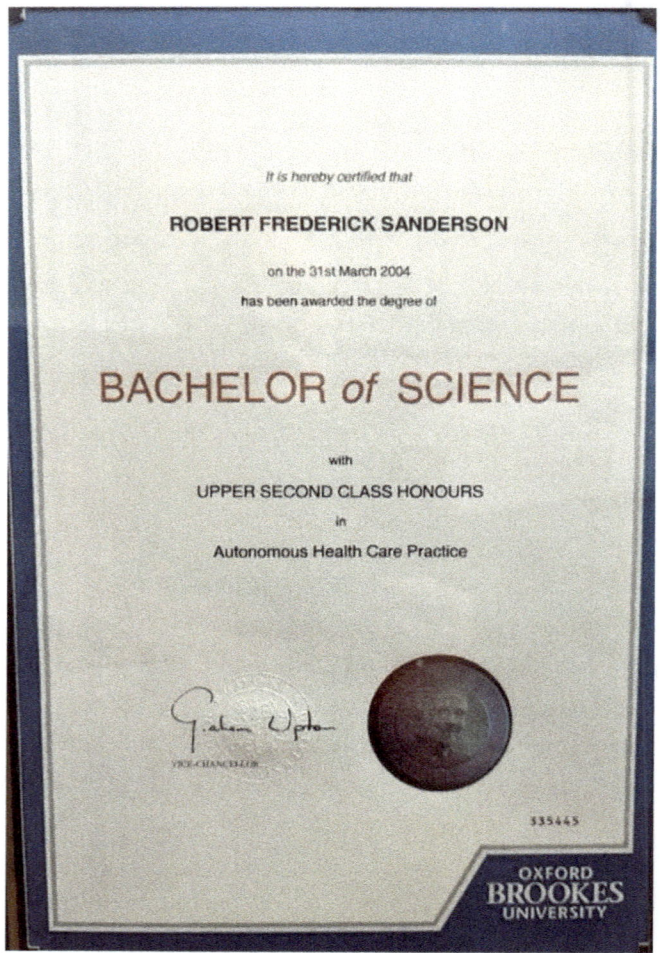

Degree 2004

__Graduation day with Mary, Andrew, Matthew and Sister Julie 2004__

I missed out on a first as I buggered up a module as I was on beta blockers. I could not think at the time but passed on resit, but the maximum you can get on resit is 40%. I was very happy with this result as all the hard work paid off. My Tutor suggested that we try to get my work published. She did a poster presentation at a conference and approached the Practice Nurse Journal, which said they would publish it. After several weeks of editing and being peer-reviewed, my dissertation was published, which was a great achievement. This was my only published work.

Bob Sanderson and Debbie Massey, *An audit of hypertension management in one General Practice*. Practice Nursing 2004, Vol. 15, No. 12

Clinical Focus: CARDIOVASCULAR DISEASE

An audit of hypertension management

Bob Sanderson and Debbie Massey present the results of an audit of hypertension management in one general practice

Coronary heart disease (CHD) is the leading cause of mortality in the UK (British Heart Foundation (BHF), 2004). Studies consistently link a number of factors to a greater risk of CHD (MacMahon et al, 1990; Neal et al, 2000), but high blood pressure (hypertension) is one of the most common. CHD is twice as common in hypertensive patients as in those with normal blood pressure (Van den Hoogen et al, 2000).

Although hypertension is a prevalent and clinically serious condition, its management remains suboptimal and fragmented (Williams et al, 2004; Wolf-Maier et al, 2004). The *National Service Framework for Coronary Heart Disease* (Department of Health (DH), 2000a) and *The NHS Plan* (DH, 2000b) task primary care organizations with responsibility for screening and managing patients with hypertension. However, evidence suggests that detection, diagnosis, treatment and blood pressure control remain inadequate (BHF, 2004).

Updated guidelines for the management of hypertension have been published by the British Hypertension Society (Williams et al, 2004). The guidelines reveal that the management of hypertension remains suboptimal, in part, because of the use of monotherapy. Wide variations in standards of diagnosis and treatment persist in primary care, in conflict with the aims of clinical governance (DH, 1998). To address standards in individual general practices, evidence is needed to determine the extent to which patients with hypertension are being managed in accordance with the BHS guidelines and to identify areas for improvement. Therefore, a retrospective audit was conducted of patients diagnosed with hypertension in one general practice.

Literature review

About 37% of men and 34% of women in the UK are hypertensive (defined as blood pressure >140/90 mmHg) or are being treated for hypertension (BHF, 2004). The prevalence of hypertension increases with age.

Inadequate management of hypertension puts patients at risk of cardiovascular complications and death from CHD and stroke (Andersson et al, 1998). Early detection and treatment of hypertension has great potential to reduce the severe health consequences of CHD. About 2 million people endure angina in the UK, and each year almost 270 000 suffer a heart attack and more than 117 000 die from CHD (BHF, 2004).

A solution to this is suggested by Williams et al (2004) who recommend that protocols for hypertension management in primary care are developed in primary care covering the following areas:

➢ Screening policy
➢ Initial evaluation and investigation
➢ Implementation of non-pharmacological measures
➢ Formal estimation of cardiovascular risk
➢ Treatment policy for antihypertensive drugs
➢ Treatments targets for aspirin and statins
➢ Policy for follow-up
➢ Methods for identifying and recalling patients who drop out of follow-up.

Once patients with hypertension have been identified, they can be treated and monitored to prevent their symptoms progressing to CHD, coronary vascular disease (CVD) or renal failure. The BHS guidelines provide an aid to more effective management of primary and secondary hypertension (Williams et al, 2004). They cover all aspects of hypertension management including guidance on the implementation of best practice and clinical audit (*Table 1*).

It can be argued that the implementation of the BHS objectives for hypertension management will depend on the efforts of practitioners working in primary care. Evidence suggests that changes in diet, reduction in alcohol consumption and smoking cessation have a beneficial effect on hypertension and reduce cardiovascular risk (Williams et al, 2004). General practice—and practice nurses in particular—has an important responsibility to encourage patients to make life-style changes that will improve their health and reduce the risk of serious cardiovascular events.

Full participation in clinical audit by all clinicians is an explicit component of clinical

Bob Sanderson is Nurse Practitioner at Swindon NHS Walk-in Centre, Swindon, and Debbie Massey is Program Leader, Critical and Specialist Care at Oxford Brookes University, Oxford

Published article 2004

I went back to work at the surgery but was not happy, so I started looking for other jobs. I applied for a position as a Patient Care Manager at the Community Trust I used to work for but did not get it as I cocked up in the interview. Just to digress, my Dad always said, 'What's got to be will be. I am a great believer in fate and destiny, as you know. I think he was right. To my astonishment, a Nurse Practitioner job was advertised, you guessed it, at the Swindon WIC. I spoke to the Nurse Manager who I had appointed before I left. She was a difficult and challenging individual, and the staff were terrified of her as she would call the WIC late at night to make sure that the staff were still at work. This happened mainly during the late shift. I was interviewed and offered the post as I was the only one with a Nurse Practitioner degree!! Priceless!! She did labour the point that there was no managerial responsibility, and I was purely clinical.

I wrote my resignation and handed it to the Practice Manager, Henry. He was a very nice guy. He knew it was coming, so he was not surprised. The next thing that happened was priceless. I was at the branch surgery when one of the Senior Partners burst into my room and said, 'You are a fucking twat' and other various expletives about me leaving. I suppose I could have had him, but to be honest, I did not have the energy for a protracted grievance procedure. Anyway, the following day, the next Senior Partner called me into her room and apologised for her colleague's behaviour, saying, 'he was out of order and by no means did the other GPs support his outburst'.

I think they knew that he was in trouble. I told her 'that before employing another Nurse Practitioner, they needed to review the role and that there needed to be adequate support in place and it would be a good idea to rotate between the Branch and the Main Surgery', which she thought was a good idea. What really pissed off the Senior Partner was that they had paid for me to complete my degree, but I had this written into my contract so that there was no payback should I leave! So, I left the surgery and started again at the WIC. My only managerial responsibility was to do the bloody off-duty, as nurses called it. It was a schedule of what shifts the nurses would be working and when they were off.

Chapter Thirty-nine
ADVANCED NURSE PRACTITIONER SWINDON WALK IN CENTRE 2004 TILL 2009

It's an oddity within nursing, but going back to when I was in the RAF, we had some sort of explanation for why it was called off duty. We had various shifts, a 5-8, a 2-5 and late morning. Each of these shifts represented your time off, e.g., a 5-8 meant you were off from 5 pm till 8 am, and a 2-5 meant you were off from 2 pm till 5 pm. You would have worked the morning and then come back in the evening after being off from 2 pm till 5 pm. The late morning meant you were off in the morning and started work at 1 p.m., all very strange, but it sort of explains the history behind the "off duty". I digress. Back to the WIC, the manager and I rubbed along for 12 months or so and then along came a new pay structure called Agenda for Change, which matched my job to a specific point on a pay scale. The scale started at 1 through 8 a/b/c for clinical roles. Most new staff nurses would start on band 5, which would replace the old grading system. Band 5 would equate to grade D/E. I was a G grade, and the manager was a H grade. Anyway, I had to describe my role, which was matched against a set of criteria of what I did and how much managerial responsibility I had. This went to a matching panel to match your job to the new pay scale. I was matched to an 8b, which was great as this was more money, and there were increments within each banding. I was happy with my banding, which reflected the level of clinical responsibility that I had.

I was also the first member of staff to compete and pass what was called non-medical prescribing. This was groundbreaking in many ways, as it meant you could see, examine, diagnose and treat your patient. Since 2000, further changes in legislation have radically altered the professional restrictions on prescribing. Since May 2006, Independent Nurse Prescribers in England have been able to "prescribe any licenced medicine for any medical condition within their competence." As time went on, it became increasingly clear that there were problems with the manager, as she was unable to do clinical work due to back problems, so the day-to-day running of the WIC was left to me (sound familiar?).

The next thing that caused a problem was the new GP contract, which meant that GPs were no longer responsible for out-of-hours care of their patients. This was taken over by the Primary Care Trust (PCT), and the current WIC manager was given the job of helping to set this up. The GP out-of-hours service was to be located on the Great Western Hospital site, which was in the Glover Centre which essentially was a large Portakabin. This move was overseen by one of the PCT managers, who was also a difficult person to work with. The PCT Manager and the WIC Manager clashed, and it turned into a war of attrition between the two of them. It became almost impossible to work in the atmosphere. What happened next was a shock. We were all called to a meeting by one of the PCT Directors to try and sort out the issues, as it was becoming clear that they wanted the WIC Manager out as she was causing major problems. It was with the usual sleight of hand that happens in the NHS that she was moved sideways (did not deal with the issues), and guess what? The WIC was mine again, and I was told to sort it out and appointed Matron!

It became increasingly clear that the nurses needed stability as they were working across two sites, so I asked all the staff where they would like to work, the WIC or the Glover Centre. It worked out well for both services, as it was a 50/50 split. Staff were working at the place they wanted to so we could get some stability again. This carried on until 2009 when our service would be put out to tender.

Chapter Forty

CARFAX HEALTH ENTERPRISE 2009 TILL 2017

Carfax Health Enterprise was the marriage of two different Primary Care Trust (PCT) services, a GP practice and the Swindon Walk-in Centre. I had been managing the WIC since the 1st of April 2000 (apart from 12 months when I was at the GP Surgery), having project managed the setup of the service from October 1999 until the 31st of March 2000.

I had lived and breathed the WIC as it was my baby if you know what I mean. I suppose I was a bit protective of the service and my staff. So, when I was told about the decommissioning of the service and that a new tender would be offered to run a new 7-day-a-week GP service working from 08:00 until 20:00 with the WIC tagged on, I was duly concerned about our future.

To be honest, I think the PCT at the time tried to maintain the current services within the new contract. Initially, there was a lot of uncertainty about exactly how the services would integrate with each other. The GP of the practice and our PCT manager had obviously been talking about the various options available, which were to do nothing and see who bids for the contract or put a bid in ourselves.

When I say "ourselves," initially, this was the GP and the PCT Manager who would resign from the PCT and take up the position of Managing Director and Medical Director with what would eventually become Carfax Health Enterprise, a Community Interest Company. When I became aware of this, I spoke to them both and said I needed to be involved with the bid as the WIC was an integral part of the service. The three of us set up a company called Carfax Health Enterprise so we could submit a bid for the new service. The Practice Manager and the Senior Nurse from the practice became aware of this and quite rightly wanted to be involved.

The five of us became the directors of the company as follows,

Medical Director, GP

Managing Director, PCT Manager

Nurse Director, Senior Nurse from the practice

Director for Scheduled Care Practice Manager

Director of Unscheduled Care, me!!

As the focus was on the GP practice, the service was called a GP-led Equitable Access Service, or "Darzi Centres", as they were the brainchild of Lord Darzi, which meant there would be a registered list of patients plus the ability to see non-registered patients. The opening hours would be 08:00 to 20:00, 7 days a week, 365 days a year. (Another great idea that was dropped a few years later.) The income would come from the registered list, plus we had to meet many key performance indicators (KPIs). There were financial penalties if we failed to meet the KPIs.

The Walk-in Centre (WIC) was a simpler service, as we were paid a tariff for each patient that we saw. Interestingly, the tariff was the same for a patient requiring a blood test or having a heart attack. In hindsight, this was a mistake by the then-PCT, but good for us. We won the contract and so Carfax Health Enterprise was established. The only issue was we had no money to pay the staff (a minor point), so the PCT advanced us the first month's payment, which resolved the issue.

The tension between the practice and the WIC soon began to surface as the WIC was seeing all the patients from the practice who could not get an appointment, as well as other patients who walked into the service. This was madness, as we did not get any income for the registered patients as we had already been paid a tariff for those patients.

We had two queues on the computer system, and the WIC staff had to flip between the two queues to see whose turn it was to be seen. This caused a massive amount of stress for the WIC nurses, as often they would be getting off work late due to the sheer volume of patients.

The WIC was seeing an increasing number of patients registered with the practice. This was adding to the tension between the WIC and the practice. The tension spilt over at the board level as the WIC staff had to deal with more complex cases. There seemed to be no desire at the board level to try and sort out this problem. The nurses in the WIC were getting increasingly fed up with getting off work late as they were dealing with practice patients. What irritated them the most was the fact that all the practice staff (Practice Nurses and GPs) were gone by 20:00 while the WIC staff had to remain until 21:00 or later.

The WIC hours were from 0700 to 20:00. When the doors closed, the staff worked till 21:00 to clear any remaining patients still in the queue. This was the theory, but several patients could book just before 20:00, adding to the queue. With the demand growing, staff were working late, up to 22:00 on a regular basis (I will come back to this later).

Following the merger in 2009, the Managing Director did as much as she could to dismantle the previous services and structure; an example of this was my secretary for the WIC. Kay (who sadly died of ovarian cancer a few years later), who had worked in the WIC for many years, knew all the staff and would sort out the off-duty if someone called in sick (which was a constant headache), so instead of leaving Kay where she was, the Managing Director moved her to cover Human Resources. This really hacked off Kay. Looking back on this now, I am more convinced this was a wilful act to impose her will on others. Kay could not sit and see the nurses struggle, so she carried on behind the scenes, helping with covering shifts, until she was caught by the Managing Director, who told Kay she had to stop doing this.

The unholy alliance of the Board of Directors was very stressful, as we were all pulling in opposite directions. My main concern was the WIC and looking after my staff. The Director of the practice and the Nurse Director were always shouting at each other generally about the same things, namely the GPs not doing their job and mainly the Quality Outcome Framework (QOF) (from which the practice was paid tariffs) not being done. This was a recurring theme during the time I was on the board.

The Medical Director was woolly. He would let the other GPs do what they wanted, e.g., filing test results, etc, were not done. He was also like a spoilt child who had tantrums if he could not get his own way, and an example of this was when we were approached by a Nursing Home Manager to look after their residents. The Managing Director, the Nurse Director, and I met with the Home Manager and outlined a proposal for the management of the residents. We were looking at a Nurse-Led service rather than a GP-led model. However, the Medical Director did not want to do this despite being told that the Nurse Practitioners would be leading the service. At the weekly GP meeting, he brought this up, so no surprise all the GPs were against it, so he scuppered it, and we had to go back to the home and withdraw our offer. This was just one example of many that happened over the years.

The worst part for me as Manager of the WIC was the staff. They all had problems that impacted the day-to-day running of the service. As well as their personal issues, there was a high level of staff sickness. I dreaded the 06:55 hour call, as generally, this was the receptionist telling me, "One of the nurses had called in sick," which meant there was no chance of covering the shift, so I had to cover the shift. This did annoy me, as it was happening on a regular basis. We also had episodes of long-term sickness lasting, in some cases, months. Mental health was a big issue, including myself. There were four other staff members who had mental health issues. Then, there were childcare issues. This always makes me laugh. When you employ staff, it is standard to go through the shift patterns with them. Funnily enough, it is never a problem as they can do anything until there is a problem with childcare. They would phone in, stating they could not come to work as the child was ill. This, again, was first thing in the morning, so there was no chance of covering the shift by agency nurses, so we would have to run one down on the shift. This drove me mad.

When we first opened, there were two single parents with children in the WIC. This caused tension with other members of staff who did not have children or whose children had grown up. In my opinion, if people take on full-time work, they need to have robust childcare arrangements in place, as it is not fair on other staff when there are problems.

Carfax Health Enterprise, or CHE, as it would come to be known, was always going to have tensions between the Directors as we all had competing agendas.

The Medical Director had been around most of the local Trusts for some time and was well known as he was the Medical Director of the previous Community Trust before a merger with Swindon. He was not that keen on seeing patients hence, he migrated to more management roles. He was pretentious and liked to get his own way. He was very two-faced and liked to talk about the other directors behind their backs. Both the Medical Director and the Managing Director felt that the Operations Director and Nurse Director of the practice would not be capable of running the business after they retired.

Again, to mitigate this, they engineered a job for one of the Directors from the local Community Trust to work at CHE two days a week as a Non-Executive Director. He had discussions with the Managing Director to fix this move. This was their way of bolstering the management team in their eyes! Interestingly, the Community Trust went bankrupt a year later, and they lost their contract with the Clinical Commissioning Group (CCG). God knows what happened, but the feeling was that they were not getting their payments on time from the CCG. The CCG is another story which I won't go into!

On one of the so-called "away days" that we had monthly at a local hotel, the Medical Director caught me in the gents' toilet. He was slagging off the Operational Director and Nurse Director. It started to feel like I was becoming Piggy in the middle of the four of them. It was clear to me that the relationships would only deteriorate.

Our contract was extended for another two years as NHS England had not gotten their act together to retender the contract. This theme would continue, but the Chair of the Clinical Commissioning Group had become hostile to our company. This followed a meeting where the Operations Director challenged the Chair of the Clinical Commissioning

Group about an issue. The one thing he did not like was being challenged, especially in a meeting. He died suddenly in September 2016.

The Managing Director was responsible for looking after the finances. It soon became clear that we were in financial trouble, and then it became "our problem". To be fair to the Operations Director who took on the finances and the remaining three of us, had to set up cost-saving measures. After a lot of work, we managed to get the finances back on track. The Medical Director retired. To be honest, he was no great loss. However, this left us with a problem as we needed a Medical Director (this was mandatory as part of the contract). So, one of the existing GPs took on this role, which eventually turned into a disaster. He was an odd character, very intelligent and a good GP, but he had a strange personality and was socially awkward. This decision would come back to haunt us later.

Chapter Forty-one

THE FIGHT BEGINS.

I have already alluded to the odd personality of the new Medical Director. He was socially awkward. He wore the same types of clothes virtually all the time: dark trousers, slightly short in the leg, an open-neck shirt with a pullover. He had problems engaging with some of the staff due to his odd personality. Having said this, he was a very good GP, and his medical knowledge was unquestionable. All was sort of well for a few months, despite a couple of run-ins on one of the "away days".

I need to digress for a moment and talk about the reception team, which was made up of full-time and part-time staff. One of the part-time staff, whom I will describe as small in height, is very loud, you could hear her miles away. She worked mainly weekends at the WIC reception, and she was well-known amongst the staff for her brashness and loudness. Having said that, in a funny sort of way, her heart was in the right place.

An example of this was when she was reported for taking condoms from the box in reception for her personal use. So, when she was interviewed about this, she said that 'we give them away to sex workers and others who attended Walk-in Centre, so she could see no reason why she could not take some as well'.

It had to be pointed out that she was a member of staff, not a client. You may be wondering why I am talking about this member of staff. Well, a very odd thing happened. As I previously said, she worked weekends, as did the Medical Director. They seemed to develop a rapport, bearing in mind that they came from opposite ends of the social spectrum. She was a single mother with two children. He was in a relationship. He lived in his own home. She lived in a council house.

If you were told that these two would hit it off, you would think the person telling you this was mad!! Anyway, they started a relationship. At first, it was covert, but several weeks later, it became common knowledge. It soon became clear that there was something more going on at work, if you get my drift. He had his own office, and she would trot up to see him several times during her shift. It was now starting to be a problem. The next thing was that they became engaged, which caused a major stir amongst the staff. I think it was a disbelief. Odd things were happening: a bottle of vodka was found on the office manager's desk by the Medical Director apparently, he was looking for a stapler! Then the Reception Manager had paint poured over her car there was lots of speculation as to who was responsible, but the police could not prove who had done it.

She started to change the way he dressed to a purple theme. God knows why purple, but when he started wearing purple shirts and sweaters, his office was transformed with purple items, including purple balloons tied to his chair. It was beginning to get out of hand. Things came to a head when the Managing Director asked to see him about the relationship and how this was impacting the other staff. Suffice it to say, he threw a wobbly and said it had nothing to do with the company. He could not see that this relationship was causing problems with some of the staff, as she would say, 'I will tell Dr*****. We had a fingerprint log-in machine for doing the timesheets and payroll. We came in one day, and the wire had been cut. We found out later that it was the Medical Director, who cut the wire, very childish.

Anyway, he went off sick with stress, and during this time, the company and the Managing Director decided to part ways with the Medical Director. A confidentiality agreement was drawn up between the company and the Medical Director, this would prevent him, or so we thought, from criticising CHE after he left. He was also given a substantial payoff. His partner carried on for a few weeks. Then, she left following another incident that resulted in disciplinary.

This would be the start of covert warfare between the two of them. The thought was that he was someone who bore a grudge. Between them, they systematically tried to bring down the company. It started with anonymous telephone calls to NHS England and the local CCG about the number of GPs. They made other anonymous calls to the Care Quality Commission (CQC) about the standard of care, and so it went on as the calls were anonymous, so they did not go anywhere as we told CQC and NHS England about the issues with him. Then they tried the General Medical Council (GMC), stating that the Medical Director was not on the Medical Register again, which was total rubbish, so this did not go anywhere. It became a war of attrition, as we did not know where the next attack would come from.

During this period, it came to light that they were carrying out their love affair using the messaging service on the clinical system. We had recently moved from Egton Medical Information Systems (EMIS) to the SystmOne (this is the correct spelling) clinical system, mainly due to SystmOne having the ability to manage urgent care as well as the GP system. SystmOne is very clever; it keeps a log of everything that the user does, e.g. The instant messaging system that is used for sending a quick message to colleagues that need a quick response then disappears, or so they thought. When we started to audit both of them and how they were using the messaging system, it soon became apparent that they were sending each other very personal messages, most of which had sexual connotations. There were references to him asking her to come to his room! It was that blatant! Personally, I would have sent this to the GMC, but for some reason, this was never done. I think everyone hoped that it would all become quiet and they would go away and get on with their lives.

Months would go by then something else would happen, things would settle again, and they would resurface. Then, they did it again just before Christmas 2015. The non-executive director took a call from the Nursing and Midwifery Council (NMC) about a complaint or concern that they had received about two Senior Nurses. I was at my desk when she took the call and just knew that this would involve me and the other Senior Nurse from the practice. When she put the phone down, she said that the NMC had received a written complaint from Ms. HD (no surprise there) about malpractice by me and the Nurse Director. Bearing in mind that this was just before Christmas, it was designed to create as much stress and anxiety for the two of us as possible.

The complaint was emailed to the non-executive director. However, what the NMC did not know was the setup of the company in that both me and the other Senior Nurse were Directors as well as clinicians employed by the company, and we were fully aware of the allegations.

This showed him at his most devious and destructive, as he was using his partner to do his dirty work and submit the complaint. It was obvious from the language used that it was not written by her, but by him, but by getting her to submit the complaint, he was not breaching the confidentiality agreement. The complaint was utter rubbish. However, both me and my colleague were aware of how the NMC operated. Nurses were often presumed guilty and had to prove their innocence, unlike the GMC, where GPs are innocent and then must be proven guilty. However, bad GPs still slip through the net, e.g., Harold Shipman, who was reported several times to the GMC, but nothing was done. The rest is history.

The first thing we did was to contact the Royal College of Nursing (RCN) (this was the first time I had ever had to use the RCN in 48 years of nursing) legal department for advice.

When this complaint came through, the Directors met to discuss the allegations, most of which were too ridiculous for words. An example of one of the allegations was that we had told the nurses to reuse disposable gloves. This was so ridiculous it hardly needed defending. It is worth recording the full list of allegations in this text to illustrate the depths some people will go to destroy individual careers. I will describe the allegations as they were written in the Nursing and Midwifery Council letter dated the 4th of January 2016. In brackets was the NMC response in a letter dated the 21st of January 2016.

- **You have humiliated colleagues in public by verbally reprimanding them in the presence of staff and the public.** (*There is no evidence to support this allegation.*)

- **You have put the health of patients at risk by allowing a member of staff to work while under the influence of alcohol on more than one occasion.** (*There is no evidence to support this allegation.*)

- **You put patients at risk by directing healthcare staff to reuse disposable gloves and cut cotton wool balls into halves for the purpose of saving money.** (*There is no evidence to support this allegation.*)

- **You verbally insulted the referrer and accused her of misbehaving with another member of staff. The referrer** advises that you were invited to examine CCTV footage and to consult with witnesses, but you refused to do so. (*There is no evidence to support this allegation*).

- The referrer also alleges that you failed to respect and abide by company grievance and disciplinary procedures. (*There is no evidence to support this allegation*)

- Fabricated evidence against employees with the intention of dismissing them from their posts. (*There is no evidence to support this allegation.*)

- There is gross discrimination in your behaviour towards employees of the company. The referee notes an incident in which one employee received a loan towards the purchase of a car for the purpose of travelling to work. However, other members of staff were refused assistance with other methods of travelling to work, such as by bus and taxi. The referee herself was advised she was denied a salary increase in line with annual appraisals, while others were given such. (*There is no evidence to support this allegation*)

My colleague was distraught as she thought she had a good working relationship with this GP, so she took this extremely badly. It was interesting that so far, both had gone for the company, never individuals, but this time, they went for the only two Directors who had something to lose and were registered with a professional body, the NMC. The other two directors were not registered with any professional body.

Although looking back on this now, it really was desperation tactics by the two of them. At the time, it was extremely stressful, especially doing this just before Christmas, as this would hang over both my colleague and me over the Christmas period. My colleague was very upset by this, often in tears, so they achieved the desired effect.

However, what they had forgotten was that they could not prove any of the allegations. The non-executive director sent in a robust defence to the NMC, fully supporting both myself and my colleague and refuting all the allegations. There was a reference to a disciplinary hearing I had conducted on the receptionist. She was alleging that I did not follow company policy, but as luck would have it, I had recorded the interview (with her consent), which destroyed her allegations.

The RCN was very good, and we were both assigned a legal team, who, once they received the company response, advised me that the case would be dropped.

The Referee was informed of this and tried to stir up more issues, but when the Non-Executive Director advised the NMC of the background to this pair's behaviour over the past months, all the allegations were dropped, and the case was closed.

This incident was very stressful for me, and my colleague and I did not feel that the other 2 directors fully appreciated how potentially serious this could have been.

The two who made the allegations were not as clever as they thought and forgot that although we were Directors of CHE, we were also employees of CHE, both employers and employees. If this had happened in a larger Trust, we would both have been suspended pending an investigation. The other noteworthy thing to say was the language that was used in the complaint document. It was obvious that it was written by the GP, not his partner in crime, as the language used was too complex for her to write. There was a lull in any more attempts to bring the company down. I feel they had played all their cards and lost the game. I was off sick with depression from July 2016 until December 2016. I went back to work for 3 months and retired on March 31, 2017.

While I was off work, the new health centre was almost ready for occupation. I had played a part in the design of the WIC rooms, but again, the practice took up a major part of the building. I never set foot in the place. The WIC was taken over by the Great Western Hospital, and eventually, the WIC was moved to the hospital site some 18 years after it had opened. The WIC is now incorporated within the Urgent Care Centre, which, to be honest, works very well.

Chapter Forty-two

RETIREMENT

I retired from nursing on the 31st of March 2017 at age 64. The job was becoming very stressful. I was an Advanced Nurse Practitioner and an Independent Non-Medical Prescriber. I was also a Director at Carfax Health Enterprise, which was becoming a complete nightmare working with the other two directors. I was also tired of dealing with staff issues; sickness levels were high, which caused major problems as they worked 12-hour shifts, so if someone went off, I had to cover the shift. I once worked 14 hours to cover sickness, and I vowed never again. The WIC was also seeing large numbers of patients from the practice, as they would just send them to the WIC if they had no appointments.

After 18 years at the WIC, bearing in mind that I had project managed the service and set it up and managed it over the past 18 years with a 12-month gap out at the GP surgery. The company, Carfax Health Enterprise, gave me a £100 voucher and a bag of tat.

My staff bought me a nice pocket watch. I did ask if they would pool whatever they collected to get me a voucher for a jeweller in Swindon, but that fell on deaf ears. This may sound ungrateful, but £100 from the company was just beyond the pale.

After I had left, I still felt that I needed to ease into full retirement, so I got a part-time job at Tesco, working on the checkouts. I worked 11½ hours a week, Friday morning from 09:00 till 12:00 and Saturday from 13:00 till 22:00. This was a long shift. I worked there for 4 years and decided to retire completely in 2021. What was interesting about 4 weeks after I left was that I received a recorded delivery package. When I opened it, there was an engraved glass gift with my name on it thanking me for my time working for Tesco and a £50 gift card, £50 for 4 years and £100 for 18 years. Yes, I am bitter. I felt that I had been valued as a worker at Tesco, unlike when I left the NHS and the RAF, where I felt completely undervalued.

We have taken up cruising as our holiday of choice. This was due to my dear friend Ray, who sadly died suddenly in 2019. He had been in hospital for planned surgery. I sent him a text on the morning of his death to see how he was. He said 'he was tired and would get back to me later' sadly, he had a cardiac arrest 2 hours later although they managed to resuscitate him, he remained unconscious. Doctors told Don, his partner, that Ray had suffered irreversible brain damage, so Don had to make the very difficult decision to turn off the ventilator. What I was not aware of at the time was I had Ray's last text he sent before he died. It was only when Don got access to Ray's phone that he realised that I had Ray's final text, which I sent to Don. This was a very emotional moment for the two of us.

I first met Ray in 1974 at RAF Hospital Cosford. I was posted there following my qualifying as a SEN. We subsequently shared a room and became very good friends, but I lost contact when I was posted to another hospital. Then, in 2011, I received a message on Friends Reunited (precursor to Facebook) from Ray. We exchanged emails, telling each other what we had been up to in the intervening years. It turned out that Ray and his partner Don lived in Romsey, Hampshire, which is only 90 minutes away from our home. Ray came to visit us for Sunday lunch so we could catch up. Ray also knew Mary, my wife, from RAF Cosford days. Ray left the RAF shortly after we lost touch to forge a career in the NHS, while I remained in the RAF.

Ray had been with Don for 30 years and got married when the law on same-sex marriages changed, which was great to hear. Now that we were in touch, we kept in regular contact. We visited them several times and Ray and Don had been to see us.

Me, Mary and Ray (right) 2015

Getting back to cruises, we went to stay with Ray and Don in 2015 for a weekend. After dinner and several glasses of wine later, we started talking about holidays. Ray was telling us that he and Don go on cruise holidays sometimes twice a year and they love them as gay men cruise holidays just work for them.

Before speaking to Ray, we had never considered a cruise, as we always went to Cornwall for two weeks, generally renting a cottage. Ray showed us some of their photos of their cruise holidays, and they looked very good. Ray said 'that a good cruise to start with is a 10-day cruise to Norway and Fjords' Ray said, 'We could stay with them the night before, and he and Don would drop us off at the terminal at Southampton, which was very generous of them.

Both Ray and Don were worried that we would not like the holiday, but they need not have. We really enjoyed the holiday, so much so that we booked a 14-night cruise to the Baltics (we went to St Petersburg, which was stunning. Sadly, this is no longer an option due to the Ukraine War) for the following year. The third cruise was to the Southern Mediterranean, which includes Spain, Scilly, Italy, Venice, Dubrovnik, and Gibraltar. We have been on four ships, Arcadia. Oriana. Arvia and Iona. Since then, we booked a 30-night trip to Canada and the USA. Unfortunately, this was cancelled twice due to COVID-19. We got the green light to go on the 6th of September 2022 until the 6th of October 2022. Unfortunately, we contracted COVID-19 on the 19th of September, so we had to be quarantined for 10 days, so we missed Boston and New York. We have three further cruises booked, January 2023 to the Canary Islands. September 2023, the Mediterranean and September 2024, the Southern Mediterranean, this is with my sister, as it is her 60th birthday. We plan to do the Canada/America cruise again in 2025, as this will be our 50th wedding anniversary and hopefully won't catch COVID again.

We are very fortunate that between us, we have our State, NHS, RAF and War pensions, our mortgage is paid off, so we are financially secure. I have three allotments, which keep me busy in the spring and summer months. Hence, we go on holiday in the autumn.

I still volunteer with the St. John Ambulance, the Royal Air Force Association, and the Royal British Legion, and I am Chair of the Princess Mary's Royal Air Force Association. I also play the cornet in a youth brass band and the Royal Wootton Bassett Brass Band. I believe it is important that you keep busy and keep your brain and body working as long as you can. About physical fitness, I see a personal trainer once a week. Even though COVID, we did our sessions online, which worked well as I bought some weights and exercise bands

Ryan and me at gym 2024

I have an exercise bike at home and do 60 minutes every night, which is around 15 miles while watching something on Netflix. Sadly, we have other issues that have impacted our lives, which I will discuss later.

Chapter Forty-three

REFLECTIONS

I was sitting on our cruise ship, having just left St. John's, New Brunswick. It's September 28, 2022. Mary and I have been in quarantine since the 19th of September 2022 due to COVID. I came in the day after, so Mary was being released on the 30th of September 2022. I got out on the 1st of October, 2022. Although it's been a complete ballache as we have missed all the key ports, I typed up my notes for this book, so it's not a complete waste of time. I had also taken my cornet with a silent mute. This is a device that you put in the bell end of the cornet (where the sounds come out). This is linked to headphones, so when you play, the sound comes through the headphones, not from the cornet. I was able to play while in quarantine, which was great.

I often look back and reflect on my younger days in the late 50s and early 60s, life was much simpler then and not always better than today. As a working-class family living in a council house (which most people did), there were low aspirations expected of you. Money was tight, so there were no luxuries as it was living from hand to mouth. Dad worked as an electric welder in the shipbuilding industry, apart from when he was doing his National Service in the RAF as a cook class 1, he spent all his service in India. He always wanted to be a chef, but he did not get any encouragement from his parents. His Father also worked in the shipbuilding industry as a riveter. They were not that close. Grandma was cold as well, but again, looking back, she lost two children and had a Stepfather, so you can sort of understand why people were like they were when you have some background and context to their lives.

It's funny looking back as Dad never talked about his relationship with his parents apart from having been hit with his Father's belt. We would often visit Grandma and Grandad on Sunday afternoons. This was always a challenge and quite traumatic for Mam because she did not like going out and hated buses, which was a little unfortunate as it was the only way to get there. It was a long process of Mam getting ready. She would faff about wasting time, and then, just as we were leaving, she would need to go to the toilet. Dad would give us a warning about our behaviour when we were out with him; we had to be on our best behaviour or else. Once out, we had to walk a short distance for the number 19 bus. As Grandma and Grandad lived in Longbenton, it took about 40 minutes on the bus. This was the only bus that got us close to their house, as there was still a 15-minute walk from the bus stop to their house. When we finally arrived, it was all tense. Sometimes, we would have Sunday dinner, but conversation was not a priority. David and I were the second-class Grandchildren, as Lil's (Dad's) sister's two Grandchildren, Ken and Ian, were the preferred ones.

I used to belong to a church choir (I know, don't laugh). I would attend church every Sunday and would often go myself to see Grandma and Grandad after the service, and it was completely different. They had a radiogram (a large piece of wooden furniture with a radio and record dec built inside) that always had the same programmes on the radio on a Sunday. The two programmes that spring to mind are Round the Horne and The Clitheroe Kid, both comedy shows that were very popular and very funny. I used to sit with Grandad and listen to the radio while Grandma made Sunday dinner. It was strange as it was a completely different experience from when we all went together. It was a pleasure to visit them by myself. If I was lucky my Uncle Alan would be there, which was great to be able to chat with him.

I have been researching my family history now for over 20 years and have all the birth, death and marriage certificates of all my ancestors. It started with Grandad (Pop), Dad's Father, who I found on the 1901 census. It's strange when you have a physical bit of paper; it brings that person to life, and you can start to trace their own background. For instance, my Godfather was a chap called Davy Dow. Dad's best friend, I could not find him anywhere until the 1901 census was released. I found my Granddad. His Father, William, was a shoemaker, and his Mother was called Margaret this was a second marriage. Then, as I looked down at the rest of the family, there was a Matthew H. Dow Stepson. This was Margaret's Son from her first marriage. He turned out to be Davy Dow's Dad. It's amazing what you can find out. I have since been in contact with a relative of Davy.

When I was a lad there were no potholes in the road as roads were resurfaced at regular intervals. They used a technique of pouring hot tar on one side of the road. A lorry with pink chippings followed, dropping the chippings into the hot tar. Then a steam roller (it's what we called them. They did not work with steam) would compress the chippings into the tar which worked. This would then be repeated on the other side of the road.

There were road sweepers who would keep the streets clean and free from litter. There were no McDonalds, unlike today when people throw their waste out of the car window onto the roadside. There was always a Police Officer walking the streets, and as kids, we were terrified of him. They were always men! We had a great public transport system which included trolly buses which were run off electric cables. There were two arms on the roof of the bus, which were connected to the cables running along the route. These were dismantled for diesel buses if we only knew then what we know now? We had gone a full circle with bringing back trams and electric trains.

We never missed school due to bad weather, and at times, we would have 12 inches of snow. We just put our wellies on and walked to school. In the senior school, in the winter, the older boys would make a slide on top of the ice that could be up to 30 feet long. The challenge was to slide down without falling over. Where we lived, there was a hospital called Walker Park Hospital. Attached to the hospital was a small accident department. This was covered by the local GPs, all of whom had experience as Medical Officers in the local mines. They could deal with most things. I remember having an ingrown toenail removed and a skin graft to a hole in the back of my thigh (fell onto a metal bar) today. This type of injury would be seen at the local A&E. The one thing that is better today is dog owners generally pick up their dog poo, not in the 60s. There was dog poo everywhere!! There were no telephones and very few cars in the street apart from Maud next door. When Mam eventually had the phone put in it took months to get the phone installed.

It's strange looking back. People looked old. Even in their 50s, my Nana looked old, they were the war generation, which may account for this. They are dressed in old-fashioned clothes, unlike today when I try and keep up with the fashions. I always wear a hat, either a trilby or fedora. I have several hanging by the front door.

When Mary and I first got married, we had nothing. The pay in the RAF was very low until Margaret Thatcher gave us a substantial increase in our pay. However, as a lower rank, life was still a struggle. We bought second-hand furniture as we had some spare cash then we were able to hand back some of the RAF furniture. When Andrew was born, I bought his carry cot for 50p which also was used when we had Matthew. Mary did not work until the boys were older, around 5 and 3 years old. She worked in a Nursing Home around my shifts. In the Summer holidays, I would request nights for the 6 weeks of the holiday, which worked out 7 nights on and 7 nights off. On my week of nights, I would go to bed till 13:00, then get up. Mary would go to work till 17:00. This worked, but I was knackered at the end of my week of nights. Once the boys were at school, Mary went to night school to learn shorthand and typing. She ended up as a very successful Medical Secretary. She worked at RAF Hospital Wroughton in the Ear Nose and Throat Department. When RAF Hospital Wroughton closed, she was successful in getting a Medical Secretary post in the Ophthalmic Department at the local NHS hospital, where she worked for some 20 years. She also managed 2 private practices for 2 Ophthalmic Surgeons.

We both know what it is like to struggle with a lack of money and material things, but we appreciate the journey that we have been on for over 50 years, and now we are in a place where we don't have to worry about money. This has been achieved through hard work and sacrifice. We can help our family and spoil the grandchildren. Well, that's what grandparents were put on this earth for. We are very proud of our children and grandchildren they have all done well for themselves. Earlier in the year, Andrew, who was head of Security for Tesco, attended a meeting a 10 Downing Street amazing.

Having worked in the military, NHS, and later Tesco (I took a job at the checkouts in 2017 and finished in 2021), it is interesting to compare the work ethic within the three institutions. In the military, there is a different work ethic with a distinct structure that all staff understand and work with. You know where you are in the "pecking order" as there is a rank system. Generally, service personnel have a significantly better work ethic and are more reliable with lower levels of sickness than their civilian counterparts. Much lower than the NHS, where certain staff will go off sick for the most trivial thing, as all they must do is make a phone call saying they are sick and won't be in. When I first took my first NHS post as a Charge Nurse in Malmesbury Community Hospital, it was a nightmare when someone went sick, as you had to cover shifts with a bank nurse if you could get one. The same issue happened in the WIC, where sickness levels were high.

If I were on an admin day, I would dread the 06:55 hour call from a certain receptionist stating, "Someone has gone off sick." She had a whiney voice, which made it worse. I would then have to put my uniform on and cover the shift, as it had to be a Nurse Practitioner and prescriber. There was no chance of getting an agency nurse to cover this. Staff worked 12-hour shifts, which are essentially two shifts. I remember one day, I covered the shift and did a 14-hour day to cover the service. I vowed I would never do this again, and I never did, as it's not safe. It's hard for others to imagine doing a shift that long and seeing one patient after another, making sure that you missed nothing and treated the patient safely. GPs would not work like this. By the end of the shift, your brain was completely fuddled. Looking back at my time in the NHS, I would say staff sickness is a major problem, mainly because staff get 6 months full pay and then 6 months half pay after 5 years' service, so there was no incentive to go back to work. Compare this to the private sector (Tesco), where there is a totally different approach to staff sickness. Generally, staff would not be entitled to sick pay and had to rely on statutory sick pay (SSP), so the incentive to go to work is somewhat higher. I have experienced both systems. I was off 6 months in 2016 with depression while working for the NHS. I received full pay for the 6 months I had no contact with anyone from work.

While at Tesco, I had my first hip replacement done. I would be off work for three months. As it was planned surgery, I had to show a letter confirming this, which was held on my personal record. I received a call from my manager weekly to check how I was. After 4 weeks off, it was classified as long-term sickness, so you had to have a face-to-face meeting, which in my case was done at home as I could not drive for 6 weeks. Once I returned to work, there was a written back-to-work plan, which was generally reduced hours, you only got paid for the hours that you worked. Unfortunately, on Mother's Day 2019, I tripped, going into my local Tesco in the village "rather ironic" and fell onto my new hip. When I got up, I could feel this crunching in my hip. I went and bought the bottle of milk, then drove home. When I got home, the crunching was worse. I called Andrew to take me to A&E, and after an x-ray, I was told that I had smashed the ceramic femoral head of the new hip. I was admitted and had another hip replacement, which I am pleased to say went very well, and I have had no problems with it, which is extremely lucky as second hip replacements tend not to do well. Mine has been great.

Chapter Forty-four
MEMORABLE EVENTS

During your lifetime, you live through world events, some good and some bad. My first clear memory of a significant world event was the Cuban missile crisis in October 1962, when I was 9 years old. For thirteen days in October 1962, the world waited, seemingly on the brink of nuclear war, hoping for a peaceful resolution to the Cuban Missile Crisis.

In October 1962, an American U-2 spy plane secretly photographed nuclear missile sites being built by the Soviet Union on the island of Cuba. President Kennedy did not want the Soviet Union and Cuba to know that he had discovered the missiles. He met in secret with his advisors for several days to discuss the problem.

After many long and difficult meetings, Kennedy decided to place a naval blockade, or a ring of ships, around Cuba. The aim of this "quarantine," as he called it, was to prevent the Soviets from bringing in more military supplies. He demanded the removal of the missiles already there and the destruction of the sites. On October 22, 1962, President Kennedy spoke to the nation about the crisis in a televised address.

No one was sure how Soviet leader Nikita Khrushchev would respond to the naval blockade and US demands. However, the leaders of both superpowers recognised the devastating possibility of a nuclear war and publicly agreed to a deal in which the Soviets would dismantle the weapon sites in exchange for a pledge from the United States not to invade Cuba. In a separate deal that remained secret for more than 25 years, the United States also agreed to remove its nuclear missiles from Turkey. Although the Soviets removed their missiles from Cuba, they escalated the building of their military arsenal. The missile crisis was over, but the arms' race was not.

Locally, we were all told at school about the possibility of a nuclear war and plans for civil defence were put in place. Our next-door neighbour, who had a furniture removal van, had this commandeered. The news was grim, as we all thought that a nuclear war was imminent. Thankfully, common sense prevailed, and a diplomatic resolution was reached.

Reference https,//www.jfklibrary.org/

Chapter Forty-five
ASSASSINATION OF PRESIDENT JOHN KENNEDY

November 22, 1963, DEATH OF THE PRESIDENT

The Assassination

Crowds of excited people lined the streets and waved to the Kennedys. The car turned off Main Street at Dealey Plaza around 12:30. As it was passing the Texas School Book Depository, gunfire suddenly reverberated in the plaza.

Bullets struck the president's neck and head, and he slumped over towards Mrs. Kennedy. The governor was shot in the back. The car sped off to Parkland Memorial Hospital, just a few minutes away. But little could be done for the president. A Catholic priest was summoned to administer the last rites, and at 13:00, John F. Kennedy was pronounced dead. Though seriously wounded, Governor Connally would recover.

The president's body was brought to Love Field and placed on Air Force One. Before the plane took off, a grim-faced Lyndon B. Johnson stood in the tight, crowded compartment and took the oath of office, administered by US District Court Judge Sarah Hughes. The brief ceremony took place at 14:38.

Less than an hour earlier, police had arrested Lee Harvey Oswald, a recently hired employee at the Texas School Book Depository. He was being held for the assassination of President Kennedy and the fatal shooting, shortly afterwards, of Patrolman J. D. Tippit on Dallas Street.

On Sunday morning, November 24, Oswald was scheduled to be transferred from police headquarters to the county jail. Viewers across America watching the live television coverage suddenly saw a man aim a pistol and fire at point-blank range. The assailant was identified as Jack Ruby, a local nightclub owner. Oswald died two hours later at Parkland Hospital.

Reference, https,//www.jfklibrary.org/

Over the years, it was said that you knew where you were when you heard the news of the death of President Kennedy. I was at home when the news came through on the wireless (radio), and as television news was still in its infancy, we eventually were updated by the television news. This was a sad day for the world, as President Kennedy was seen as a man who could have made massive changes in the world despite his own personal flaws. The one thing he did promise was to land a man on the moon and return them safely to Earth by the end of the 1960s, which was done. Sadly, he would not witness this momentous event.

Chapter Forty-six

FIRST MOON LANDING

I was fascinated by astronomy, as was my friend Joseph. We would spend hours outside looking for constellations, shooting stars and planets, and looking at the moon through our telescopes. We both had refractor telescopes that were powerful enough to see Jupiter, four of its moons, and Saturn's rings. We were both captivated by the moon, as we could see all the craters up close. When the National Aeronautics and Space Administration (NASA) announced the Apollo program, also known as Project Apollo, which was the third United States human spaceflight program carried out by NASA, it succeeded in preparing and landing the first humans on the Moon from 1969 to 1972.

It was first conceived in 1960 during President Dwight D. Eisenhower's administration as a three-person spacecraft to follow the one-person Project Mercury, which put the first Americans in space. Apollo was later dedicated to President John F. Kennedy's national goal for the 1960s of "landing a man on the Moon and returning him safely to the Earth" in an address to Congress on the 25th of May 1961. It was the third US human spaceflight program to fly, preceded by the two-person Project Gemini, conceived in 1961 to extend spaceflight capability in support of Apollo.

Kennedy's goal was accomplished on the Apollo 11 mission when astronauts Neil Armstrong and Buzz Aldrin landed their Apollo Lunar Module (LEM) on the 20th of July 1969 and walked on the lunar surface, while Michael Collins remained in lunar orbit in the command and service module (CSM). All three landed safely on Earth in the Pacific Ocean on the 24th of July 1969.

The Apollo 11 moon landing happened on the 20th of July 1969, at 16:17 Eastern Daylight Time (EDT). The UK's time zone is Greenwich Mean Time (GMT), which is 4 hours ahead of EDT, so the time in the UK was 20:17 on the 20th of July 1969. At 02:56 UK time on the 21st of July 1969, American astronaut Neil Armstrong became the first person to walk on the moon. He stepped out of the Apollo 11 lunar module and onto the moon's surface in an area called the Sea of Tranquillity.

The moon landing was a historic event that was watched by millions of people around the world, including in the UK. The BBC broadcast live coverage of the event, its main presenter was Cliff Michelmore, with James Burke and Sir Patrick Moore concentrating on scientific and technical explanations and analysis. There were public gatherings in cities and towns across the country to watch the historic event on TVs in shops. I remember staying up for hours to watch the live feed of Neil Armstrong taking his first steps on the moon. The whole world was gripped by this event, as I was as a 16-year-old boy. Interest waned in the Apollo missions as it was becoming all too routine, and most people had switched off, that is, until Apollo 13. Apollo 13 was the third moon mission, crewed by Fred Haise, James Lovell, and John Swigert.

During the mission, there was a dramatic series of events. An oxygen tank explosion almost 56 hours into the flight forced the crew to abandon all thoughts of reaching the moon. The spacecraft was damaged, but the crew was able to seek cramped shelter in the lunar module for the trip back to Earth before returning to the command module for an uncomfortable splashdown. Many are familiar with Apollo 11, the mission that landed humans on the Moon for the first time, but there were 14 missions in total during the Apollo Program (1961-1972).

Apollo1/4/5/6/7/8/9/10/11/12/13/15/15/16/and17. They were all launched using the Saturn V rocket apart from Apollo 1. During a preflight test on the 27th of January 1967 for what was to be the first crewed Apollo mission, a fire claimed the lives of three U.S. astronauts: Gus Grissom, Ed White and Roger Chaffee. After the disaster, the mission, which had previously been referred to as Apollo-Saturn 204 (AS-204), was officially designated Apollo 1, which was the name for the mission the crew had intended to use.

Rocket scientist Wernher Von Braun is hailed as the founder of American rocketry and the designer of the Saturn V launch vehicles.

By late 1944, it was obvious to Von Braun that Germany would be defeated and occupied, and he began planning for the post-war era. Before the Allied capture of the V-2 rocket complex, Von Braun was sent south, eventually to Bavaria. He surrendered to the Americans in the Austrian Alps, along with other key team leaders.

In 1960, President Eisenhower transferred his rocket development group at Redstone Arsenal from the Army to the newly established National Aeronautics and Space Administration (NASA). Its primary objective was to develop the giant Saturn rockets. Accordingly, Von Braun became director of NASA's Marshall Space Flight Centre and the chief architect of the Saturn V launch vehicle. This super booster would propel Americans to the Moon. The NASA Launch Operations Centre was renamed the Kennedy Space Centre Florid in December 1968.

Chapter Forty-seven
VIETNAM WAR

During the 1960s, the television news was dominated by the Vietnam War. Quite graphic scenes would be beamed into your home. The Vietnam War was a long and bloody conflict that lasted from 1955 to 1975. It was fought between North Vietnam (with the support of the Soviet Union and China) and South Vietnam (with the support of the United States). The war began as a civil war between the communist North and the anti-communist South. The United States entered the war in 1965 to prevent the spread of communism. There was one image that has stayed in my memory banks, which is the young child running naked following a Napalm attack. The picture became iconic and synonymous with the Vietnam War.

Chapter Forty-eight
THE TROUBLES

The Troubles in Northern Ireland began in the late 1960s and lasted until the Good Friday Agreement, which was signed in 1998. The conflict was primarily political and nationalistic, fuelled by historical events. It also had an ethnic or sectarian dimension, but despite the use of the terms "Protestant" and "Catholic" to refer to the two sides, it was not a religious conflict. The key issue was the status of Northern Ireland.

One of the worst events in the "Troubles" was Bloody Sunday, a demonstration in Londonderry (Derry), Northern Ireland, on Sunday 30th of January 1972, by Roman Catholic civil rights supporters that turned violent when British paratroopers opened fire, killing 13 and injuring 14 others (one of the injured later died)

There is not one definitive answer to the question of when the Troubles started. Some historians point to the events of 1968 when a civil rights movement led by Catholics began to protest against discrimination by the Protestant-dominated Government and Police Forces. Others argue that the conflict can be traced back to much earlier events, such as the partition of Ireland in 1921 or the Plantation of Ulster in the 17th century.

The following are some of the key events that took place in the years leading up to the Troubles,

- 1921, The Government of Ireland Act is passed, partitioning Ireland into Northern Ireland and the Republic of Ireland.

- In 1968, The Northern Ireland Civil Rights Association (NICRA) was founded.

- 1969, The Battle of the Bogside takes place in Derry.

- 1972, The British government imposes direct rule on Northern Ireland.

- 1973, The Sunningdale Agreement is signed, but it is rejected by unionists.

- 1979, The IRA bombs the Grand Hotel in Brighton, England, during the Conservative Party conference. Nearly wiping out the British government.

- 1993, The Downing Street Declaration is signed by the British and Irish governments.

- The 1996 Manchester bombing was an attack carried out by the Provisional Irish Republican Army (IRA) on the 15th of June 1996. The IRA detonated a 1,500-kilogram (3,300 lb) lorry bomb on Corporation Street in the centre of Manchester, England. It was the biggest bomb detonated in Great Britain since the Second World War.

- 1998, The Good Friday Agreement is signed, bringing an end to the Troubles.

The Troubles were a time of great violence and loss of life. Over 3,500 people were killed, and many more were injured. The conflict also had a profound impact on the people of Northern Ireland, both physically and psychologically.

The Good Friday Agreement was a major step towards peace in Northern Ireland. The agreement established a power-sharing government between unionists and nationalists, and it also created several cross-border institutions between Northern Ireland and the Republic of Ireland. The agreement has not been without its challenges, but it has largely held, and it has helped to create a more peaceful and prosperous future for Northern Ireland. The power-sharing government has not been working due to political issues. On February 4, 2022, Givan resigned as First Minister, which led to O'Neill automatically ceasing to hold office as Deputy First Minister. The offices have since remained vacant until now. Due to an agreement with the Democratic Unionist Party (DUP) and the UK Government over post-Brexit trade between the UK mainland and Northern Ireland, the Northern Ireland Assembly was reinstated on the 3rd of February 2024, with a Sinn Fein First Minister.

Chapter Forty-nine
THE COLD WAR

The Cold War was a period of geopolitical tension between the United States, the Soviet Union, and their respective allies, the Western Bloc and the Eastern Bloc, lasting from the late 1940s to the early 1990s. The term Cold War is used because there was no large-scale fighting directly between the two superpowers, but they each supported major regional conflicts known as proxy wars.

The conflict split the temporary wartime alliance against Nazi Germany and its allies, leaving the USSR and the USA as two superpowers with profound economic and political differences. A neutral faction arose in the form of the Non-Aligned Movement, with countries that chose not to align themselves with either the US or the USSR. The Cold War came to an end with the collapse of the Soviet Union in 1991, leaving the US as the world's sole superpower.

Some of the key events of the Cold War include,

- The Berlin Blockade in 1948–1949
- The formation of NATO in 1949
- The formation of the Warsaw Pact in 1955
- The Cuban Missile Crisis in 1962

- The Vietnam War from 1954 to 1975

- The fall of the Berlin Wall in 1989

- The collapse of the Soviet Union in 1991

The Cold War had a profound impact on the world, shaping political, economic and social developments for decades. It also had a significant impact on the development of technology, as both sides competed to develop new weapons and military systems. The Cold War was a complex and multifaceted topic, and there is no single answer to the question of who "won" the Cold War. However, the end of the Cold War was a major turning point in world history, and it has had a lasting impact on the global order.

During my time in the RAF the Cold War and the prospect of nuclear war was a dominant factor. We did regular exercises simulating a nuclear attack. These were called Tactical Evaluations (TACEVAL) to test our readiness to survive and sustain combat readiness following a nuclear attack. Some of these would last for 48 to 72 hours. When I was a RAF Lyneham, we had a couple of TACEVALS. Generally, we would be woken at around 01:00 hours with a load claxon and TACEVAL being broadcast over a loudspeaker. All personnel had to report to their place of work with their full nuclear biological and chemical (NBC) kit, including respirator. During the Cold War, these exercises were taken seriously, as your life could depend on getting it right.

Sources

en.wikipedia.org/wiki/Cold

Chapter Fifty
THE FALL OF THE BERLIN WALL

The construction of the Berlin Wall was commenced by the government of the German Democratic Republic (GDR) on the 13th of August 1961. It included guard towers placed along large concrete walls, accompanied by a wide area (later known as the "death strip") that contained anti-vehicle trenches, beds of nails and other defences. The primary intention for the Wall's construction was to prevent East German citizens from fleeing to the West.

The fall of the Berlin Wall on the 9th of November 1989, during the Peaceful Revolution, was a pivotal event in world history that marked the destruction of the Berlin Wall and the figurative Iron Curtain. It was one of the series of events that started the fall of communism in Central and Eastern Europe, preceded by the Solidarity Movement in Poland. The fall of the inner German border took place shortly afterwards. An end to the Cold War was declared at the Malta Summit three weeks later, and the German reunification took place in October of the following year.

Chapter Fifty-one
EUROPEAN UNION

The United Kingdom joined the European Economic Community (EEC), also known as the Common Market, on the 1st of January 1973. The EEC was formed in 1957 by six countries: Belgium, France, Germany, Italy, Luxembourg, and the Netherlands. The UK first applied to join the EEC in 1961, but its application was vetoed by France in 1963 and again in 1967. In 1970, the UK government renewed its application to join the EEC, which this time was successful.

The UK's decision to join the EEC was controversial at the time and remains so today. Some people believe that the UK was right to join the EEC, as it has helped to boost the UK economy and create jobs. Others believe that the UK was wrong to join the EEC, as it has led to a loss of sovereignty and has contributed to the decline of British manufacturing.

The UK's membership in the EEC was a major turning point in British history. It marked the end of the UK's long history of economic and political isolation and brought the UK into closer alignment with its European neighbours. The UK's membership in the EEC also had a significant impact on British politics, as it led to the rise of the Eurosceptic Movement. Over the years, what was once an economic alliance has become a more political union and was renamed the European Union (EU). Due to political pressure in the UK, mainly from the United Kingdom Independence Party (UKIP), led by Nigel Farage, the then

Conservative Prime Minister David Cameron announced an EU referendum, which was held in June 2016.

Most of the political elite thought that this was going to result in the Country remaining in the EU. However, politicians like Boris Johnson put their weight behind the leave movement, along with Dominic Cummings, who allegedly masterminded the leave campaign. The referendum result was a majority to leave the EU (52% leave, 48% remain). David Cameron resigned, and Theresa May became the new Prime Minister. What followed were years of political wrangling and High Court rulings. The then Conservative Government was relying on the Democratic Unionist Party to maintain their majority in the House of Commons.

There was another leadership challenge: Boris Johnson was elected by the Conservative membership as leader and Prime Minister. There was the Fixed Term Parliament Act (brought in by the Coalition Government), which took away the Prime Minister's option of calling a general election when they felt it was beneficial to the government winning. This was revoked, and Boris Johnson called for a general election on the 12th of December 2019, against all predictions. Boris Johnson's Conservative Party won an 80-seat majority, mainly gaining what were solid Labour seats (named the Red Wall) with the slogan "Get Brexit Done." The UK left the European Union on the 31st of January 2020.

Chapter Fifty-two

MINERS' STRIKE

The UK miners' strike was a major industrial action within the British coal industry to prevent colliery closures. It was led by Arthur Scargill of the National Union of Mineworkers (NUM) against the National Coal Board (NCB), a government agency.

The strike began on the 6th of March 1984 and lasted for 14 months until the 3rd of March 1985. It was the longest industrial action in British history, which had a profound impact on the UK economy and society. The strike was triggered by the NCB's announcement that twenty pits would be closed, resulting in the loss of 20,000 jobs. The NUM argued that the closures were unnecessary and would damage the British economy. The government, led by Margaret Thatcher (the first woman Prime Minister), argued that the closures were necessary to make the coal industry more efficient.

The strike was deeply divisive, and it led to widespread violence and disorder. The police were accused of using excessive force against pickets, and there were numerous clashes between miners and the police. The strike also had a significant impact on the communities that depended on the coal industry. Many miners lost their jobs, and their families were forced to go on welfare. The strike eventually collapsed after the NUM was expelled from the Trades Union Congress (TUC). The government had also succeeded in breaking the strike by using a variety of tactics, including using scab labour and bringing in troops to guard the pits.

The UK miners' strike was a major turning point in British history. It marked the end of the power of the trade unions in the UK, and it led to the decline of the coal industry. The strike also had a significant impact on British politics, as it led to the rise of the Conservative Party and the decline of the Labour Party.

Chapter Fifty-three
DEATH OF PRINCESS DIANNA, AUGUST 31, 1997

During the early hours of the 31st of August 1997, Diana, Princess of Wales, died from injuries sustained earlier that night in a car crash in the Pont de l'Alma tunnel in Paris, France. Diana's partner, Dodi Fayed, and the driver of the Mercedes-Benz W140, Henri Paul, were found dead inside the car. Dodi's bodyguard, Trevor Rees-Jones, was seriously injured but was the only survivor of the crash. This event almost brought down the monarchy, as the Queen was slow to respond to what turned out to be the largest outpouring of public grief. The flowers outside Buckingham and St. James Palace were unbelievable. The Royal Family were ensconced in Balmoral (protecting William and Harry) and were heavily criticised for not returning to London sooner.

The funeral of Princess Dianna took place on the 6th of September 1997. The coffin was followed by the Duke of Edinburgh, Prince William, Earl Spencer, Prince Harry and Prince Charles. Hundreds of thousands of mourners lined the streets of central London to watch the funeral procession. This event has had a lasting impact on the Royal Family, in particular Prince Harry, who blames the press for his mother's death. The shadow of Dianna hung over the relationship of Prince Charles and Camilla Parker-Bowles as the public was unforgiving of the relationship.

However, time has a way of healing, and King Charles III and Queen Camilla seem to be accepted by the British public.

Chapter Fifty-four
GULF WAR 1

Saddam Hussain invaded Kuwait in August 1990 in an unprovoked attack to take control of the oil fields. Iraq's leader, Saddam Hussein, ordered the invasion and occupation of Kuwait with the apparent aim of acquiring that nation's large oil reserves, cancelling a large debt Iraq owed Kuwait, and expanding Iraqi power in the region. It was the first major international crisis of the post-Cold War era, and the U.S.-led response would set important precedents for the use of military force over subsequent decades. A coalition of 42 nations joined together to remove Saddam Hussain from Kuwait. The troop build-up began in August 1990. The air war started on the night of the 17th of January 1991, called Operation Desert Storm, with Kuwait being liberated on February 28, 1991

Chapter Fifty-five
9/11

I was at the NHS conference on the 11th of September 2001 at Exeter. It was an all-day affair. During the afternoon coffee break, we were in a large room, as there were various trade stands scattered around. At the far end of the room was a large flat-screen television, not like we have today, but a Sony rear projection television. Like all breaks, there was a hum around the room with people talking in huddles. Suddenly, the hum started to diminish, and the room fell silent as the news channel was on television and the first plane had hit one of the Twin Towers of the World Trade Centre. This was the same as knowing where you were when President Kennedy was shot. I remember this event as it was yesterday. It is very clear in my memory that the meeting concluded soon after the second plane hit the other tower. I had a 2-hour drive back home, and I listened to the news on the car radio. It was a devastating terror attack on the United States of America, which would have far-reaching repercussions for years to come. This resulted in the war on terror with the bombing of Afghanistan and the search for Osama Bin Ladin.

Chapter Fifty-six
Iraq War

In 2002, the United States (now led by President George W. Bush, son of the former president) sponsored a new United Nations (UN) resolution calling for the return of weapons inspectors to Iraq. U.N. inspectors re-entered Iraq that November. Amid differences between Security Council member states over how well Iraq had complied with those inspections, the United States and Britain began amassing forces on Iraq's border.

Bush, without further U.N. approval, issued an ultimatum on the 17th of March 2003, demanding that Saddam Hussein step down from power and leave Iraq within 48 hours, under threat of war. Hussein refused, and the second Persian Gulf War, more generally known as the Iraq War, began three days later.

On the 19th of March 2003, the United States, along with coalition forces primarily from the United Kingdom, initiated war on Iraq. Just after explosions began to rock Baghdad, Iraq's capital, U.S. President George W. Bush announced in a televised address, 'At this hour, American and coalition forces are in the early stages of military operations to disarm Iraq, to free its people, and to defend the world from grave danger'. President Bush and his advisors built much of their case for war on the spurious claim that Iraq, under dictator Saddam Hussein, possessed or was in the process of building weapons of mass destruction.

After an intense manhunt, U.S. soldiers found Saddam Hussein hiding in a six-to-eight-foot-deep hole nine miles outside his hometown of Tikrit. He did not resist and was uninjured during the arrest. A soldier at the scene described him as "a man resigned to his fate." Hussein was arrested and began trial for crimes against his people, including mass killings, in October 2005. On the 6th of November 2006, Saddam Hussein was found guilty of crimes against humanity and sentenced to death by hanging. After an unsuccessful appeal, he was executed on the 30th of December 2006.

No weapons of mass destruction were found in Iraq. The U.S. declared an end to the war in Iraq on the 15th of December 2011, nearly ten years after the fighting began.

Chapter Fifty-seven
7/7 2005

We were on holiday in Cornwall and just got up and put on the news. It was the 7th of July 2005, and there was coverage of bombs going off across London—the day before, it had been announced that London would host the 2012 Olympics. The celebrations of the bid's success were partly silenced the day after the announcement when the 7th of July 2005 London bombings killed 52 people and injured hundreds more. There was no confirmed link between the International Olympic Committee's (IOC) decision and the attack, which also coincided with the G8 Summit in Scotland. The 7th of July 2005 London bombings, also referred to as **7/7**, were a series of four coordinated suicide attacks carried out by Islamist terrorists that targeted commuters travelling on London's public transport system during the morning rush hour.

Three terrorists separately detonated three homemade bombs in quick succession aboard London Underground trains in inner London. Later, a fourth terrorist detonated another bomb on a double-decker bus in Tavistock Square. The train bombings occurred on the Circle line near Aldgate at Edgware Road and on the Piccadilly line near Russell Square.

Apart from the bombers, 52 UK residents of 18 different nationalities were killed, and more than 700 were injured in the attacks. It was the UK's deadliest terrorist incident since the 1988 bombing of Pan Am Flight 103 near Lockerbie and the UK's first Islamist suicide attack.

Chapter Fifty-eight

COVID-19

In late 2019, a mystery virus broke out in China in Wuhan Province. Initially, not a great deal of interest was shown by the Western Media until China quarantined millions of people in their homes. China has been the source of severe acute respiratory syndrome (SARs) and other coronaviruses over the years, which is thought to be due to animal-to-human transmission, mainly bats. Initially, it was thought that the source may have been through the Wuhan wet markets, where animals such as pangolins, snakes, and bats were being sold for human consumption.

The virus soon spread outside of China and was popping up all over the world, including in the UK. The government was a little slow on banning flights from China despite knowing that the virus was emanating from China. Italy was the next country to see a dramatic increase in numbers, and their hospitals started to become overwhelmed. As the cases increased across the world, the World Health Organisation (WHO) eventually called it a global pandemic. The virus was identified as a novel coronavirus, and scientists throughout the world were frantically trying to establish what this virus was, as it was attacking the respiratory system and was especially lethal in older age groups and those with weakened immune systems and other long-term conditions. There also seems to be a link between obesity and those from the black and Asian communities.

It was clear from what was happening elsewhere in the world that the virus was spreading quickly and easily between human-to-human contact. Lots of other countries started to lockdown their societies as a means of controlling the spread. Again, in the UK, the Cheltenham Festival (a horse racing event) was allowed to take place in early March 2020, followed by a European football match, where there were thousands of people in very close proximity to each other, both events caused a surge in infections. It took the government until the 23rd of March 2020 before the Country was put into lockdown, which meant we had to stay at home apart from exercise and essential activities like shopping. There were two further national lockdowns in England on the 5th of November 2020 and the 5th of January 2021.

Exercise was allowed, as was shopping, but the supermarkets put in stringent measures to manage the risk. Early on, there was a lot of panic buying, and bizarrely, toilet rolls were cleared from the shelves. There were sanitising stations at the entrance to supermarkets to clean your trolley and then sanitise your hands with alcohol gel. New words entered our everyday language like social distancing, social isolation, shielding, lockdown, sanitising gel, lateral flow tests, PCR testing, face masks and furlough.

I was lucky enough to have my allotment, which was exempt from any restrictions, so I was able to get down there every day. The weather for the first lockdown was amazing: crystal-clear blue skies and sunshine, no planes in the sky, limited traffic on the roads, and birds singing. It was heaven. But at a cost to the economy, which shrank by 20%, the government introduced a furlough scheme to support people financially while at home.

While most of the population adhered to the strict rules, it soon became clear that Dominic Cummings and the staff of Number 10 Downing

Street played by a different set of rules. Cummings went up to Durham with his family, then drove to Barnard Castle to test his "eyesight," which he tried to justify at a press conference in the Rose Garden of Number 10 Downing Street.

It soon became apparent that the staff at Number 10 were having parties, which later became known as "Party Gate." Boris Johnson tried to wriggle out of this when questioned in Parliament, but as ever, photographs emerged of the parties. Matt Hancock, the then Health Secretary, who was telling the nation what we could and could not do, was caught on CCTV snogging his secretary. Unbelievably, Boris did not sack him. He tried again to hold on to Hancock, but the media pressure finally forced his resignation.

The sleaze and lies finally brought Boris Johnson down. Then we had Liz Truss, the Prime Minister with the shortest tenure in history. She and Chancellor Quazi Quatrain crashed the economy with a mini-budget, causing untold harm to the country's economy.

At least the scientists were on the ball in the making of a vaccine against COVID-19. There were two main contenders in the UK. Astra Zeneca (AZ) and Pfizer, both companies, developed a vaccine in months rather than years. Both vaccines were different in how they worked. The AZ vaccine was a more traditional type of vaccine, whereas the Pfizer vaccine was an RNA type and had to be kept at minus 70 degrees C, then thawed, mixed and drawn up. AZ was able to be kept in a standard vaccine fridge (5C).

The UK was one of the first countries to roll out a mass vaccination programme for the population, starting with the elderly and those vulnerable groups first, then the rest of the population. COVID-19 was a wake-up call for the world, as it showed just how precarious our existence on this planet is. During COVID-19, we went through lockdowns, social distancing, social isolation, a very high death rate within care homes, inadequate personal protective equipment, furloughs, clapping the NHS staff, compulsory mask-wearing in public places and vaccination—a track and trace service which cost billions of pounds which did not work.

Where we are today in 2024, there are no restrictions at all. We have all returned to normal living, but COVID-19 is still here, and we are having to live with it just like influenza. Currently, there is a new strain as the virus mutates, as does influenza. Hopefully, the scientists will come up with a more effective vaccine in the future.

Chapter Fifty-nine

DEATH OF QUEEN ELIZABETH 11

Death of Her Majesty Queen Elizabeth II 8th September 2022

Queen Elizabeth II, the UK's longest-serving monarch, has died at Balmoral aged 96, after reigning for 70 years.

She died peacefully on Thursday afternoon at her Scottish estate, where she had spent much of the summer.

The Queen came to the throne in 1952 and witnessed enormous social change.

Her son, King Charles III, said the 'death of his beloved mother was a moment of great sadness for him and his family and that her loss would be deeply felt around the world'.

He said: 'We mourn profoundly the passing of a cherished sovereign and a much-loved mother'. He continued, 'I know her loss will be deeply felt throughout the country, the realms and the Commonwealth, and by countless people around the world.'

During the coming period of mourning, he said, 'he and his family would be comforted and sustained by our knowledge of the respect and deep affection in which the Queen was so widely held.'

Chapter Sixty

CORONATION OF KING CHARLES III

The coronation of Charles III and his wife, Camilla, as king and Queen of the United Kingdom and the other Commonwealth realms took place on the 6th of May, 2023, at Westminster Abbey. Charles acceded to the throne on the 8th of September, 2022, upon the death of his mother, Elizabeth II.

Chapter Sixty-one
CURRENT WORLD EVENTS

On February 24, 2022, Russia invaded Ukraine, which was supposed to last a few weeks, but the Ukrainians, with the support of NATO, pushed the Russians back to the Donbas Region. President Zelensky has been the main driving force to gain support and weapons from NATO and the West. Following the invasion, Finland and Sweden applied to join NATO. Finland's application was approved. Sweden's application has just been approved on February 24. It is now the 2-year anniversary of the war, and the Ukrainians need more Western munitions. The American Congress has just passed (after months of wrangling in Congress) a further military aid package worth billions of dollars, which is greatly needed by the Ukrainians. The UK has also pledged several billion in military support. The other major issue is that there are Presidential Elections in November 2024 with the prospect of Donald Trump becoming President again. He has been giving off some very negative vibes about NATO and Europe and American support for both NATO and Europe. This will embolden Putin if he senses there are cracks in the Western Alliance. Oh, guess what? Putin has just been re-elected for another 5 years with over 80% of the vote. What a load of tosh, as there is no opposition in Russia. However, this may have consequences for the rest of the world he will become more emboldened. Given that the US and UK will be having elections later in the year, he may use this period of political turmoil to attack Ukraine further. Another development has just occurred, which may make the US elections a more close-run contest. Joe Biden has withdrawn, and Kamala Harris, the Vice President, is now the nominated Democratic candidate with her running mate Tim Walz, the Governor of Minnesota. This has revitalised the Democratic campaign time will tell if she can win the Presidency.

Donal Trump has been elected as the next President of the United States of America with a resounding win. Let's see what the next 4 years bring.

Chapter Sixty-two
MIDDLE EAST

The Middle East has flared up again. It started when 1200 Israeli citizens were murdered at a music festival by Hamas on the 7th of October, 2023. 250 hostages were taken. Israel responded by bombing Gaza and stating that they would eradicate Hamas. It is now August 2024. Gaza has been reduced to rubble, and there are issues getting humanitarian aid into the area. Some of the hostages have been released, and some have died. Iran seems to be supporting Hamas, Hezbollah in Lebanon and the Houthis, who have been attacking ships in the Red Sea and the Gulf of Aden since November in what they say is a campaign of solidarity with the Palestinians and against Israel's continuing war on Gaza. Israel attacked an Iranian consulate building in Syria on the 1st of April 2024, killing two Iranian Generals, General Mohammad Reza Zahedi and General Mohammad Hadi Hajriahimi and five other Iranian military officers. Iran responded with Operation True Promise (several hundred drones and missiles were launched the vast majority were intercepted by air defences), a further attack on the 13th of April 2024 against Israel by the Islamic Revolutionary Guards Corps, a branch of the Iranian military, in retaliation for the Israeli airstrike on the Iranian embassy in Damascus on 1 April. More recently, Israel assassinated the Hamas leader Ismail Haniyeh. Iran has promised a substantial response to this event, so the world awaits to see what the Israelis do in terms of a military response to any attack by Iran. The fear is that this could lead to a wider regional war.

Chapter Sixty-three
ENERGY AND COST OF LIVING CRISIS

Because of the Ukraine war, the cost of energy rocketed so much that the Government had to intervene by giving extra payments to help with the cost of energy. This had a knock-on effect of causing inflation to rise to 11% and increasing food prices, again, the Government stepped in and gave cost of living payments to those on welfare benefits. There are food banks across the country where those on low income can get food for free, which has been donated by the public and supermarkets. Warm banks have also been set up where people can go and get warm. In many ways, I feel that, as a country we are going backwards. We have all the modern technology, but the basic needs of the people are being challenged as never before. We have smartphones, the internet, flat-screen televisions and satellite TV, but people cannot afford to eat or heat their homes. The Country looks shabby, with weeds growing along the kerbs and roundabouts covered with weeds. There is litter and graffiti everywhere, and public services are being cut back. My local council in Swindon is in financial difficulty and is going to reduce the power to streetlights (all streetlights have been converted to LEDs) by 50% overnight. Apparently, they have tried this, and it makes little difference to the lighting but has a massive effect on the cost of electricity. My council tax bill has just arrived, and it's £1996.38. There will be a General Election in 2024, and I am certain that the Conservatives will be thrown out, but will Labour fare any better as there is no money? I think bold and drastic action will be needed to get the economy growing again. We also need to have energy security and become less reliant on imported gas. The steel industry is once again in trouble. We must have a steel industry in case Putin causes a major conflict.

All in all, it is quite depressing the Country is lacking leadership and sadly, there is no current politician that has the leadership qualities needed at this time. What is needed is a Churchillian leader. Sadly, the options offered at the General Election on the 4th of July 2024 will not deliver such a leader. The current opinion polls suggest Labour will win with a landslide. Labour has won with a large majority so that it will form the next government.

Chapter Sixty-four
ST. JOHN AMBULANCE

In 1989, I was made a Serving Brother of the Most Venerable Order of St. John of Jerusalem. This is an award system of the Order of St. John of Jerusalem. I attended the investiture in the Church of St. John in Clerkenwell, London, to receive the award.

Investiture into the Order of St John 1989

It was a great honour to receive this award, as I was a sergeant in the Princess Mary's Royal Air Force Nursing Service. I was awarded the honour for the charity work I had been doing in the Royal Air Force at RAF Hospital Wroughton which cumulated in the annual hospital bed push. This is where teams of hospital staff adapt hospital beds and trollies in a race around the hospital. It is a fun-packed afternoon with water bombs and other substances like flour and coloured water bombs that are thrown at the opposition. I organised this event and raised substantial funds for local charities

Consultant Orthopaedic Surgeon RAF Hospital bed push

RAF Hospital Wroughton bed push team

The order has various levels, which have now been brought into line with the civil honours, which are,

- Member of the Order (MStJ)
- Officer of the Order (OStJ)
- Commander of the Order (CStJ)
- Knight/Dame of the Order (KStJ) (DStJ)
- Bailiff/Dame Grand Cross (GCStJ)

The Order of St. John is a British Royal Order of Chivalry constituted in 1888 by Royal Charter from Queen Victoria and dedicated to St. John the Baptist. It is a Christian order founded on Christian principles, motivated by Christian ideals. However, their services are open to everyone, and their members and volunteers come from all faiths or no faith. Christian clerics look after the welfare of St. John staff and volunteers, as do Imams and Buddhist monks in some of the countries where they operate.

The order traces its origins back to the Knights Hospitaller in the Middle Ages, which was later known as the Order of Malta. The modern Order of St. John is perhaps best known for the health organisations it founded and continues to run, including St. John Ambulance and the St. John Eye Hospital in Jerusalem. As with the order, the membership and work of these organisations are not restricted by denomination or religion.

The Order of St. John is a registered charity under English law. Its headquarters are in London. The current Grand Prior is Prince Richard, Duke of Gloucester. The current Lord Prior is Rear Admiral Simon Williams CB CVO KStJ. The King is the Sovereign Head of the Order.

The Order of St. John is committed to helping others in need. They provide a range of medical, social, and humanitarian services around the world. They also work to promote peace and understanding between different cultures and faiths.

The Order of St. John is a respected and influential organisation that has been awarded the Nobel Peace Prize and the Queen's Award for Voluntary Service and is also a member of the International Red Cross and Red Crescent Movement.

Sources

1. wikipedia.org/wiki/Order_of_Saint_John_(chartered_1888)
2. stjohninternational.org/Trder#,~,text=The%20chivalric%20Order,The%20Order%20of%20St%20John.

I joined St. John Ambulance as a volunteer in 1989 with Swindon Division as the Divisional Nursing Officer. In those days, there was no control over who joined, as you could just walk through the door of any Division and join. It was up to the Divisional Superintendent to sort out any new recruits. There were no checks on the individual, unlike today, where all new recruits go through a robust application process, including interviews, references, and Disclosure and Barring Service (DBS) checks.

St. John was broken down into Counties, and each County was responsible for managing its own affairs. There were numerous small Divisions within Wiltshire with small numbers of people. Over time, these smaller Divisions closed and merged to make larger Divisions.

There was a County Commander and County Commissioner (a role I held) who were responsible for managing the volunteers. Following a reorganisation in 2011, the Country was split into 8 regions. Wiltshire is in the Southwest of England. My current role is District Manager for Wiltshire, where I am responsible for all the adult and youth volunteers within Wiltshire. I have been in St. John Ambulance for 34 years.

Here are some of the key events in the history of St. John Ambulance,

- 1080, The Knights Hospitaller are founded in Jerusalem.
- 1836, The St. John Ambulance Association is founded in England.
- 1887, The St. John Ambulance Brigade is founded in England.
- 1888, The Knights Hospitaller are granted a Royal Charter by Queen Victoria.
- 1908, St. John Ambulance ceases operating in Scotland.
- 1920, St. John Ambulance Cadets are founded.
- 1958, The First Aid Manual is published.
- 1974, The St. John Ambulance Association and the St. John Ambulance Brigade are merged.

- 1990, St. John Ambulance launches its youth programme, Ambulance Cadets.

- 2000, St. John Ambulance launches its community programme, St. John Active.

- 2012, St. John Ambulance celebrated its 140th anniversary.

St. John Ambulance is an asset to the UK and to other countries around the world. They provide essential first aid and emergency medical services, and they work to improve health and well-being in communities. St John Ambulance has evolved over the years from volunteers wearing the distinctive black uniform with a peaked cap and a white bag slung over their shoulders into a modern, well-trained healthcare provider with a modern service delivery uniform, which is now a green shirt with black trousers no hats or white bags!

There are various roles within St John Ambulance. The mainstay is the First Aider, who is now trained to a higher level; the Advanced First Aider, who has additional skills to a First Aider and the Emergency Ambulance Crew, who work on our ambulances. These volunteers are trained to a high level on par with the NHS.

St. John Ambulance is now the official NHS reserve ambulance service. One of the great things about St. John Ambulance is the friends that you make. I have two good friends whom I have known for many years. Shirley Cox and Jan Baker—these two ladies are remarkable. Shirley is 83 years old, and Jan is 86 years old, and both are still active in St. John Ambulance, where they are my Area Managers. I often joke that we are the oldest management team in St. John, as I am now 71!!

Unfortunately, due to post-Covid problems, St John Ambulance is in financial difficulties, currently losing 1 million pounds a month, so once again, we are going through another major reorganisation. There have been redundancies, and we are reducing our estate and fleet to save money. The hierarchy is confident that these measures will get the organisation back on track. Time will tell!

We are going back to where we started with something called Community Networks, which is embedding St John Ambulance in the local community that they serve, which is what we used to do. The wheel has a habit of turning a full circle. In February 2024, the Princess Royal came to St John HQ Devizes to dedicate our new Community Support Vehicle. I was the joint host for the event. Princess Ann was delightful and spoke to everyone who attended the event.

Bob with Princess Ann St John Devizes 4th Feb 2024

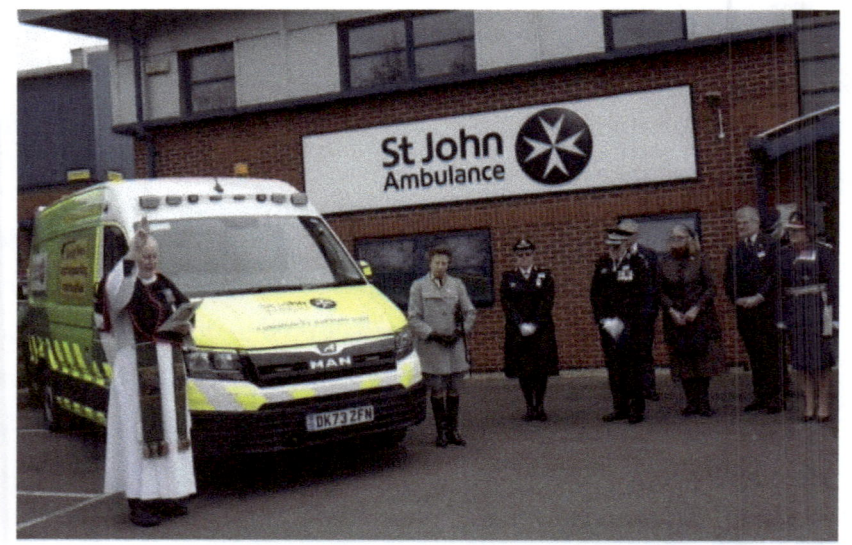

Dedication of Community Support Vehicle with Princess Ann 4th February 2024

Chapter Sixty-five
FINALLY

Throughout your life, there are various milestones that we all must pass through, from early childhood to starting your own family and hoping that they do better than you. I think I have certainly done better than my parents; that's not a criticism of them. It is what should happen depending on individual circumstances. I own my house. My parents remained in council accommodation until they died but were happy with their life despite the issues described in previous chapters.

When you get married and start a family, you want to do your best for your children. We have 2 sons, both very different. Andrew is a Director with Tesco now managing the takeover of 10 stores on the Isle of Man (he will be living there for the next 12 months), and Matthew is Autistic, which has its challenges for him, Mary and I, but they both are great parents. We have 4 Grandchildren. Andrew's children are Joe, 26; Hannah, 24 (has cerebral palsy) Beth, 24 (they are twins and were born at 26 weeks). Hannah

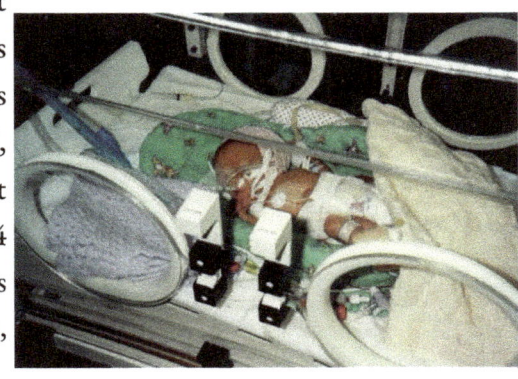

Hannah just after she was born

had hydrocephalus, which needed a shunt put in her brain to drain the fluid when she was just weeks old, which was done in Oxford.

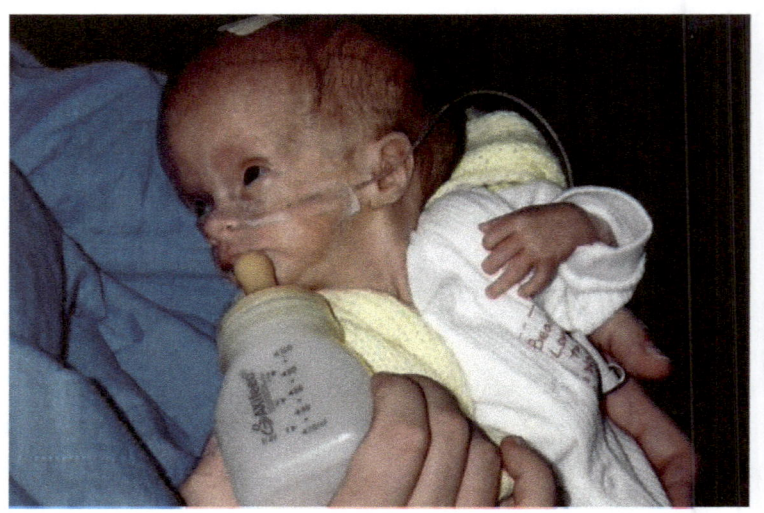

Hannah looking poorly after having shunt inserted

Hannah grown up

Thankfully, she is now 24 with all her faculties but has some physical disabilities. T is 8 years old he is Matthew's son. We were young grandparents aged 45 but had to start again when T was born. I also have 2 Nieces (my sister's children) and 2 Great Nephews and 2 Great Nieces this makes you feel old!

Reaching 60 years of age was such a milestone. As you get older, the years you have left are diminishing with the passage of time, unlike when you are young time seems endless. There were a couple of things I wanted to do when I reached 60 years of age, nothing too dramatic. The first was to get a tattoo, and the second was to learn to play the trumpet, an odd combination, some may think, but don't knock it till you have tried it. Mary does not like tattoos, but both my lads and grandchildren have them, it is not seen as a seedy thing anymore.

So, to start the process of acceptance, I decided to get a small tattoo on my left upper arm of my birth sign, Aquarius the water bearer. Although it was small, Mary did not like it. My master plan was to get a full sleeve done on the right arm, so with meticulous planning, I dropped Mary off at work and headed off to the same tattooist who did my first one. When I went for the first tattoo, I had not met the tattooist as I booked the appointment when he was off. My first impression when I finally met him was Oh My God, he had long, straggly hair, loads of piercings, and multiple tattoos; however, don't make judgments on appearances. He was a lovely lad and an extremely talented artist. Back to the full sleeve, I wanted a music-themed tattoo, so I found several on the internet and sort of combined them all together. I showed him what I wanted, and he reproduced the design perfectly. I even had the Grandchildren's names added.

The only problem was Mary finished work at 17:00, and I was still in the tattoo studio, so I had to say I was stuck in traffic. He eventually finished at 17:30 I had been there since 10:00. The good thing was my right arm was covered in cling film, so Mary could not see it straight away. However, you can't hide it forever, so the great reveal came later that evening I won't repeat what she said. What was interesting when I went to work, there was stunned silence at "What had the boss gone and done?" Once they got over the shock, all was well. The number of patients who made positive comments or wanted to compare tattoos was numerous, and they never had a negative comment.

My Tattoo

One down, one to go, the next thing was the trumpet. Part of my reason for wanting to learn to play the trumpet is I love swing music and the sounds of the big bands of the 1940s Glenn Miller, Bennie Goodman, Harry James, and numerous others. So, in my naivety I thought how hard it can be. There are only 3 things to press down (that is all I knew to call them things to press down). I now know they are called valves they are numbered 1/2&3. The other major issue was I could not read music (a minor issue, so I thought). I found a music teacher a couple of miles away and arranged to see him at his home. He gave me a trumpet and told me to blow. He said, 'that's a G' I said, 'I will take your word for it' I had no idea what he was talking about.

So, he said, 'Let's give it a go'. He was very talented but eccentric, I would say hyper intelligent with poor social skills. His wife was the local Vicar, and they had a 4-year-old little girl who was confined to another room to watch a video while he was teaching not ideal as she often came in to interrupt the lesson. Then they bought a dog which was in a cage in the same room as the lesson, which was not ideal competing with the noise of a whining puppy. I bought a very basic Learn Yourself the Trumpet book and a trumpet and started to read about music as I had to master this if I was going to be able to play anything. As it turns out it's quite logical there are various notes ABCDEFG which repeat either higher or lower. The next thing to learn was which valves played which note. This is where my ignorance of the trumpet came to haunt me.

It seems that you must use a combination of valves to play the note or press no valves to play several notes. With all the valves open, you can play bottom C, then go up G C E and top G. I began to think I am never going to get this, then in a twist of fate (remember I am a great believer in fate) Joel's wife the Vicar was being moved to East Anglia, I had been with Joel for about 12 months and had made some progress but not as much as I had hoped.

Joel knew another music teacher locally called Matthew, who he asked if he would take me on, which he did, and I have never looked back. Matthew is a brilliant teacher. I have learnt so much from him. I can say now that I can read music, including the flats and sharps (I nearly forgot about them) fluently.

Matthew is a completely different person to Joel, much more people-friendly, he teaches children as well. I have been playing now for some 11 years and have learnt so much. I now play the cornet and have joined a band on Saturday morning which is a youth band. Playing with others is a completely different genre. You must learn how to count, especially the rest (this is when you are not playing), as these are the hardest things to learn. If you get it wrong, you will come in too early or too late. I still have music lessons once a week and I always learn something new.

Playing with the band has taught me a more disciplined approach, as playing by yourself can lead to bad habits which are hard to shake off. I am still learning and will carry on for as long as I can as I find it a very enjoyable time. I play at home every day and I have converted the small bedroom into a music room with all my instruments and music and an armchair. Well, comfort is essential! I have just invested in a laptop which folds into a tablet, and I have been putting my music into a music program on my laptop. I have a foot pedal which changes the pages much better than loads of music in paper form. I am slowly working through my music to scan them into the program. I have just decided to do a music grade exam in March 2025. The awarding body is Trinity College, Matthew has recommended I go for grade 4. I will have to play 3 pieces of music then there are some exam pieces. I choose one and the examiner chooses one, and there is an exercise that you must learn to play from memory. On top of this, there is a test of your musical knowledge. So, I will be practising these over the coming months.

I remember my Dad would say, 'Televisions will be hung on walls in the future' How right he was. One of the great innovations in my lifetime is the flat-screen TV. I have a 65-inch TV hung on the wall with my speakers and amplifier all connected to it. I think my Dad would have been in his element if he was still alive. Technology has developed at lightning speed with the internet, which was initially called the World Wide Web, invented by Tim Berners-Lee in 1989, an English computer scientist.

 Today the internet is an essential part of your home as so much now is online, banking, insurance, council tax, online shopping, yes you can do your shopping online and have it delivered to your door. Companies like

Amazon have developed online shopping to another level. There is nothing you cannot buy from Amazon and have it delivered, in most cases, the next day. We do our online grocery shopping with Tesco and have it delivered. Wonderful!

I have managed to keep up with the technology. I have a smartphone, yes, the smartphone, which now is a computer in your pocket. You can do everything on a smartphone that you can do on your computer. I would be lost without mine. I am into Google Pixel phones (up to a Pixel 9 XL) they are great bits of kit with superb cameras built into the phone. With each new phone, the technology gets even smarter and with the development of artificial intelligence (AI), the technology is developing at breakneck speed. I even have a smartwatch with my debit card on so I can pay with my watch. You often hear about the "elderly" (I hate this phrase) being disenfranchised as everything is now online to a degree that is correct, but my generation has sort of grown up with modern technology when we were in our 50s and 60s (I still have the same mobile phone number when I got my first mobile phone the one with the aerial!) so I believe that my generation of "elderly" will be much more tech-savvy than the current "elderly" population. However, that does raise the question of when you are classed as "elderly"? I have two friends, both in their 80s and are very tech-savvy. I am in my 70s, and I have all my banking/credit cards/utilities online using email and, Microsoft Teams/Zoom and Google Meet. I get very irritated if I am called "elderly." Age is just a number. It's about health and ability.

I have a satellite television. My Dad would have been in his element as he loved watching cricket. I remember as a young boy, when the test matches were on, he had the cricket on all day Mam would go mad as she hated it. There were the old commentators Peter West, Brian Johnston, Jim Laker and John Arlott. Today, the cricket coverage is amazing. With all the different matches to watch and the in-match analysis, the camera coverage is great, so you don't miss anything. The other gadget I can't live without is the satellite navigation system in my car. It has never let me down yet.

I suppose I have to reflect on my life. Has my journey from a young lad of 15 leaving school with no qualifications, starting an engineering apprenticeship as a centre, later turner in a boilersuit, then changing to an RAF blue suit been a success? I was able to have a second career in the NHS and, complete a Nurse Practitioner degree and became an Independent Non-Medical Prescriber. Looking back on my life, am I proud of my achievements? I would say yes, I have had a successful career in the RAF and as a nurse of 48 years, I have two great Sons and four lovely Grandchildren. I have a great relationship with my Sister Julie. I have two Nieces who are both Nurses. Julie is a Health Visitor I would like to think they have followed in my footsteps. Mary and I have been married for 50 years, I don't know where that went seems like yesterday since we got married in 1975. Mary and I are Great Aunt and Uncle to two Great Nieces and two Great Nephews' family is very important the older you get. Life has also had its ups and downs, but I have managed to deal with them despite living with

Me and Mary on a cruise

depression. I have lived through two centuries and one Millennium, which turned out to be a damp squib. There was a thought that all computers would crash when the year moved to 2000. I was duty manager at Malmesbury Community Hospital just in case things went pear-shaped. When it was obvious that the world did not end, I went home around 03:00 and then went into bed.

I own my house, which is an achievement. It was hard at first, as interest rates were 15%. I also feel that I have had a positive effect on the wider community and, hopefully, have been a role model for my sons and grandchildren. Time will tell. I feel content with my life and the journey that I have taken, all thanks to the fickle finger of fate. However, life has a habit of throwing a curved ball at you, which is what has happened to Mary and I and the rest of the family. This should have been the end; however, I have called the next chapter *"so you think it's all over,"* which is very apt, as you will see.

Chapter Sixty-six
SO, YOU THINK IT'S ALL OVER!!!

When you reach a certain age in your life, your kids are grown up, grandchildren come along, and you can start to enjoy your life. Sadly, for many, us included, events can take over your life. Our situation started in 2016 with the birth of our fourth grandson, T. Matthew, his Dad. Unfortunately, got mixed up with a young woman who was significantly younger than Matthew but turned out to be a control freak. It turned out to be a complete nightmare and has had a significant impact on our lives and Matthew and T's lives. At this point in time, Matthew did not have a diagnosis of Autism, which came much later when we had him assessed privately.

Matthew is easily led and can be influenced by the wrong types of people, including this woman. The warning signs were there early on and lots of lies were being told to us. Matthew, at the time, was working for Tesco, collecting the trollies, earning about £800 per month. She had never worked, then out of the blue, he told us that he was moving in with J as she had a family friend who was renting them her flat (lie number 1). The rent alone was around £600 a month, leaving £200 a month to pay all the bills and live on. This was not going to work out. Then she became pregnant, which was full of drama during the pregnancy morning sickness, but she could wolf down a full Sunday roast.

It was not long before they fell behind with the rent, but the owner, who was an elderly lady, let them off with paying the rent. We had helped them out by getting them shopping, as they had no money. Unfortunately, we could see this was a car crash waiting to happen, but she was able to control Matthew to such an extent that he just went along with whatever she said, including that she would look after the money! (I will come back to this later).

When T was 3 months old, we went around to visit one Sunday, and we noticed two large suitcases in the living room. This seemed a little odd, to say the least. When challenged, she said, 'Oh, we have been given a holiday to New York for 2 weeks by my aunt. She works as a travel agent, and she has developed a heart condition, so she can't go' (lie number 2). Mary and I looked at each other and were thinking the same thing, what a load of tosh. Surely if this mysterious Aunt were working as a travel agent, she would have had travel insurance? Given that they could not pay the rent or buy groceries, how were they going to survive for 2 weeks in New York? Most people go for 5 days. Oh, what about the 3-month-old baby? A minor point. We were told that T was being left with J's parents. J booked the hotel but did not book a bed and breakfast, just the bed "muppet.".

They had no passports, so they had to get emergency passports, which cost several hundred pounds. I will tell you later how this was paid for.

As I was still working, I emailed the Health Visitor Manager to express my concerns about this whole situation, as I did not believe this was a good idea. I was asking the manager to see if they could investigate this as it was concerning. To my utter astonishment, she emailed back and said, 'I hear your concerns, but I can't disclose any information'. I was not asking her for any information. I was giving her information. Despite my best efforts, she was not budging. I can now see how children slip through the net as professionals hide behind data protection and confidentiality, and then you end up with a "baby P" or "Alfie." As it turned out, T was not seen for 4 months by a Health Visitor. His red book had an entry for February 2016, then nothing until July 2016.

This was a disaster waiting to happen. On their return, we went around to see Matthew, and T. T did not look well. He was pale-looking. We expressed our concerns and asked if he had been seen by the Health Visitor. Matthew sent me a photo of the centile chart from his red book. We were shocked to see that he was below the bottom centile when he should have been midway up the centile chart. I showed my sister the chart (she is a Health Visitor), and she immediately said that this was a cause for concern, and she called children's services in Swindon to report her concerns. Julie lives in Newcastle.

That's when the trouble really started. Unbeknownst to us, Social Services got involved immediately. This caused a massive rift between Matthew and us as J blamed us for Social Services being involved. The first thing we knew about what had been going on was when we got a call from a social worker called Tamsin. She asked, 'if she could visit us to explain what had been going on with T'. Tamsin came to our house and said, 'she would have to get Matthew's permission for her to tell us what had been going on'. She called him, and he said, 'He was happy for Tamsin to tell us everything'. It read like a horror show as to what had been going on. Matthew and J had moved to another property, which was more expensive than the previous one (that they could not afford). J had convinced Matthew to leave Tesco and take a job with a company that supported Honda, but that did not work out as planned. To cut a very long story short, it was a complete nightmare. Tamsin said, 'There was going to be a child protection conference to which we would be invited' She then said, 'If T needed to be taken away from Matthew and J, would we be willing to take him'? We both said, 'No, as we were too old to take on a 12-month-old baby. We hoped that it would not come to this.

The first child protection conference was an eye-opener for us, as we had never been to one before. It's all about the safety of the child and what needs to be put in place to maintain the safety and well-being of the child. There was a conference chair who would lead the meeting and ask all the professionals present for their reports. Also present were J's mother, Mary, and I, and Matthew and J. It was clear that T had not been looked after, as he was underweight and had not reached any of his milestones for a 12-month-old. What was also clear was that Matthew was working 12-hour shifts, and J was at home with T, so in my book, she should have been looking after T for much of the time. What also emerged over the coming months was that Matthew was being coercively controlled by J; she had completely isolated him from his family. The final straw came when J was caught having an affair with the landlord to whom they owed rent.

When we finally prised Matthew away from J, the full extent of the finances was laid bare. Remember the 2-week trip to New York? We could not understand how they could afford this. It was bank loans. J talked Matthew into taking out loans in his name, one for £7,000 over 10 years (I know, don't ask) and another for £3000 over 5 years. Bearing in mind that they were behind with the rent and could not afford food!

I took Matthew to the bank, and he got 6 months of bank statements, which I went through forensically. They were always overdrawn by £2000 per month (remember that J did the money), then suddenly there was a deposit of £23000 into the account, which was blown in 3 weeks, and they were back to being £2000 overdrawn. When I asked Matthew about this, he said that J had been given this money by the previous landlord to pay off their debts (sounds great in practice), but they only paid one loan off the £3000. The rest was spent on handbags, jewellery, and other consumer goods, including over £800 at Pets at Home (oh, I forgot about the dog, the 4 cats, and the rabbits). When I finally added up all the debt, it was over £40,000, all in Matthew's name.

The only option was to make Matthew bankrupt, which I did as it was the only way to wipe off the debt. Obviously, Matthew could not stay in the family home due to J's behaviour and having an affair with the current landlord. Due to the debt, he could not stay with us just in case the bailiffs came knocking, and we had to provide ownership of our belongings, so he had to move into a shared accommodation while J was given a council house and was assigned a family support worker.

The other thing I had to do was navigate around the benefits system and learn how to get Matthew on the housing list. Due to his difficulties, he finds this aspect of life very challenging. To be honest, it took me some time to get my head around the complexity of Universal Credit (UC). It is not an easy process. Once the forms are submitted, there is a 5-week wait before any payments are made. I am not sure what people are expected to do in the interim. You can get an advance, but that is clawed back over several months, which in many ways compounds the situation. Personal Independence Payments (PIP) is something else. The questions are so ridiculous for words. PIP has two components: mobility and daily living. There are two rates: lower and higher. You can get one without the other. Currently, Matthew is on the higher rate of PIP £101.75 per week. The other benefit was council tax, which is administered by the local council, so you must apply to them for exemptions, which I did, and Matthew does not have to pay any council tax.

That was the benefits sorted just and to go through several more child protection meetings with J and her very sanctimonious Family Support Worker. Eventually, T was downgraded to a child in need. Tamsin, who we can't speak highly enough, told us she was leaving, which was a great blow as she had a handle on everything, including J, which was very helpful. A new social worker called David was assigned to the case. He was in his early 50s and was not that interested in the case. He was just going through the motions, and within a couple of weeks, he said 'there was no longer any need for social services involvement', which pleased J no end as Social Services were "off her back," in her words.

Over the next 5 years, we had to work out a schedule for Matthew's contact. It was difficult when he was living in shared accommodation, but he was offered a new build one-bedroom flat in October 2018. We had to purchase all his white goods and furniture as he was not in a position to do this himself. Andrew sorted out the carpets for Matthew. This made contact much easier as he had a safe place in which to take T, which started with alternate weekends. As Matthew has no transport, we had to ferry around Matthew's to collect T from J's.

On Sundays, when T and Matthew came to our house, he would have a bath before being returned to Js'. We still had concerns about T's development, as he was not reaching his milestones and had delayed speech and walking. Then, in 2020, J met another man called D. She fell pregnant soon after and had another baby in 2021. We started to have further concerns as T was telling Matthew about how he was being treated at home, e.g., being sworn at being sent to his bedroom without any food. Then we saw a photograph of T sitting on the sofa with a python around his neck (this was Ds pet), and he looked terrified. We kept reporting our concerns to Children's Services, who, to be honest, were not that interested, but my Health Visitor Sister said, 'It did not matter. They had to log all concerns, and should there be an issue at some point in the future, all these concerns would be pulled'.

It was obvious that T needed to be in a special needs school as he was not able to cope with mainstream school. This was our next hurdle. T needed a Health Education and Care Plan (EHCP). This is a legal document for an individual child or young person aged 0–25 with special educational needs and disabilities (SEND), which sets out a description of their educational, health, and social care needs and the provisions that must be implemented in order to help them. T was awarded an EHCP. The next step was getting him into a specialist school, which was easier said than done.

Having been told by J that she would apply for specialist provision, we took a step back, bearing in mind there was a deadline for applications to be in, so with 2 weeks to go, J told Matthew that she could not do this to get your Mum and Dad to do it. Mary spent hours on the phone discussing this with various agencies prior to a meeting with the local authority to seek funding for a place. Thankfully, T was awarded a place at a Special Education School in Swindon. Matthew, Mary, and I had a visit prior to T starting. The staff were so committed to helping these children that it was hard to put into words what the provision was like. The main difference was the smaller class sizes—eight children in a class with a teacher and several teaching assistants (TAs). All was going fine and dandy until the 21$^{st\,of}$ April, 2023.

This was a Friday afternoon; it was Matthew's weekend. On arrival at school to pick up T, Matthew and Mary were asked to see the Special Educational Needs Coordinator (SENCO). It had been noted that T had two suspicious marks on his back, and we were advised to have T seen by his GP (good luck with that on a Friday afternoon). Matthew sent me a photo of the marks, which were around 5mm in diameter in the middle of his back, 10 centimetres apart. I said to Mary, 'Take him to the Urgent Care Centre' which they did, and T was eventually seen in a Paediatric

Accident & Emergency. The A&E doctor thought they looked suspicious, she wrote in the note's cigarette burns (to be honest, that's what I thought when I first saw the photographs), and she referred T to the Paediatric Team. By this time, it was 23:00, so they said he would be kept overnight and reviewed by the Consultant Paediatrician the following day.

T was seen by the Consultant Paediatrician, who said that the marks looked highly suspicious and she could not think of a situation where these marks could have happened by accident, so she called the Duty Social Worker (DSW). This then set in train a sequence of events that none of us were fully prepared for.

This invoked something called Section 47, which is a child protection investigation to assess if the child is at significant risk of harm. Following an interview with the DSW at the hospital, Matthew was asked to take T into his care until the investigation was carried out. Unbeknownst to us, the police and the local authority were also involved. We were all interviewed at Matthew's flat on the evening of the 22nd of April 22. They then went to inform J of what was going to happen. When the DSW, Police, and Local Authority arrived at J's house, they looked through the downstairs window, and according to the report, "G the 2-year-old was unsupervised in a highchair with a sandwich, his head resting on the tray. J&D were upstairs and took 5 minutes to answer the door". T had school transport, but as the address had to be changed, we had to reapply for pickup at Matthew's address. This took 3 weeks. I just thought of a quick phone call to change the address, but no chance. So, we had to pick up T to take him to and from school for 3 weeks, which meant an early start at 06:45!!

J was informed about the marks, and they were being looked at as a non-accidental injury (NAI) and that T would be staying with his Dad,

Matthew, until further notice. This was the initial safety plan for the immediate future until further investigations by social services and the police were undertaken.

A Child Protection Conference was scheduled for early May, and both parents were told to engage legal advice as this was likely to go to a custody hearing. What came out of the conference was that both children, T and G, were on a Child in Need Plan. J had not bargained for G being dragged into this, but he was.

Over the past 6 months, we have been interviewed by the police, who were great when they spoke to T. They had a specialist worker to assist them. On our first visit, they had arranged a police car for T to sit in and operate the lights and sirens, which were all designed to gain his trust. Unfortunately, T was not able to articulate how these marks occurred. He does know, but we all feel he is frightened to disclose it in fear of retribution. What did come out of the discussions was that there were concerns around D, which would support what T had been saying about him.

Getting legal representation on legal aid is not an easy process. We tried numerous solicitors in Swindon, but as soon as legal aid was mentioned, they said no. We did have a stroke of luck as the solicitors that we have used for our wills did family law. We called and were promised a call back in 30 minutes, which did not happen. We then called again late in the afternoon and were told the person who should have called us back was on a call, but they would message her with no callback. I called again the next day and was assured that she would call back. No surprises, no call. I decided to email our solicitor to see if she could help. I explained what had happened, and although she did not deal with family law, she would put us in contact with one of her colleagues who dealt with family law. We had a call back within the hour and had a solicitor and paralegal assigned to the case. They applied for legal aid for Matthew, which was granted, and the custody papers were lodged with the court in early September 23. We were waiting for the first court hearing, which was set for the 7th of December, 2023.

In the middle of all of this, we had a cruise holiday booked from the 17th of September until the 1st of October 2023. Should we go or not? Eventually we agreed to go, as nothing would be happening yet regarding the court. We went on the cruise and had a lovely time, but it all seems like a distant memory now as we look back with fond memories of the trip.

At the first court hearing on the 7th of December 23, the court asked for a Section 7 report. A Section 7 report may be required in cases where an application has been made to the court for an order under Section 8 of the Children Act 1989, in respect of which the parents cannot agree. This can take up to 10 weeks to compile. This would be done by the local authority rather than by the Children and Family Court Advisory and Support Service (CAFCASS). They have also asked for school and police reports. Both Matthew and J must complete an online learning programme and have a group session with other parents before the next court date on April 24. At this hearing, it will be decided where T will reside until he is 18 years old.

We were due to go on a cruise in January but had to cancel due to me catching COVID-19, which was a blessing as T had an autism assessment date in mid-January 2024 when we would have been away. The Local Authority did not start the section 7 report on time and asked for an extension to complete the report. They must file their report by the 7th of May 24. The court date is now set for the 30th of May 24. On the plus side, a new Social Worker has been assigned to the case. She has visited Matthew and T at home and wants to speak to Mary and me, which is great. The section 7 report concluded that T's best interest would be served by living full-time with Matthew and J having alternate weekends.

As expected, J has contested the section 7 report in court, and the court has asked for a review of the section 7 report. Unfortunately, the next course date is not till the 21st of October. This will be the final hearing. T will still be staying with Matthew until the next court date. This must be sorted out as we as a family are stressed out with this whole thing that has been going on, so we need a resolution.

We have a holiday booked for September 24, a two-week cruise around the southern Mediterranean, which will be very welcome. Julie, my Sister, is coming with us as it is her 60th birthday we are all looking forward to the holiday. This will recharge our batteries prior to the final hearing, which we hope will go in Matthew's favour. At no time has J expressed any remorse for what happened and her actions. Matthew has acknowledged that he made mistakes and has learned from them.

We have just booked another cruise for February 2025 I will be away for my birthday. We decided to go for two 14-night cruises next year rather than the 30-night cruise to Canada and New York as we don't want to risk getting COVID-19 again.

Chapter Sixty-seven

AND IT'S DEFINITELY THE END!

When you strip everything away from the daily grind of life the question then becomes one of what is important? I feel that this is an easy question to answer. It's people, both family and friends. The other question for me is have I done the best I could for my family and myself as an individual? I can say yes to both questions.

My journey through life has taken me from living on a council estate in Newcastle, working in a factory, to a career in the Royal Air Force, trained as a Nurse in what turned out to be a 48-year vocation. I continued as a Nurse in the NHS for a further 18 years until I retired. During this journey, there have been the trials and tribulations of life which I have described in previous chapters. I have done better than my parents, which is how it should be, and I hope my children will have a better life than me, which I hope they will.

Mam, Dad and Nana, despite the issues we had, did their best for me Julie and David. They had a tough life with little money. We always had food and clothes and were cared for in a loving but strict environment. In a funny sort of way, they were content with their lives, which is fine. I have a greater understanding of Mam and Dad since they died by researching my family history and finding out more about their lives. For me, I want to remember them in two photographs, one of Mam and Nana

Mam and Nana

and the other photograph of Mam and Dad at their front door they look so happy in these photographs and show their true personalities. I have also included a photograph of Nana and Uncle Alan.

Mam and Dad

Nana and Uncle Alan

This is such a lovely photograph and captures their love for each other.

I was the first person in our family to go to University. I have my BSc (Hons). I also own my own home. Thankfully, the mortgage is now paid off. When we were working, we had the house extended back and front and a larger bathroom created, which is great now we are retired. We have some lovely views from our house. The one I love is a photo of the Church poking through the tree line, very quintessentially English.

Front of my house

View from House

We still have the village Carnival every July which brings all the village together. I feel very lucky to live where I do. I could not live in a city again. Having said that, we visit London in November for Remembrance weekend. We stayed at the Union Jack Club (UJC) which is opposite Waterloo Station. On Saturday night, we attend the Festival of Remembrance at the Royal Albert Hall. Sunday, we are part of Princess Mary's Royal Air Force Nursing Service Association contingent to march past the Cenotaph, followed by lunch in the RAF Club. After lunch we meet up with my friend Pete and his partner Dan and their two friends Martin and John. We leave around 21:00 and stagger back to the UJC via a tube from Green Park to Waterloo. Then on Monday evening, we will see a show in the Westend. I am very familiar with London and happily navigate the underground. Although we enjoy the long weekend, we are always happy when we return home to the peace and quiet of our village. As you can imagine, the UJC is extremely busy

Bob and Mary on Remembrance Sunday

over the Remembrance weekend, so I booked our rooms 2 years in advance just booked 2026 must be an optimist!

Our two sons are very different. Andrew has done very well for himself through hard work and commitment. He did not go to university, started at Tesco at 16 on the checkouts, and now is at the Director level it goes to show what you can achieve without a University education. Andrew went to Number 10 Downing Street for a security meeting and took the opportunity to have his photograph taken outside the door. Andrew has three children: Joe, Hannan and Beth.

Andrew outside Number 10 Downing Street

Grandson Joe

Hannah and Andrew (Dad)

Andrew and partner Mitzi

Matthew and Grandson T

Joe, Hannah, Andrew & Mitzi, Beth & Luke all are well rounded young people and are starting out on their journey through life. Matthew is Autistic, which has its challenges for him, but he is a great Dad to T, who also has learning difficulties, which can be challenging. Matthew is a very caring person but still needs support from Mary and me. He is very close to my Sister Julie and her two daughters.

Granddaughter Beth and partner Luke

Niece Rachel left Sister Julie's centre. Niece Sarah

I am the only Grandad Joe, Hannah, and Beth have as Andrew's partner. Mitzi Dad died suddenly of a heart attack in his forties when the children were still little.

Nanny Pat and Grampy Mike deceased

which was a shock at the time. So, I try to give advice, support, love and guidance, which is what Grandads should do. Mary is a great Grandma to all our Grandchildren.

I have two very good friends, Shirley and Jan, as well as my best friend Ray, who is sadly no longer with us.

Shirley and Jan 2024

Me, Mary and Ray (deceased) 2018

Writing this book has been a monumental task which I started some 7 years ago on a beach in Cornwall where I penned the first words of the manuscript sitting in the sun at Holywell Bay. As I chose to write the book by hand, it has taken a long time to come to fruition. Today as I write the final chapter, it has been a long road to get here. This is my story in script and pictures. I hope my children and Grandchildren will be able to read this and understand my journey from a young boy in a boiler suit to a young man in a blue RAF suit and everything else that has happened along the way. I have also enclosed my final RAF annual confidential report, known as (RAF form 6442) my last boss in the RAF did this, and he was very honest about

First Reporting Officer

9. Guidance on the structure and content of narrative reports is given on Form 6442A. If there are no 2nd/3rd Reporting Officers, para 12 is to be completed.

Of medium height and build WO Sanderson is well groomed and invariably smart. A dry sense of humour compliments his quiet and correct manner. The toll of a particularly difficult period manifests in a reduction of his normal vitality and energy.

For a year now he has assumed the role of Senior Primary Nurse on one of the two orthopaedic wards. This role is in keeping with a system of care delivery recognising professional and personal qualities rather than Service rank hierarchy alone. It was fortunate that an individual of his competence happened to be in the right place at the right time to facilitate and ensure the success of this endeavour. Undoubtedly his contribution proactively and in support of the Unit Manager is at the forefront of the successful way in which care is delivered and staff development and motivation through especially difficult months has been sustained. It is unique for a Staff Nurse even at the rank of WO to work at this level. He sets a very high personal standard and expects the same of his subordinates, he does though devote time and energy in enabling others achieve that standard.

He enjoys the respect of his subordinates and of those Junior Officers working under his guidance; with both he is firm but fair. As his immediate superior I recognise and value the support he gives me and to the Unit overall. He is adept at knowing the individual strengths and weaknesses of his team, utilising those positive factors to uplift the performance of individuals. He sets realistic goals and follows through to establish if they have been met.

It is inescapable even given the excellence of his overall performance, that events of the past year have impacted on him as an individual and are likely to lead to a diminution over time. At the start of the year traumatic health problems left him frightened and vulnerable. It is testimony to his depth of character and normal commitment that on the surface at least he has overcome and faced up to these difficulties. It is not unlikely that his efforts at work have impeded his recovery but he would have it no other way.

More fundamental though is his realistic belief that in the reorganised nursing service his role as a WO Staff Nurse will never again enable him to work at the level he both desires and demands. The future for him in the Service then is viewed very negatively. It is unlikely that his commitment to the Service is sustainable when his personal and professional needs are unfilled. At best his performance is likely to become lack lustre and averagely acceptable. This is not the desire or potential of a man who has always shown an outstanding performance across the board.

10. I certify that:
   a. The [x] airman [ ] airwoman has served under my command for `1` years `5` months.
   b. I [x] am [ ] am not a specialist in the duties being performed by the [x] airman [ ] airwoman.
   c. The action required at serials 1 and 2 of the table at para 17 of F6442A has been taken.
   d. I have reviewed the subject's eligibility for "X" annotations (vide AP 3392 Vol. 2, Chap. 5, Leaflet 525) and taken action where appropriate.

Appointment/Post	ORTHOPAEDIC UNIT MANAGER	Signature	*GHolliday*
Unit	PA RAF(H)	Station	WROUGHTON
Date	24 OCT 95	Rank	SQN LDR
Name in block letters	HOLLIDAY	Branch/Trade	PMRAFNS

Confidential Report Page 1

Staff in Confidence

5. Duties on which engaged
Primary: STAFF NURSE – ORTHOPAEDIC UNIT
Secondary:

Personal Assessment

Note: In making personal assessments place an "X" in the appropriate box in accordance with the guidance in Form 6442A. Assessments are to be based on the substantive or normal paid acting rank held.

6. Trade Proficiency
		9	8	7	6	5	4	3	2	1
a.	Trade Knowledge		X							
b.	Resourcefulness as a Tradesman		X							
c.	Proficiency in Current duties		X							

General Assessment for Trade Proficiency: 8

7. Supervisory Ability (Corporals and above only)
		9	8	7	6	5	4	3	2	1
a.	Acceptance of Responsibility		X							
b.	Ability to Organize		X							
c.	Effectiveness in Control		X							

General Assessment for Supervisory Ability: 8

8. Personal Qualities
		9	8	7	6	5	4	3	2	1
a.	Common Sense			X⊗						
b.	Reliability			X⊗						
c.	Self Confidence (☐ under ☐ over) (tick box if assessment below "4")				X					
d.	Co-operation					X				
e.	Sense of Duty			X⊗						
f.	Appearance and Bearing				X					
g.	Determination				X					

General Assessment for Personal Qualities: 7

Transcribe assessments to appropriate ABC boxes on page 1

Certificate of Recording Action

Final Check		Form 280A	
Initials	Date	Initials	Date
			23"95

RAF PMC use only		P Man 7
Initials		
Date	1996	

Staff in Confidence

Confidential Report page 2

Staff in Confidence

Second Reporting Officer

11. I accept the assessments and recommendations of the 1st reporting officer, subject to my amendments in red. In addition I have the following comments:

> WO Sanderson is an exceptionally determined and highly professional individual who has certainly risen to the challenges of his present unique ward role. Whilst fully supporting the comments of the first Reporting Officer, I consider the numerical assessments for Common-Sense, Reliability and Sense of Duty are not an accurate reflection and therefore I have amended these accordingly. A man who clearly enjoys responsibility and taking the lead, WO Sanderson will undoubtedly be frustrated in a less demanding and less responsible role than that which he currently enjoys. After much thought, he no longer sees his future within the PMRAFNS and has successfully applied for PVR; he leaves the Service in Sep 96.
>
> Although not a keen sportsman, WO Sanderson maintains his fitness through regular running.

12. a. I consider the ☐ airman ☐ airwoman has the potential to reach 2 ranks higher than ☐ his ☐ her present substantive rank:

    ☐ Yes   ☐ Not sure   ☐ No

    b. I consider this [X] airman ☐ airwoman potentially suitable for a commission.

    ☐ Yes   ☐ Not sure   [X] No

13. I certify that:
    a. The [X] airman ☐ airwoman has served under my command for `1` years `11` months.
    b. The action required at serials 1, _____ of the table at para 17 of F6442A has been taken.

Unit	Appointment	Signature and Rank
PA RAF(H) WROUGHTON	DEP OCNW	*(signed)* SQN LDR
Date	Name in block letters	
21 NOV 95	E B PROUD	

Third Reporting Officer

This part must be completed by the Station Commander if the report is (a) on a WO, (b) includes a special recommendation for promotion or (c) includes a general assessment below 4.

14. I accept the assessments and recommendations, ~~subject to my amendments in red.~~
    In addition I have the following comments:

> I endorse the above assessments and comments as amended by the 2nd Reporting Officer. Though understanding entirely WO Sanderson's reasons for leaving, I consider the Service will be the poorer for the loss of his professional expertise and experience, as well as his valued contribution over the years to life in the Sergeants' Mess.

15. I certify that:
    a. The award of a general assessment below 4 has been noted and QR 529 or formal warning action will be considered.
    b. Any variation of the conduct assessment has been made in accordance with QR 2024(3)
    c. The action required at serials 1, _____ of the table at para 17 of F6442A has been taken.

Unit	Appointment	Signature and Rank
PA RAF(H) WROUGHTON	OC MED WING AND ACTING STN CDR	*(signed)* WING COMMANDER
Date	Name in block letters	
22 NOV 95	K R DANIELS	

Confidential Report page 3

How I felt. Geoff also gave me an excellent reference which has been discussed earlier. I will always remember Geoff who sadly died suddenly some years after leaving the RAF, as he gave me the opportunity to manage Ward 4 Male Orthopaedics at RAF Wroughton as a Warrant Officer against opposition from the Nursing Management, which I will be forever grateful for this would not happen in the new world of the Princess Mary's Royal Air Force Nursing Service.

When I left the RAF, I was sent my discharge papers

Discharge Papers

which I have also enclosed in the book this is what can be sent to a prospective employer. RAF Hospital Wroughton will always hold a special place in my heart as I spent 15 years at the Unit, which is unheard of. I was present at the closing ceremony when the RAF Ensign was lowered for the last time

Lowering of the RAF Ensign for final time RAF Hospital Wroughton December 1995

The other place that is dear to my heart is the Swindon Walk-in Centre. I have found two newspaper cuttings, one from 2000 and the other from 2020.

WIC article 2000

WIC article closure 2020

when the WIC opened, we were short-listed for the Nye Bevan Awards. Although we did not win, just to be shortlisted was a great achievement. The WIC was open 365 days of the year. I cooked Christmas dinner (for the first Christmas we were opened) at home and took it in for the staff that were working on Christmas Day that's what I call going over and above!

Regardless of the outcome of the custody case, Mary and I must get on with our lives as we are both 71. The years just tick away before your very eyes. No one knows what is around the corner, so you must grasp life by the throat and saviour every second, minute and hour, which is what we intend to do. We will be having two cruises a year for as long as we can, as this is something that we enjoy. I have my allotments, exercise and cornet playing, which keeps my mind, body, soul and brain going. Mary is into card making which keeps her occupied, but this has been put on the back burner with the issues with T and the custody case. Hopefully, once the case is over, Mary can get back to her hobby, and we can get some normality back in our lives.

And finally, it's the 4th of July 2024, polling day for the General Election. I must admit I do enjoy General Election night as I stay up most of the night watching the results come in. It looks like there will be a Labour Government if the exit polls are to be believed. As I normally do, I stayed up till 04:00 (with a supply of crisps, whiskey and crumpets) to see the election results, then went to bed. We now have a Labour Government. Let's see what they can do to sort out the Country we can only live in hope!

As I have said throughout this book, I am a believer in fate, and I don't know what the fickle finger of fate may have in store in the future, but I am sure there will be a reason for whatever lies ahead in the fullness of time for Mary and me. Let's hope the Gods are looking down upon us, and we have a happy and healthy rest of our lives.

The end

ACKNOWLEDGEMENTS

This is my first attempt at writing; I am grateful for the support of my wife, Mary over the past years while I have been getting my handwritten notes into a book. I also would like to recognise all the nursing colleagues both in the military and NHS that I have worked with over the years that have been part of my life since 1972.

I need to pay tribute to my parents and Nana, without whom I would not be able to write my story. I would like to thank Jan Baker DStJ for proofreading this manuscript several times. Her help has been much appreciated.

www.ingramcontent.com/pod-product-compliance
Lightning Source LLC
Chambersburg PA
CBHW061228070526
44584CB00030B/4035